Socializing the Classroom

Socializing the Classroom

Social Networks and Online Learning

Susan B. Barnes, PhD

Associate Director, Lab for Social Computing

With Experts from the Lab for Social Computing

LEXINGTON BOOKS

Lanham · Boulder · New York · Toronto · Plymouth, UK

Published by Lexington Books
A wholly owned subsidiary of Rowman & Littlefield
4501 Forbes Boulevard, Suite 200, Lanham, Maryland 20706
www.rowman.com

10 Thornbury Road, Plymouth PL6 7PP, United Kingdom

First paperback edition 2013

The hardback edition of this book was previously
cataloged by the Library of Congress as follows:

ISBN: 978-0-7391-4013-0 (cloth : alk.paper)
ISBN: 978-0-7391-8823-1 (pbk. : alk. paper)
ISBN: 978-0-7391-4015-4 (electronic)

British Library Cataloguing in Publication Information Available

Library of Congress Cataloging-in-Publication Data
Barnes, Susan B.
Socializing the classroom: social networks and online learning / Susan B. Barnes.
p. cm.
Summary: "Socializing the Classroom: Social Networks and Online Learning, by Susan B. Barnes, examines how social media can be used in education through two research grants and real-world applications. Barnes analyzes social media including Facebook, Courseware, and Second Life, while providing a theoretical foundation for examining social software. A new generation of students is surrounded by digital technologies, leading scholars and teachers to consider virtual worlds to engage students."—Provided by Publisher.
Includes bibliographical references and index.
1. Internet in Education. 2. Social Media. 3. Education—Effect of technology innovations on. I. Title.
LB1044.87.B36 2012
371.33'44678—dc23

2011050049

Contents

Acknowledgments

The research described in this book would not have been possible without the generous support of the Rochester Institute of Technology and the National Science Foundation. To both organizations, I am deeply grateful. The support from the Rochester Institute of Technology came from several sources. The major support came from a Provost's Learning and Innovation Grant and I thank Jeremy Haefner for his support of my work. Funding was also provided through the College of Liberal Arts in the form of Faculty Research Funds. These monies were spent on my graduate research assistants including Bonnie McCracken who deserves special recognition. I thank James Winebrake and the previous Deans for their willingness to fund my research.

No research is ever completed without the help of others. Some of these people are contributors to the book. As co-principle investigators on the National Science Foundation grant, Chris Eggert and Steve Jacobs were terrific collaborators. The project could never have been completed without them. Chris Eggert especially deserves recognition for his tireless hours of setting up the computer system and collecting the data. I appreciate all the ways in which he has been supportive. On the Provost's grant, Neil Hair deserves special recognition. He also is a wonderful collaborator. Starting something new is not easy and with his efforts the course we taught was a great success and we even won a Rochester Institute of Technology award. Liz Lawley and the member of the Lab for Social Computing deserve thanks for their efforts on researching social media. Our lab was one of the first to explore these new technologies.

Finally, I would like to thank the different editors from Lexington Press, who have worked with me through the process of publishing this book. With the support of all the organizations mentioned and friends, we have been able to conduct innovative research in social media and I have been able to present our work in the form of a book.

Introduction

Neil Postman (1995) is not the typical source for starting a book on computers and education because during his lifetime, he gained a reputation for being a Luddite. Postman (1979) writes about the ancient conflict of the word versus image. He reminds his readers of the following two biblical ideas: "in the beginning there was the word" and "thou shalt not worship graven images." Postman's reputation for being a proponent of the printed word was a key reason why he was a popular public speaker, especially in places such as Meinz, Germany, where the printing press was invented. Postman (1979) spoke about the power of the book and print-age mentality as a way to counterbalance the impact of visual television on society. When Postman (1985) wrote *Amusing Ourselves to Death,* he was concerned about the role of education in developing citizens for running a democratic society.

He was concerned because the visual impact of television is very different from the impact of word-oriented print. In the past, academics generally considered information received from books or text-based materials to be superior and more reliable than information presented visually on television. For example, Postman (1985) argued American television was primarily an entertainment medium, all information received from television tended to be entertaining. Additionally, television has been cited as being responsible for a larger educational issue—the decline of alphabet literacy. Educators argue that the widespread use of television has eroded traditional literacy skills because students spend more time watching television than they do reading books, newspapers, or magazines. Healy (1990) argues, "children immersed from birth in the spicy sensory bouillabaisse of visual immediacy will not become readers unless they have also soaked up the rich broth of language and reflection" (p. 234).

As a result, there is a bias against the use of television and visual media for general educational instruction. However, this bias against the image is not just a conflict between text and image, it is also based on how people perceive verbal versus visual information. Postman (1979) describes the difference as follows:

> Language is, by its nature, slow moving, hierarchical, logical, and continuous. Whether writing or speaking, one must maintain a fixed point of view and a continuity of content; one must move to higher or lower levels of abstraction; one must follow to a greater or lesser degree rules of syntax and logic. . . . Imagery is fast moving, concrete, discontinuous, alogical, requiring emotional response, its imagery does not provide grounds for argument and contains little ambiguity. There is nothing to debate about. Nothing to refute. Nothing to negate. There are only feelings to be felt. (p. 72)

American cultural connotations associated with "logical" text versus the "emotional" image, not only influence our educational systems, they also impact on media design. For example, serious academic Web sites tend be text-oriented rather than image-oriented, although this is changing. Conversely, advertising and commercial sites use more images to attract viewer attention

In a television culture, Postman (1979) argued that schools need to preserve culture and he advocated the use of traditional verbal forms of representation to promote critical thinking skills. Moreover, Healy (1990) contended that television viewing has contributed to the decline of traditional literacy and critical thinking skills of students in the United States. As a result, television is considered a negative influence on education.

All of these arguments against television revolve around visual and verbal forms of information. On the computer we have both. However, underlying this visual/verbalist debate was Postman's concern for building a democratic society. Postman (1985) believed that democracy was developed and supported by print-based skills. People have to develop reading and critical thinking skills, a concern of Healy's (1990). However, today we live in a truly electronic culture. We have moved past television, the computer is now the major form of communication in American life (see Graham, 1999; Lenhart, Madden, & Hitlin, 2005). Moreover, computers are a requirement for most universities to execute homework and present classroom instruction. Thus, computers are a primary medium used in education, a role that television never achieved. Discussions about education and computers are now part of American culture.

For example, academics are now arguing that the multimodal discourse of image and word combined can expand meaning (O'Halloran, 2008). O'Halloran (2008) contends: "Digital technology opens up the path to explore semiosis [the theories of signs and symbols] in new ways because static and dynamic visual images can be easily manipulated" p. 460). Computer scientists, Alan Kay and

Adele Goldberg (2003 [1977]) understood that the dynamic visual nature of the computer is a central feature of digital media that will influence education. The dynamic nature of the machine enables the simulation of processes and ideas to occur. Today, the characteristics of computer technology impact culture in a very different way than television culture.

Ong (1982) describes some of the differences between print-based and electronic cultures. "Print encourages a sense of closure, a sense that what is found in a text has been finalized, has reached a state of completion" (p. 132). The opposite is true of the flexible Internet, where information is constantly changing. For instance, YouTube videos are regularly evolving and new ones are uploaded every day. Users are generating content without formal editing processes. As a result, the Internet is not a fixed or final medium, it is always in fluctuation.

Messages on the Internet are both visual and verbal. Ong (1982) contends that in electronic culture verbal expression is transformed into a new type of "secondary orality." Secondary orality is more informal and self-conscious than primary orality. It is based on the use of writing and print, which is essential for the operation of technologies that use secondary orality, including radio, television and the computer. For example, Lee (1996) states, "E-mail merges the literate emphasis on sight with the breezy informality of talk, with its many variations of sound" (p. 287). E-mail, chat rooms, and discussion lists are perceived as places where people talk to each other, not type to one another. Ong (1982) says:

> Like primary orality, secondary orality has generated a strong group sense, for listening to spoken words forms hearers into a group, a true audience, just as reading written or printed texts turn individuals in on themselves. But secondary orality generates a sense for groups immeasurably larger than those of primary oral culture. (p. 136)

The Internet has the potential to bring large geographically dispersed groups together and share commerce and services around the world (see Friedman, 2005). People now talk to each other through the Internet in similar ways as they spoke in oral cultures. The difference is that people do not have to be co-present to be part of the Internet community or group. As a result, we can form a global village through the use of the Internet (see McLuhan & Powers, 1989). In a global village people come together into community networks that are participatory by nature. Ong (1982) contends, "Primary orality fosters personality structures that in certain ways are more communal and externalized, and less introspective than those common among literates" (p. 69). There is a tendency for electronic culture to maintain some of the features of an oral culture, although it is through secondary orality rather than primary orality.

As quoted earlier, secondary orality generates a strong group sense, which is characterized on the Internet through the creation of communities. The formation of community networks has been an Internet topic for a number of years. (Graham, 1999; Schuler, 1994). In the early beginnings of the Internet, scientists shared their working papers and ideas with each other. Since that time, Schuler (1994) describes community networks, Rheingold (1998) coined the term virtual community, and social networking sites have emerged (boyd & Ellison, 2008).

Virtual communities are "informational and emotional support groups that form the same type of bonds as geographic communities where people share their experiences" (Barnes, 2003, p. 226). Rheingold (1998) describes them as "a group of people who may or may not meet on another face to face and who exchange words and ideas through the mediation of computer bulletin boards, and networks" (p. 116). Garton, Haythornthwaite, and Wellman (1997) state: "just as a computer network is a set of machines connected by a set of cables, a social network is a set of people (or organizations or other social entities) connected by a set of social relationships, such as friendship, co-working or information exchange" (p. 2).

Finally, boyd and Ellison (2008) describe social networking sites as "services that allow individuals to (1) construct a public or semi-public profile within a bounded system, (2) articulate a list of other users with whom they share a connection, and (3) view and traverse their list of connections and those made by others in the system" (p. 211). Essentially social networking connects people together and it is now referred to as social media, including twitter, Facebook, Second Life, Wikis, blogs, and YouTube.

"Individuals who enter adolescence today in the United States will likely grow up in an immersive media environment, but one based on the Internet more than television" (Schrock, 2009, para. 25). The idea of media as environments was a concept that Postman wrote about. He called his critical form of media analysis—media ecology. Postman (1992) stated, with regard to how technology is incorporated into society, that "technological change is not additive; it is ecological" (p. 18). What Postman means is that when a new technology is introduced into a culture, it changes everything, including education. As generations grow-up with the technology, the culture is modified along with the use of the technology itself. Postman argues "that embedded in every tool is an ideological bias, a predisposition to construct the world as one thing rather than another, to value one thing over another, to amplify one sense or skill or attitude more loudly than another" (p. 13).

For example, a bias of social media is its development of social connections and relationships. Today, unlike previous generations, young people known as the millennials or "Generation Y" have a tendency to place less value on money and more on connections, knowledge and freedom of expression (Degraffenreid, 2006 & 2007). Social Networking programs, such as Facebook, MySpace, and

LinkedIn, are places where Millennials maintain and develop relationships. As a result, relationship development is an important aspect of their culture.

However, Millennials have grown up using computer technology in relatively limited social capacities, such as Instant Messaging, creating and monitoring Facebook pages, and watching television programs and movies. Using computers as a teaching medium seems natural for them and one would think that they can use this tool for educational purposes. Often a misunderstood generation, Millennials are described as being non-linear thinkers, highly adaptive to new technology and well connected, especially due to the rise of social networks. They live in a world surrounded by music, images and video games. Concerns have been raised about the reading habits of these young people because they read less than prior generations. While the time they spend with books and newspapers has declined, the time they spend reading email, instant messages, text messages, and material on social networking sites has grown to an approximately thirty-one hours per week (see Telegraph Media Group, 2009). In addition, "children also use the internet to help them with homework, with at least three hours a week spent searching for such information" (para. 5). This information is presented in a multimodal format to connect people together.

The collaborative nature of the Internet to connect people and share information is changing educational culture. David Warlick (2009), in *Redefining Litercary 2.0* explains that online communities are changing because "the Internet has become, once again, a highly collaborative environment" (p. 165). Online tools such as blogs and wikis have created a new "spirit of information democracy."

By connecting people and information together, social media provide opportunities for civic participation. In the past, television has been considered a barrier to civic participation (see Schuler, 1994). In contrast, the Internet "contains the potential of increased knowledge, tightened relation and wired communities of coordination and cooperation" (Shaw, McLeod, & Yoon, 2001, p. 465). For example, Howard Dean's campaign for president utilized an obscure website called MeetUp.com to organize 600,000 supporters (see Trippi, 2004). Similarly, the election of President Obama used social networking to reach citizens. The Internet has already played a major role in American politics and civic participation.

Civic participation has been popularized by Putnam's (2000) term *social capital.* Social capital as defined by Shaw, McLeod, and Yoon (2001) is "the resources of information, norms, and social relations embedded in communities that enable people to coordinate collective action and to achieve common goals" (p. 467). A goal of social media is "the design of systems that supports groups with an underlying value proposition of building social capital" (Rowland, 2004, para. 5). Social capital is the development of an individual's personal social network (Van Der Gaag & Snijders, 2004). According to Wellman, Haase, Witte & Hampton (2001), social capital is increased offline interpersonal contact, organizational and political participation, and commitment to community. Simply stated, social software is software that enables people to interact with each other and build social networks that increase their social capital.

Forming social networks, relationship building, and creating social capital are the new focal points of social media and the development of social software. A key area of social software development is in social networking sites and education. However, it was revealed in a National Science Foundation Grant (Theoretical and Applied Approaches to teaching Social Computing in STEM Education), described throughout this book, that commercial social networking sites are influencing the ways young people perceive educational courseware. Students find the social networking sites more engaging than educational ones. Thus, the introduction of social media into American society is already changing student's perceptions of online education. Today, education needs to become participatory, similar to the Internet. Educators need to understand social media and its relationship to educational teaching, learning, objectives, and tools.

Social media is a new type of message system that has already had an impact on education. Postman (1980) contends, "a complex message system which imposes on human beings certain ways of thinking, feeling, and behaving. It structures what we can see and say and, therefore, do. It assigns roles to us and . . . specifies what we are permitted to do and what we are not" (p. 161). Social media encourages the behavior of participation, which is a concept that needs to be better understood.

Social networking was begun in 1997 and became popular in 2002 (boyd & Ellison, 2008). However, the idea of social media was discussed in an educational text five years before the use of these popular sites. In *Sociomedia: Multimedia, Hypermedia, and the Social Construction of Knowledge,* Edward Barrett (1992) argued for the social aspect of computing and its role in education. Barrett (1992) stated, "'Sociomedia' forces us to look outward from the machine into the complex interaction of human relationships which define 'university' and 'education,' human relationships that are the real content of all educational technology" (p. 9).

Human relationships are the key to new educational systems. "The old world of education often consisted of listening to lectures, memorizing facts, using drill and practice to acquire skills, and accessing information in books to complete worksheets" (Shneiderman, 1992, p. 17). The old world that was suited for an industrial age, needs to be altered for the electronic age. Shneiderman (1992) argued "the purpose of learning is not to store facts in the student's head, but to *engage with people*" (p. 18). This engagement can be extended into political discourse and the building of a democracy. It also fits with the concept of constructivist learning.

Postman's (1985) primary concern in education was building a democratic society. He argued for this through the logic of print. As previously described, today, we can build democracy through the multimodal technology of the Internet.

This book provides insight into the technology of social media. It utilizes the expertise of a number of scholars from the Lab for Social Computing who have been working with these tools for a number of years. The Lab for Social Computing (LSC) is part of the Rochester Institute of Technology, Wallace Center and offers a wide range of educational programs and lectures on social computing and social media topics. Additionally the LSC conducts research on social media topics including online games, Second Life, educational courseware, teaching social media, and designing research tools for social media applications. Research from these projects is incorporated into this book. The influence of social media tools on education is a complex issue. The themes of each chapter represent different approaches to unraveling the issue of social networks and education.

The visual/verbalist debates taking place during the widespread use of television need to be revived in the age of the computer because reading print-based texts is being replaced by computer interaction. Teachers need to find new methods for teaching old ideas. In this text, we describe both our successes and failures teaching with technology, but more important is the framework used to examine the changing world of social media itself.

The framework[1] is based on the technical, social and usability issues described by Egert (2003). The technical dimension addresses the hardware, software, and network requirements necessary to realize a collaborative system. The technical dimension addresses aspects such as web browsers, rich Internet application software (RIAs), client-side and browser programming languages, server-side technologies and programming languages, as well as database systems. In addition, the technical dimension deals with issues such as support for different models of communication, including support for same time and different time communication as well as same location and different location communication (Johansen, Sibbet, Benson, Martin, Mittman & Saffo, 1991). The technical dimension also has to address issues of session management and maintenance, which delineates the start and the end of a user's interaction with a system (Kristofferse & Ljungberg, 1999). Session management has to be flexible to support shared artifacts, shared activities, and virtual co-location (Kristofferse & Ljungberg, 1999). The technical dimension must also provide support for search and filtering, providing the user with mechanisms to manage multiple criteria over many data sets. Finally, the technology dimension has to address issues of access, control, security, and persistence to make sure that information is secure, accessible by the correct people, and is accurate and immutable over the lifetime of a social media system.

The social dimension addresses how people interact as well as their organization (Kollock, 1998). The social dimension examines both modes of communication, including discourse-centric and artifact-centric approaches as well as tasks, roles, and expectations of individuals and community. The social dimension defines what users know about themselves and their relation to their communities (Dyson, 1997; McMillan & Chavis, 1986). Social considerations include concepts such as appropriate access and control (Jones, 1998). Access and control implies a balance between individual and group access and responsibility and is reliant upon societal factors such as reputation, intended role, and community status to regulate its form (Donath, 1999; Dyson, 1997; Jones, 1998; Hiltz & Wellman, 1997).

The usability dimension addresses the notion of whether a particular application satisfies the needs and requirements of the stakeholder groups as well as end users (Nielsen, 1993). Usability can take numerous forms including guidelines and aesthetics for the design of web applications and Internet enabled tools (Forsythe, Grose & Ratner, 1998; Johnson, 1997; Spool, Scanlon, Schroeder, Snyder & DeAngelo, 1997; Borges, Morales & Rodrigues, 1998; Whitaker, 1998; Nielsen, 2000), quantitative analysis of usage patterns through observation or instrumentation (Ivory, Sinha & Hearst, 2001), administration of instruments designed to measure user satisfaction and efficacy with a particular software system (Harper & Norman, 1993), or application of usability inspection techniques (Bias, 1994; Nielsen, 1994; Wharton, Rieman, Lewis & Polson, 1994).

The theoretical foundations for this book are based on Postman's work on Media Ecology that focus on characteristics of media and Egert's framework on the technical, social and usability dimensions of a technology. Throughout this book a National Science Foundation grant is mentioned. It is grant #0633401—Theoretical and Applied Approaches to Teaching Social Computing in STEM Education and the research is based on Egert's framework. Susan B. Barnes, Christopher Egert, and Stephen Jacobs conducted the NSF research. Susan B. Barnes and Neil Hair conducted research on Second Life and they received an additional grant. The grant was awarded as a Provost Learning and Innovation Grant from the Rochester Institute of Technology.

The National Science Foundation project had two primary goals and one secondary goal. The first primary goal was to improve technology education by introducing the new discipline of social computing into the science, technology, engineering and mathematics curriculum. A measurable outcome of this goal was the level of student understanding of social media before and after they have taken the course. The second primary goal was the preparation of undergraduates for positions in the social media sector of the technology industries. A measurable outcome of this goal was a student's perceived awareness of career opportunities in this new sector of the technology marketplace. Data was collected through pre- and post-test surveys to measure these two goals.

A secondary goal and benefit of this project, was the tracking of the formation of social network building within three different online learning environments. Analysis of this data provided a case study for the course and insight into how students build social networks. Our case study of the social aspects of learning environments helped to demonstrate, how the software tools included in these programs support (or sometimes impede) student participation and social network formation, which leads to the building of social capital.

To investigate this phenomenon of social networking, the researchers of the National Science Foundation Grant created an undergraduate college course titled "Social Media Theory and Practice" as a means of exploring both the technical and social ramifications of social media integration into courses as well as courseware and course management technologies. Before developing a college course based upon social media theories and practices, the authors deliberated upon organization and presentation techniques for the materials. One unique design aspect of the course was that it was to be taught by three faculty with diverse backgrounds. Perspectives and themes that frequency occurred in developing materials included media ecology, communications, web technologies, usability, aesthetics, popular culture and practice, social norms and acceptable behaviors online, as well as unconventional and serendipitous use of technology.

To this end, the authors organized content based upon two different organizational scales based upon prior work in Media-Enabled Collaboration (Egert, 2003). One scale approached the material from the perspective of technology, social, and usability concerns, based upon prior concepts in socio-technical systems theory (Bostrom & Heinen, 1977; Cummings Srivasta, 1977. The other scale was based upon work, communication, and learning functions drawn from the Computer-Supported Collaborative Work (CSCW), Computer Mediated Communication (CMC), and Computer-Supported Collaborative Learning (CSCL) communities. Thus, a combined theory of information technology and computer-mediated communication informed the work. The following chapters describe what we found out about social media and education.

Today, we live in a multimedia world and need to find a new balance between all forms of literacy. We have gone way beyond visual/verbal discussions that compare print literacy to television. Social networking is so pervasive in the lives of young people that we need to better understand how these tools can be harnessed for educational purposes. Instead of counter-balancing popular media with print-based media, we need to incorporate these new visual tools into education. However, these new tools are based on interpersonal relationships, rather than texts and printed words, which adds a social dimension to the classroom.

Note

1. The description of the technical, social and usability dimensions of Egert's framework was adapted from *When Social Worlds Collide: Charting the Intersection of Social Tools and Courseware Systems* by Christopher Egert, Stephen Jacobs and Susan B. Barnes, 2009.

Chapter One

What Are Social Media?

Since the introduction of television, media have increasingly created a sense of interpersonal relationships through mediated environments. With the introduction of computer networks, people can now create their own sense of presence to communicate with others. A major change between older media outlets and today's social media revolution is in the content. Media have evolved from one-to-many message distribution systems into a many-to-many system that supports the sharing of content between individual people. Social media networks make the connections between people visible and create the feeling of talking face-to-face. Social media can enhance our face-to-face educational activities and support distant relationships.

Today, social media are generally known as sites such as Facebook, MySpace, Second Life, and YouTube. The popularity of these websites illustrates how people have embraced the idea of social media. Although people think the technology is new, a number of ideas going back to the 1950s helped to make social networking a reality. The development of social media can be traced back to a number of different concepts, including: parasocial relationships (Horton & Wohl , 1986 [1956]; Meyrowitz, 1986), personalization of media (Beniger, 1987; Gumpert & Cathcart, 1986), personal computing (Kay & Goldberg, 2003 [1977]; Lüders, 2008), social networking (Barrett, 1992; Licklider & Taylor, 1968), presence theory (Short, Williams & Christie, 1976), and the power of many (Crumlish, 2004; Rheingold, 2002). Today, social media is instigating political revolutions in the Middle East and enabling a ten-year-old to win a Guinness World Record for being the youngest video gamer to achieve a perfect score on *Dance Dance Revolution* (duLac, 2011).

Para-Social Relationships

Horton and Wohl (1986), first examined communicating through media on an interpersonal level. In 1956, they conducted an early exploration of the interpersonal relationship created between actors and viewers. They coined the term para-social relationships because people engaged in the actor/viewer relationship created by television and radio, act as if the relationship is not mediated. These para-social relationships are carried on as if they were face-to-face encounters. Horton and Wohl (1986) stated:

> When the camera pans down on a performer, the illusion is strong that he is enhancing the presumed intimacy by literally coming closer. But the person's image, while partial, contrived, and penetrated by illusion, is no fantasy or dream; his performance is an objectively perceptible action in which the viewer is implicated imaginatively but which he does not imagine. (p. 187)

Television programming has the ability to create the feeling of an intimate, face-to-face association with a performer. Meyrowitz (1986) asserted: "Electronic media allow for a unique form of interaction that dislocates the traditional relationship between physical setting and social situation, rearranging social forums so that individuals find themselves in contact with new persons in new ways" (p. 379). The mediation tends to be transparent in both television and computer-mediated communication relationships. For example, computer mediation creates the feeling of talking, not typing to someone. What is unusual about electronic media is the ability to "offer the illusion of face-to-face interaction with performers and political figures" (p. 119). This is one reason why social networks are so successful. The technology is not a barrier because participants ignore the medium and are able to express themselves through blogs, videos, and pictures.

However, a difference between the Internet and mass media is the fact we are communicating with other people. Social Networks have different approaches to how people can interact on their network. For instance, MySpace allows users to sign up using a real name or a pseudonym. As a result, film companies can create pages for characters in their movies. In contrast, Facebook makes all users place their real names on the site. People have the opportunity to engage in parasocial relationships, similar to television, on MySpace, but in Facebook, the names represent actual people. Thus, mass media becomes more interpersonal.

Interpersonal Mass Media

The idea of not paying attention to the medium combined with the personalization of media adds to the socialization of media. We internalize media when we forget it is there. For instance, reading is internalized because experienced readers don't have to look at every word. Moreover, the computer programs on the Internet that place people's names on websites, personalizes the medium. Beniger (1987) argued that mass media has increasingly supported the relationships between people and machines to simulate human communication. In an attempt to make mass media appear more personalized, industrial society developed specialized magazines, targeted mass mailings, neighborhood-edition newspapers, and phone-in radio shows. Efforts were made to obscure the size of the audience receiving the message to create the illusion of a personal message. Beniger (1987) stated: "Gradually each of us has become enmeshed in superficially interpersonal relationships that confuse personal with mass messages and increasingly include interactions with machines that write, speak, and even 'think' with success steadily approaching that of humans" (p. 354). For many years, computers have been used to create the appearance of interpersonal, rather than mass messages being sent to large audiences. Direct mailing envelopes with your individualized name and address is an example of this trend.

The interpersonal nature of mass media is the topic of Gumpert and Cathcart's (1986) book, *Intermedia*. This edited volume describes interpersonal relationships with television, radio, magazines, film, photography, and person-computer interaction. Turkel (1986) warns of the phenomenon of anthropomorphism and computers, how people tend to treat computers as other people. She stated: "anthropomorphic imagery, supported by the computer's projective capacity, seems deeply embedded in the nature of computation" (p. 457). Cathcart and Gumpert (1986) state, "Humanizing the computer is also prompted by the physical and electronic properties of the computer and by the nature of programming which uses the interpersonal dyad as an operational model" (p. 329). Human-like responses are programmed into the machine, such as "Do you want to save the changes you made to 'document X?.'" Computing is a social act and people tend to treat computers like other people (see Reeves & Nash, 1996). Reeves and Nash (1996) said: "*All* people automatically and unconsciously respond socially and naturally to media" (p. 7). Computers mimic social conversation with individuals and people respond by communicating back to the computer, as if it was a person.

A classic example of how computers are treated as people is the ELIZA program created by Joseph Weizenbaum. In reality, ELIZA is a conversational natural language program that simulates the reactions of a Rogerian psychotherapist, who would mirror patient responses back to the patient. People's reactions to the program drew them into closer relationships with the computer. Individuals became personally involved with the program, forgetting that it was software, not human. In this case, individuals were interacting with the machine and not other people. Here is an example of ELIZA:

> Men are all alike. [person]
> IN WHAT WAY [computer]
> They're always bugging us about something or other.
> CAN YOU THINK OF A SPECIFIC EXAMPLE
> Well, my boyfriend made me come here.
> YOUR BOYFRIEND MADE YOU COME HERE
> He says I'm depressed much of the time.
> I AM SORRY TO HEAR YOU ARE DEPRESSED
> (Weizenbaum, 1976, p. 3)

When communicating with other people through the computer, individuals tend to ignore the medium of the computer. Cathcart and Gumpert (1986) contended: "for the mediated exchange to work as interpersonal communication, there must be a tacit agreement that the participants will proceed as though they are communicating face-to-face" (p. 325). This aspect of computing makes it easy to use the computer for interpersonal communication instead of other media like the telephone, which emphasizes the distance between people. Lüders (2008) stated: "the development and use of digital media technologies have destabilized the traditional dichotomy between mass communication and (inter)personal communication" (p. 690). The ability of the computer to enable people to be both senders and receivers of information is the primary difference between mass and personal media.

Personal Media

The idea of using computers as personal media started with Alan Kay. After seeing interactive computing demonstrated by Douglas Engelbart, the Logo program used by children, and reading Marshall McLuhan, Kay realized that children should be able to program a computer (see Barnes, 2007). Engelbart "is best known as the groundbreaking engineer who invented such mainstays of the personal computer as the mouse, windows, e-mail, and the word processor" (Packer & Jordan, 2001, p. 65). The Logo programming system is important in the evolution of computers in education. "Logo was developed as a mathematical tool and also a tool for engaging in and enhancing thinking" (Clements & Sarama, 1997, p. 21). It helped develop types of problem-solving behaviors in children. Combined with McLuhan's (1964) ideas about media, Kay (1990) created a new paradigm shift in thinking about computing. He described his concept as follows:

> The ability to 'read' a medium means you can access materials and tools created by others. The ability to 'write' in a medium means you can generate materials and tools for others. You must have both to be literate. In

> print writing, the tools you generate are rhetorical; they demonstrate and convince. In computer writing, the tools you generate are processes; the simulate and decide.
>
> If the computer is only a vehicle, perhaps you can wait until high school to give 'drivers ed' on it—but if it's a medium, then it must be extended all the way into the world of the child. (p. 191)

Kay understood that computers were a medium of communication, not just a tool for performing tasks. As a medium, people would use it for personal communication. Therefore, he began designing "personal computers" that were easy enough for children to use. Kay and Goldberg (2003 [1977]) described the computing device as follows:

> Imagine having your own self-contained knowledge manipulator in a portable package the size and shape of an ordinary notebook. Suppose it had enough power to outrace your senses of sight and hearing, enough capacity to store for later retrieval thousands of page-equivalents or reference materials, poems, letters, recipes, records, drawings, animations, musical scores, waveforms, dynamic simulations, and anything else you would like to remember and change. (p. 176)

Today, "the parallels with the way in which personal media are used three decades later are apparent" (Lüders, 2008, p. 684). For example, Apple Computer's release of the iPad fits Kay's description of future computers. However, Kay's account about personal media does not stress the interpersonal nature of the medium or its role in education.

When the computer was first introduced into education it was viewed as a tutor, tool and tutee. A 1998 Rand Report described computers in education as applications that "help students learn concepts more effectively to applications that change the kinds of ideas students learn, and how they learn them" (McArthur & Lewis, 1998, p. 23). The report describes the Internet as a virtual World Lecture Hall with a repository of online course materials. However, the report also described how the Internet connects people together into online learning communities.

Online Communication

The idea of connecting people together through computer networks was first described by Licklider and Taylor (1968). They talked about the creative use of computers and described how human processes can be conducted through a computer.

> Such a medium is at hand—the programmed digital computer. Its presence can change the nature and value of communication even more profoundly than did the printing press and the picture tube, for, as we shall show, a well-programmed computer can provide direct access both to informational resources and to the *processes* for making use of the resources. (p. 22)

Licklider and Taylor (1968) used the example of a meeting to demonstrate how a computer would be used as a communication medium. They described how the meeting of many interacting minds could solve problems and engage in creative informational activities. It was argued, "to move forward the development of interactive *communities* of geographically separated people—is to set up an experimental network of multi-access computers" (p. 30). At the time when this was written, experiments with the Advanced Research Projects Agency Network (ARPAnet), the beginnings of the Internet, were just starting. Today, we have multi-access computers and it is called the World Wide Web.

Computers as Social Constructions

Looking at the Web in 1992, Barrett realized that computers were inherently social. His edited book *Sociomedia* described simulations, story telling, program design, virtual classrooms, computers in engineering education, the construction of knowledge, and intergenerational education. Barrett (1992) argued: "'Sociomedia,' as a term, underscores the fact that computer media are ultimately social constructs themselves" (p. 1). The term calls attention to the ultimate value of computers, which is to exist for social purposes, such as exchange and collaboration, comment upon, modify, and remember thoughts and ideas. His work builds on the idea of the social construction of knowledge in education. Education is a social act rather than a place to memorize facts and formulas. Social construction involves activity such as synthesis of ideas.

> Thinking becomes a casting of a net (which is language), not merely a juggling of fixed objects—it is tentative (but testable), social both in the sense of grouping many things and of being articulated to an audience (and therefore responded to), 'synthetic' or unifying (and therefore a personal possession—'original'—even in its social construction). (p. 3)

Barrett and the authors in his edited book believe in constructivist education. Computers should be used as a method to engage students in the learning process. Knowledge is constructed socially as people interact with each other. Interaction online requires a sense of the presence of the other.

Presence Theory

In order for people to communicate through computers, they must have a sense of the other person. We must think that a person is there and not just a machine. In 1976, Short, Williams, and Christie explored the social psychology of telecommunication and argued that media have various degrees of social presence, which influence the ways in which individuals will interact. This theory, social presence theory, laid the groundwork for research and theories on computer mediated communication. The theory is based on the idea that humans need connection with other human beings. When people have limited cues in an interaction, they add features to improve the social communication, such as emoticons. Social presence is part people and part technology. The technology introduces the limited cues into the communication process. Moreover, the concept revolves around the idea that a medium's social effects are caused by the degree of social presence, which it creates through people interacting with a partner. Essentially, social presence is a communicator's sense of awareness they are communicating with a person, not an impersonal object. For example, presence is determined in instant messaging by making other users aware of who is online and when they are online. When we have a sense of the other, we can communicate on an interpersonal level. In contrast, MySpace, users, who are threatened by anonymous people, feel terrified in real life (Burnette, 2007). There is a sense of presence, however the person is unknown, which can create fear.

Lombard and Dutton (1997) described the conceptualizations in the literature about presence. Their definition of presence is media designed "to provide media users with an illusion that a mediated experience is not mediated, a perception defined here as presence" (p. 1). Moreover, "they suggest that mediated experiences that closely mimic nonmediated ones cause difficulties for the reality-monitoring process so that when memories are retrieved, mediated and nonmediated experiences are confused" (p. 3). People can confuse their mediated and real encounters. Doctors use this when virtual reality environments are designed to help people with phobias, such as fear of airplanes or small spaces.

Reviewing the literature on presence, Lombard and Dutton (1997) found six conceptualizations about the concept of presence: 1) presence as social richness; 2) presence as realism; 3) presence as transportation; 4) presence as immersion; 5) presence as social actor within a medium; and 6) presence as medium as social actor. Presence can be related to social richness theory using the concepts of intimacy and immediacy. In online communication people use emoticons and language to establish a feeling of intimacy. Immediacy depends upon the type of Internet environment. Synchronous environments, such as chat, instant messaging, Twitter, and Second Life, provide almost real-time responses to messages. In contrast, e-mail, discussion lists, and online course discussion systems, have a delayed response time. According to media richness theory, environments that provide real-time responses would have a higher level of presence than environments that do not. Therefore, twitter has a higher level of intimacy than e-mail.

Presence as realism is the degree to which a medium can represent objects and events. For example, Second Life builds a world with avatars that look like people and virtual objects, such as clothing, houses and automobiles. It creates a parallel virtual life to real life. Second Life creates the feeling that people get together in a shared space. This is the transportation aspect of presence. Individuals have the awareness of being transported to a shared space, the user's space, or another space entirely. Online environments provide that feeling that we are some place. Or, total immersion can be established when a user wears a helmet and goggles to cover the eyes. This creates the feeling of physically being immersed into another space (see chapter 3 on Space and Place).

In contrast to the sense of space, presence can also be created through "virtual actors." The parasocial feelings created by virtual actors can have the same effect as television actors. Social interfaces, such as Microsoft's "Bob," attempt to use characters to direct software usage. Instead of reading a list of commands, the characters would help to tell people how to use the computer. Similarly, the more popular characters, such as cyber pets, have been known to have their own fan clubs (see Lombard & Dutton, 1997). However, the medium itself can create a sense of presence. Lombard and Dutton (1997) state: "basic social cues exhibited by the medium lead users to treat the medium as a social entity" (p. 9). This can be seen in the work of Reeves and Nass discussed earlier. Lombard and Dutton (1997) state:

> The illusion of nonmediation can occur in two distinct ways: (a) the medium can appear to be invisible or transparent and function as would a large open window, with the medium and user and medium content (objects and entities) sharing the same physical environment; and (b) the medium can appear to be transformed into something other than a medium, a social entity. (p. 10)

When a medium presents us with social cues that are parallel to cues we receive from other humans, the medium can be viewed as an independent social entity. This new social entity can be used to help people meet each other and form groups. Social media has also been used to organize people, including political rallies and the creation of smart mobs.

Power of Many

Smart mobs is a term used by Rheingold (2002) to describe "people who are able to act in concert even if they don't know each other" (p. xii). Using portable mobile devices, they can communicate across geographic spaces and then come together in one physical location. Using this method, demonstrations and public protests can be coordinated. Smart mobs in Manila overthrew the presidency of President Estrada by using text messages and cell phones to organize demonstrations.

In software development, an example of the smart mob concept, was the development of the Linux operating system. It was created by thousands of programmers from around the world and this homegrown program now competes with Microsoft in the marketplace for control over the operating system software market.

In June 2005, *BusinessWeek* ran a feature on the "Power of Us." The magazine stated:

> BEHOLD THE POWER OF US. It's the force behind the collective clamor of Weblogs that felled CBS anchorman Dan Rather and rocked the media establishment. Global crowds of open-source Linux programmers are giving even mighty Microsoft Corp. fits. Virtual supercomputers, stitched together from millions of volunteer's PCs, are helping predict global climate change, analyze genetic diseases, and find new planets and stars. (Hof, 2005, pp. 75-76)

Bringing together people and computers can build a virtual supercomputer with the computing power to solve scientific problems. The Internet has a force all of its own to share resources, but to move past assets and engage in human activity is a different issue. Crumlish (2004) identifies three stages of involvement to move people from the virtual to the real world:

- Using the virtual world to connect with like-minded people.
- Meeting in the face-to-face world.
- Taking the steps to perform the collective action. (p. 66)

These strategies are extremely useful for a political candidate and political activism. For instance, Trippi's (2004) *The Revolution Will Not Be Televised* described how the Internet worked to coordinate people for the Howard Dean campaign. Similarly, social media, such as twitter and Facebook, has fueled incidents in the Middle East of demonstrations and political unrest. Social network is influencing many aspects of life, including politics and education. However, education is not politics or protests. Managing the "power of many" in education takes a different direction.Instead of getting people to perform a collective action, students need to learn a set of new concepts and skills. The classroom extends out into the real world to provide new types of interactive learning experiences for students and professors.

Social Networking Classroom

Today, the classroom has become a hub of activity not just a place where you get a grade and go home. It is a place where you start to build your career and make connections with people professionally and within the community. This new type of classroom is the *Social Networking Classroom*. "A social network is defined here as relations among people who deem other network members to be important or relevant to them in some way" (Lange, 2007, p. 362). Adding social networking tools to the traditional classroom transforms the room into a worldwide learning experience. When the walls of the classroom are expanded into the real world, we can build social networks that not only help students with the course work, but also help them to make networking connections in their professional lives after college. Therefore, the central idea of the Social Networking Classroom is to prepare students for the real world and professional life.

However, this concept of the classroom is new. In the past, concepts about online learning have included: collaborative learning (Macdonald, 2003; Slater-Lawrence, 2006); changing role of teachers (Wheeler, 2001); technological issues (Gao & Wong, 2008; Halper, Kelly, & Chang, 2007; Park, Lee & Cheong, 2007) and collaborative communities (Cassell & Tversky, 2005). These older ideas do have implications for the newer concept of the Social Networking Classroom. In Social Networking Classrooms, the learning environment is more collaborative in terms of assignments and cooperation with classmates, professionals, and teachers.

The role of the teacher changes because teachers need "to acquire new skills in order to promote quality learning opportunities in an information and communication rich learning environment" (Wheeler, 2001). Teachers need to reach out into the community to find professional resources and they must be willing to guide students through projects rather than memorizing facts, or using drill and practice to acquire skills. They need to learn about the new social media programs that students are using to keep up with popular culture. Also, the classroom needs to be thought about in terms of a learning community rather than a room of students. When using the Social Networking Classroom, a sense of presence needs to be established between remote correspondents and students. This can be done by having people present lectures in Second Life and using a screen to project the session. Thus, the classroom is opened up to the real world through the use of a virtual one.

Online Learning

Computer-mediated environments create a sense of presence to compensate for the lack of physical interaction. A number of articles have been written about online learning and online presence (Anderson, Rourke, Garrison, & Archer, 2001; Hughes, Ventura & Dando, 2007; Picciano, 2002; Rourke, Anderson, Garrison & Archer, 2001). Anderson, et al. (2001) describes *teaching presence*, which includes individuals who collaborate to carry out the role of a teacher. They state: "Another part of the challenge [in online teaching] is to overcome the difficulty of conceiving the role of the teacher in online courses within the long established conceptual framework that we have built in the context of conventional, face-to-face teaching" (p. 14). In the social networking classroom, a professional who is lecturing or helping students with a project can establish teaching presence.

In contrast, Hughes, et al. (2007) was concerned with the presence of students and how they maintain social cohesion in an online classroom. Rourke, et. al. (2001) define social presence "as the ability of learners to project themselves socially and affectively into a community of inquiry" (p. 2). Social presence is a variable in online learning environments. To examine this variable, Picciano (2002) examined the interactions between students. However, Picciano was not able to find a relationship between social presence and performance in the course. However, a relationship was found between social presence and participation in the course. In many online and blended courses, students need to participate in weekly discussions and socialize with their colleagues.

The social aspect of learning is one of the elements that social media brings to the classroom. As previously mentioned, social media is commonly known by a number of software programs, such as Facebook, MySpace, YouTube, and Second Life. These programs with Wiki and blogging tools are now entering the classroom (see Du & Wagner, 2007; Eijkman, 2008). A social network analysis of an online class was conducted by Russo and Koesten (2005). They examined the amount of messages a student received (prestige) and the amount of messages a student sent out (centrality). This topic will be discussed further in chapter 5: Awareness and Notification.

Social Networking

Today, pre-college students are immersed in social computing technologies and they are part of a high school student's social life. As a result, students have a dramatically different relationship to technology than students had ten years ago. "The children in our classrooms are changing—largely as a result of their out-of-school experiences with technology—and are no longer satisfied with an education that doesn't immediately address the real world in which they live" (Prensky, 2010, p. XV). The increased use of technology is "changing the ways we produce, consume, communicate and think" (Collins & Haverson, 2009,

p. 5). A media ecological principle is that changing technologies have a cognitive impact on people. Thus, students learning with the Internet will think differently from students taught with books.

According to a Pew Internet and American Life report, teens are Internet savvy (Lenhart, Madden, Macgill & Smith, 2007). Approximately 94 percent of teens ages twelve through seventeen are using the Internet or e-mail. They have more access to higher speed connections, personal computers, and computers at home. Additionally, teens have more accessibility to friends and family through social networks and cell phones. Similarly, the research conducted by the authors for a National Science Foundation grant revealed that 94 percent of the students stated that they used social networking for communication.

Table 1.1 Classification of social media systems, student recognition of software group as social media, and usage of the system class, and examples from student reponses (N=34 students).

Classification	Recognized as social media	Used by student	Examples
Social Network / Friend Systems	88.8 percent	85.3 percent	Facebook, MySpace, Ning
Asynchronous Messaging/E-mail	85.3 percent	100 percent	E-mail, Distribution Lists
Instant Messaging Systems	82.4 percent	88.2 percent	AIM, Trillian, Meebo
Blogs	76.5 percent	67.6 percent (Consumer) 17.6 percent (Authoring)	(various blogs)
Forum / Discussion Board Software	67.6 percent	85.3 percent (Consumer) 52.9percent (Authoring)	(various communities)
Content Sharing/Anchored Collab.	41.1 percent	88.2 percent (Consumer) 17.6percent (Authoring)	Flickr, YouTube

Classification	Recognized as social media	Used by student	Examples
Course Management Systems	14.7 percent	88.8 percent	myCourses
Professional Networks	14.7 percent	32.4 percent	Linked In, Monster
MMO and Community Games	11.7 percent	41.1 percent	WoW, Yahoo Games
Text messaging	11.7 percent	64.4 percent	Cell phone, SMS apps
Web page / online content creation	8.8 percent	29.4 percent	(various wikis)
Podcasts	2.9 percent	55.8 percent (Consumer) 2.9 percent (Authoring)	iTunes Podcasts
RSS Feeds / Aggregators	2.9 percent	23.5 percent	(various feeds)

Academic articles on social networking are limited because researchers have just begun to examine the topic. Researching on social networking includes social networking privacy issues (Barnes, 2006; Gross & Acquisti, 2005); identity (Livingstone, 2008); space (Papacharissi, 2009); knowledge transfer (Cheuk, 2007); social norms (Kazmer, 2007; Williams & Merten, 2009); narcissim (Buffardi & Campbell, 2008); interpersonal impressions (Tong, Van Der Heide, Langwell & Walther, 2008); social network analysis (Garton, Haythornthwaite, Wellman, 1997); adolescent social networks (Bryant, Sanders-Jackson, & Smallwood, 2006); dynamics (Golbeck, 2007); uses and gratifications (Bumgarner, 2007) and civic discourse (Byrne, 2007). None of these articles focuses on the issue of social networks and education. Today, the impact of social networks on education comes from the use of social networks in popular culture.

Lenart (2009) states that 35 percent of American adults have social networking profiles and the number jumps to 65 percent for American teens. She states: "Overall, personal use of social networks seems to be more prevalent than professional use of networks, both in the orientation of the networks that adults choose to use as well as the reasons they give for using the applications" (p. 1). What the RIT researchers learned in their National Science Foundation Research (2007) on social networks is students now compare online course systems to their social networks and they want online courseware to have some of the features of personal social networking. "What makes social networking sites unique is not that they allow individuals to meet strangers, but rather they enable users to articulate and make visible their social networks" (boyd & Ellison, 2008, p. 211). One of the issues is that classroom relationships tend to end when the class is over. Students want to be able to connect with their friends and keep the connections after the course is done.

One social network space where this can happen is Second Life. "*Second Life* is populated by avatars; virtual representation of *SL* members. The SL world also contains a great variety of objects" (Rymaszewski, et al., 2007). SL residents created the objects and they range from houses to a cup of coffee. Much has been written about SL and education (Bugeja, 2005; Grassian & Trueman, 2006; Jennings & Collins, 2008; Kelton, 2007; and The New Media Consortium, 2007). A number of universities have purchased land in Second Life and set-up virtual classrooms with spaces for meetings and lectures. "Beyond gamers and social networkers, there is a large and growing educational community involved and active in Second Life" (Kelton, 2007, p. X). A student has to create an avatar and Second Life name to become part of the educational SL community. Once the avatar is created it can be used for schoolwork and play. To connect with people in Second Life you need to know the other person's virtual name.

Universities, including the Rochester Institute of Technology, have taught full and blended (face-to-face and online) courses in the virtual environment of Second Life. In the Spring 2007 Survey on Second Life conducted by the New Media Consortium, 43 percent of the respondents had taken a class in SL and 29 percent had taught a class in SL. Additionally, respondents had also held virtual office hours, mentored student research projects, hosted student services and supported activities, and collaborated with local/regional partners in Second Life. Because Second Life avatars provide a stronger sense of presence than other online tools, it is an environment that supports many different educational activities and it provides a space for people to maintain continued relationships.

Another social networking environment where people can continue relationships is YouTube. Garfield (2006) describes YouTube: "When you put together a million humans, a million camcorders, and a million computers, what you get is YouTube" (p. 224). YouTube enables people to share their own videos with millions of people around the world. The videos are also embedded into other social networking sites, such as MySpace and Facebook. "YouTube began as a video sharing platform, but it also offers users a personal profile page—which You Tube calls a 'channel page'—and enables 'friending'" (Lange, 2007, p.

362) Popular articles (Garfield, 2006; McGrath, 2006; Seelye, 2007) and academic papers (Lange, 2007) have been published about YouTube. Lange (2007) generally describes YouTube, and focuses on issues of technical and symbolic mechanisms for the delineation of different social networks. She states, "Beyond profile-based friendship connections, the analysis showed how video sharing can become an important way for participants to negotiate membership in social networks" (p. 376).

In addition to friendships, YouTube is a space where "the hitherto futile aspirations of the everyman to break out of his lonely anonymous life of quiet desperation, to step in front of the whole world and be somebody" (Garfield, 2006, p. 224). McGrath (2006) describes how Stevie Ryan became an alternate-reality star through segments that she recorded for YouTube, using the name Little Loca. Little Loca is a composite character who is part tough-talking, and strong willed, similar to *cholas* [spunking getto kids] that Ryan used to admire in her home town. Shortly after previewing the videos on YouTube the videos became her full time pursuit. Stardom on YouTube can be obtained by young people wanting to become actresses or seventy-nine-year-old men addicted to watching the videos.

A man named Peter, started to post his own videos, which came to the attention of YouTube's product management department. They were selected to be on the top featured list. From his chair in the English countryside, Peter now has numerous followers from around the world. Users create their own videos to aspire toward stardom or just dabble at making computer-based movies._Moreover, some people are making a living developing "how to" videos and other types of popular programming. YouTube shares the advertising revenue with these users.

User-Generated Content and Literacy

YouTube brings up the issue of User-Generated Content and new types of literacy skills. A key difference between older mass media, such as television, newspapers, and magazines, is the interactive nature of the Internet and the ability for individuals to create their own content. Each individual user can contribute to the content available on the Web. In 2004, the Pew Internet & American Life Project began researching content creation online. They "found that more than 53 million American adults have used the Internet to publish their thoughts, respond to others, post pictures, share files and otherwise contribute to the explosion of content available online" (Lenhart, Horrigan & Fallows, 2004, p. 2). A year later, Pew Internet researchers discovered that "57 percent of online teens created content for the Internet" (Lenhart & Madden, 2005, p. 2). The types of activities teens reported were creating blogs, a personal webpage, sharing original artwork and photographs, creating videos, and remixing content they find online into a new creation. These types of activities lead to new types of literacy skills where students express themselves through multimedia creations called remix (see chapter 10).

In 1998, Cynthia Selfe attempted to make academics aware of changing literacy skills in her keynote address to the National Council of Teachers of English. She stated, "technological literacy—meaning computer skills and the ability to use computers and other technology to improve learning, productivity, and performance—has become as fundamental to a person's ability to navigate through society as traditional skills like reading, writing and arithmetic" (Selfe, 1998. p. 1). Today, students are using multimedia skills in their personal lives to create content for the Internet. It makes sense for educators to redirect these skills for educational purposes. Social networking can help to bridge the gap between popular culture and learning. Using social networking tools, content created by students can be shared with others.

Constructivist Learning

Sharing content fits into the concept of constructionist learning. "Constructivist learning occurs when learners actively construct meaningful mental representations from presented information" (Mayer, Moreno, Boire, & Vagge, 1999, p.638). Numerous articles have been written about constructivist learning, including: Cheung, 2006; Hale, 1985; Irwin, 1983; Mayer, et al, 1999; Neo, 2007. The earlier two articles discuss theoretical communication issues, while the three later articles focus on classroom learning. Hale (1985) identifies four basic assumptions associated with the constructivist perspective:

1. humans are active perceivers and interpreters of their environment; (p. 524)
2. through perception and interpretation, individuals create their own concepts of reality; (p. 526)
3. through communication, individuals attempt to create a shared concept of reality; (p. 527)
4. competent communication is dependent on understanding how others define their realities. (p. 527)

The purpose of Hale's research was focused on the discovery of the relationship between interpretations (meanings) and communication. Meaning making is an issue for understanding visual media, such as YouTube videos and remixed images. In contrast to written language, visual media does not have a dictionary to understand symbols and images. However, many people understand the nonverbal meaning or body language, which create social images, without formally being taught these skills.

Social images are the central idea behind an article written by Irwin (1983). Irwin believes that in interpersonal communication specifically social situations involving strangers, the perception that each party has of the other based on verbal and nonverbal behavior is a constructed "image." Constructed images lead to certain human behaviors. It should be noted that the lack or visual social images can also influence behavior, for example there is a problem with misbehavior on the Internet because people don't see the other person. People are separated from their words. Conversely, in social environments, such as Second Life, constructed images play an important role in creating a stronger sense of presence between participants.

Multimedia images are the subject of Mayer et al.'s (1999) article. Their research tested different learning styles and they found that multimedia presentations are the most effective. However, there needs to be a balance between the visuals and audio in a given project. Too many visuals or too many words can make it more difficult for students to remember the information being presented. Similarly, Neo (2007) studied the multimedia learning process and created the *Multimedia Development Process (MDP)*. The six steps in the process are:

1. planning the application,
2. acquiring the resources,
3. converting the media elements to digital,
4. editing or creating the media,
5. multimedia authoring, and
6. packaging for delivery. (Neo, 2007, p. 153)

This process is for creating a multimedia project. In education, planning the constructivist activities is always important. However, social media is available and easy to acquire and social media is already digital. Participation is required and individuals need to create content. In Second Life, the environment has already been developed. Students need to only set-up an avatar to participate. The MDP could be used as a guideline for making a YouTube video to distribute on social networks.

Additionally, social networks and the Social Networking Classroom support the idea of constructivist learning. Students can become more active in the learning process by developing user content. These can be individual or group projects and be created by students face-to-face or online. Because a sense of presence is created in online environments, people can work together as if they were face-to-face.

However, the challenges of constructivist learning revolve around the changing of the classroom from a teacher-center space to a learning-centered place (see chapter 3). Hanlin-Rowney, et al. (2006) "We worked with the challenges of moving from colearners to cofacilitators of a collaborative inquiry" (p. 331) This research gave the researchers an experience of embodied knowing. "[The researchers] experienced what it is like to engage a question using all of our faculties: emotional, creative, rational, transpersonal, and practical, among others" (p. 330). Due to the change in the structure of learning, trust also became an issue for the class of graduate students in the study. Trust is an issue that will be covered in chapter 9. Trust, co-learning, and collaborative inquiry are all aspects of constructivist learning, which can make education more related to the real world.

Summary

Computer-mediated communication has a number of features that contribute to the popularity and widespread use of social networking. Para-social relationships, first observed in television usage, explain how people form relationships through media. This idea combined with the personal usage of computers enables people to communicate with each other as if they were meeting face-to-face. Additionally, people treat computer as if they were other people, not machines. As a result, online communication remotely connects people together, while people act as if they were co-present. Moreover, online communication creates a sense of presence, which adds to the personal nature of the medium. People feel as if they are meeting with other people in some type of place.

The networking aspect of social media enables people to form interpersonal relationships, participate in online coursework, and organize strangers, which we have seen happen in the Middle East. Social networking tools can be used to organize mobs of people into political action. Presidential elections in the United States demonstrate the power of these tools. The same type of tools can be used to organize online classrooms. Using Second Life and social networking, the classroom can be adapted into the Social Networking Classroom. The classroom becomes an environment where the space opens up to industry experts, user-generated activities, and constructivist learning.

Constructivist learning is the pedagogy that works with social media. The students must take responsibility for learning by participating in classroom activities. For example, students can make their own YouTube videos that are shared over the Internet. Original content creation is a key aspect of social networking. Harnessing this idea with the tools incorporated into social media, can transform education into a co-operative learning experience for both students and teachers.

Note

1. Research reported in this book was sponsored in part by the National Science Foundation grant #0633401 Theoretical and Applied Approaches to Teaching Social Computing in STEM Education.

Chapter Two

Self-Identity and Awareness

with Lyle Wetsch and Neil Hair

Social networks, online learning systems, and virtual Worlds are online media environments. These virtual spaces enable people to present themselves to others in a mediated form. Online environments simulate face-to-face interaction and theories developed prior to the Internet can be used to explain how people present themselves in virtual space. For instance, Goffman's (1959,1974) dramatist view is one perspective that applies today. This chapter combines student interviews with theory to explore how avatars represent the self. To establish a presence online, identity, personal branding, and how you represent yourself on the Internet are important. Self-identity is the first step in representation on social networks and in online learning systems.

Early theories on computer-mediated communication were pessimistic about how people would use these tools to form relationships. Many of the early researchers in the 1970s and 1980s focused their research on the question: "How do technologies influence communication?" The answer was the cues-filtered-out theory, which argued that computer-mediated communication had low social presence because the prominent social cues found in face-to-face communication were missing (see Barnes 2003). Due to the low social cues, individuals would find it difficult to form relationships. However, as people used computers to communicate, they found new ways to enhance the communication, such as emoticons. Eventually, avatars were designed by software developers to create new tools to aid the online communication process.

Avatars are used to represent the individual in Second Life. Avatars are a "character that interacts in a 3D virtual environment" (Kelton, 2007, p. 2). Second Life was inspired by Neil Stephenson's description of the Metaverse in the science fiction novel *Snow Crash.* The Metaverse is a computer-mediated reality in which people interact through avatars, visual representations of self. Linden Labs released the Second Life software program in 2003. It was designed to be a virtual world in which everything could be digitized (Jennings & Collins, 2008). The world is virtually designed and constructed by the users themselves. Moreover, Second Life has its own currency: the Linden dollar. Linden dollars can be exchanged for real-life dollars and they buy objects in Second Life. Most of the objects in Second Life are created or built from 3D geometric shapes called prims. Prims can be transformed into virtually any shape, such as houses, clothing, guitars, and cars. A number of educational institutions have built virtual campuses in Second Life by using prims (Gronstedt, 2007).

With the introduction of virtual worlds into computer-mediated communication, individuals can now develop a sense of self through the use of avatars. These visual representations of self provide a new method for individuals to interact on the Internet. How self is manifest by new entrants into a virtual world is described through the use of quotes from blog entries and interviews of undergraduate business students from two mid-sized North American Universities. The students were enrolled in an Internet marketing course and an Internet advertising course, where elements and class assignments were completed, organized or focused on the virtual world Second Life.

Interaction Mechanisms and Self

Virtual worlds create the sense of being face-to-face because we see visual representations of others that mimic real world interactions. Often, avatars are created to be idealized versions of the individual. Avatars can be human or any other type of creature. Second Life provides an avatar library that contains a body and outfits, which can be customized for hair, eye colors and shape of face. Clothes can be purchased from online vendors that have used prim's to make objects for sale. Avatars can be based on real-life, movies, comic strips, or furry animals. A student exploring Second Life stated:

> I also realized that there was a way to cutomize[1] your avatar, I suspected there was but was unsure of how to do it. So going in world, my first goal is to customize my avatar, I wan't to make it look like me. I am amazed at how much detail there is. Every single piece of the body. It's not just eye color and pupil size but upper corner curls and lower corner curls. This is a saturday night and three hours after going in world my friends are wondering what I am doing at home. I am still working on my avatar and he honestly looks nothing like me, but I must have done okay because I'm pretty sure I was virtually hit on and I also think I like it. (Student, Internet Marketing Class)

Another student stated:

> Talking to people thus far has been fun. I am not surprised in the least that there are some individuals who grace me with comments such as "you're hot" etc. Of course I am, my avatar is 6'1" with the body of Claudia Schiffer, way to be original dude. Just about every female I've seen so far has been either of supermodel proportions or an animal with supermodel proportions. (student, Internet marketing class)

Throughout history, physical proximity has been an important aspect of human communication and face-to-face interaction and proximity has influenced theories about identity formation. However, now we can apply these theories to the virtual world because, as stated above, the virtual world mimics the real world. In virtual environments, people interact in a simulated face-to-face situation that presents a sense of self.

During the first half of the twentieth century, George Herbert Mead (1932, 1934) formulated his theory about how the self develops. In the first stage of self-development, individuals internalize objects. An individual consciously realizes there is a relationship between holding an object and the effort of pressure in the action of holding. When the individual internalizes the physical object with the act of holding, the object becomes part of the individual's inner experience. In the next stage, transference occurs when the individual realizes that he or she is also an object that exists with other objects in an environment. As an individual becomes self-aware, he or she is simultaneously becoming aware of others. Similarly, we are aware of other people interacting with us in virtual worlds.

Mead argued that the self arises through social interactions with objects and other people. Mead applied a pragmatist perspective to social behavior. In American scholarship, the pragmatist philosophy can be found in the writings of Dewey (1920/1948) and Peirce (1998), who argue that human social behavior is based on problem-solving adaption to the physical environment. In contrast to animals that instinctively adapt to their environments, human beings understand their environment consciously and through their communication with one another. Humans use their senses to understand the world and social behavior has a symbolic character. For instance, people understand their world through language, visual symbols, and gestures. Thus, avatars would be considered a form of visual communication that people use to understand their phenomenal world—or in this case the virtual one.

Symbolic Interactionism

This American pragmatic approach to philosophy was later known as symbolic interactionism. Symbolic interactionists contend that the formation of social worlds involves inter-communicative symbolic interaction. In addition to exploring how individuals create their social worlds, symbolic interactionism has been used to explain the human communication process. According to Julia Wood (1995), symbolic interaction approaches to communication, examine the shared phenomenal world of the participants involved in the communication exchange. In the symbolic interaction model, communicators interpret messages based on their individual phenomenal worlds. "To the extent that these worlds overlap (that is dual perspective), [communicators] will have relatively similar understandings and meanings" (Wood, 1995, p. 27). The ability to conceptualize the self with others in social settings is key to identity formation and effective interpersonal communication on and offline.

Since the time Mead developed his theory, communication technologies have gone through a radical transformation. Many individuals now interact with each other through mediated rather than face-to-face environments. In virtual worlds, students can type or use a microphone to communicate. The choice of technological intermediary may influence the rules of interaction and how the object of the interaction is perceived. This can be seen in the following student quote:

> I know that you can activate the microphone in order to use your voice when speaking to others in Second Life, but for the present I would feel uncomfortable doing so. It would feel too personal at this time. It's cool, but at the same time a little scary when you realize that every Avatar in Second Life actually is a real human being. I think I'll use the chat application for now to dehumanize the other." (Student, Internet Marketing Class)

In cyberspace and real space, people understand the other person through the symbolic interaction of language. Building on the ideas of symbolic interactionists, media scholars, such as Paul Levinson (1997), Joshua Meyrowitz (1986), Neil Postman (1992), and Lance Strate (1996), have studied media environments. Viewing media as environments rather than communication technologies attempts to make the influence of media structures more explicit. This is an ecological view that considers how communication media influence human perception, understanding, feeling, and value. "The shift from medium as message to media as environment and ecology constitutes both a clarification and a correction of the perspective by changing the focus from the individual medium to the collective media environment" (Barnes & Strate, 1996, p. 183). For instance, Giese (1998) argues that in a sense, "the Internet is more a cultural phenomena than a technological one" (p. 2). Consider the following two student testimonials. They are describing a media environment rather than a technology.

> After leaving the party after a few minutes, myself and (name removed) felt like we were leaving a real party early and that we were missing out on the fun.
>
> I began to make an emotional connection between SL and reality: loneliness. While the sites suggested were entertaining (particularly skiing at the Weather Network) I am beginning to become frustrated with my lack of interactions with others. This also opens the door to allow me to think that in a similar way, people playing SL must feel other emotions in this virtual world: friendship? love? sadness? distress? (student, Internet marketing class)

Electronic Environments

Virtual worlds create a new type of social environment in which people can meet and interact. Prior to the introduction of the Internet, Meyrowitz (1985) argued that the arrival of electronic media dramatically changed social interaction. Electronic media, including the telephone, radio, and television, enable people to communicate across geographic distances, which create "no sense of place." He states: "Before electronic media, there was ample reason to overlook the difference between physical places and social situations. Places defined most social information-systems" (p. 116). Travel time was required to move from one place-situation to another. As a result, communication and transportation where associated with each other.

However, this changed with the advent of electronic media, which enable individuals in New York to simultaneously communicate with people in Los Angeles. According to Meyrowitz (1986), electronic messages "do not make social entrances; they steal into places like thieves in the night. . . . Once a telephone, radio, or television is in the home, spatial isolation and guarding of entrances have no effect on information flow" (p. 117). These messages come directly into the home and they alter our social situations. As described in chapter 1, Horton and Wohl (1956) suggested that people develop a special relationship with mass media performers, which creates the illusion of face-to-face interaction. They described this relationship as a para-social interaction because television is a mediated experience that psychologically feels as if it is a face-to-face interaction. Similarly, virtual worlds create a place where people connect and make friends. Students in the virtual class describe their feelings of friendship:

> I have finally made some friends! One day I was searching around fashion sites and shops they have in SL. I stumbled upon a club. There was only one female avatar there . . . It was simple conversation such as you would

> have with a friend if you were just hanging out and chatting. This made me realize that these people aren't discussing their real lives in SL but their fabricated ones.
>
> My new friends and experience shed some new light on my views of SL. Today when I logged on, one of my new friends IM'ed me and invited me to go to a store shopping with them. Having someone else to hang out with in SL is fun. (Student, Internet Marketing Class)

A difference between building a relationship with a performer and developing one over the Internet is the difference between fantasy and reality. Performers are playing roles and people have to fanaticize the relationship. On the Internet we meet real people and interact with a person, not an actor. With the widespread use of sites, such as Match.com or E-Harmony, people are using electronic media to form real relationships.

Goffman and Avatars

Meyrowitz (1986) bases his arguments about the impact of electronic media on social settings by utilizing the situationist research of the sociologist Erving Goffman (1959, 1974). Situationists contend that social behavior and communication is shaped and adjusted depending upon the socially defined circumstances in which people interact. Moreover, Goffman (1959) describes social situations by using a drama metaphor, which breaks social behaviors into two broad categories called back region (backstage) and front region (on stage). When people are on stage, they are generally polite and respectful. In contrast, people in backstage settings will complain and criticize others. While on stage, people communicate two types of information: information is deliberately communicated through language and information is inadvertently expressed through gesture, tone, and appearance.

Goffman (1959) states: "the expressiveness of the individual (and therefore his capacity to give impressions) appears to involve two radically different kinds of sign activity: the expression that he gives, and expression that he gives off" (p. 2). Expression is given through the use of verbal symbols or their known substitutes that communicate information, such as avatars. Expression is given off by a wide range of nonverbal actions that others can treat as symptomatic of the person, including posture and facial expressions. Moreover, there is an expectation that these nonverbal actions were performed for reasons other than the information being conveyed, such as nervous gestures or habits. Goffman's work is interested in social order and interaction. In virtual worlds, bad spelling and poor grammar are expressions that people give off. For example, spam messages are often recognized because they inadvertently contain misspelled words. In contrast, students are expressive by deliberately spending a tremendous amount of time designing their avatars to "give off" a good appearance.

> First off, I took the opportunity to play around with the appearance of my avatar which was definately a fun feature; I was surprised by the amount of detail that I was able to change on my avatar. (student, Internet marketing class)

> So I went into Appearances . . . I learned how to change my clothes (chose the NightLife costume . . . interesting Plummers Butt! haha) and watched a seemingly useless video about changing clothes . . . and I got "hit on" by a male avatar who appeared to like my new outfit . . . interesting! (student, Internet marketing class)

The dramatist metaphor combined with the idea that expressiveness involves two different types of symbolic activity, has important implications for the presentation of self in social settings. First, people want to create socially meaningful impressions when they present themselves to others. As a result, they consciously perform social roles. Second, in face-to-face encounters, information about the self is communicated through both intentional information sharing and involuntary actions. Facial expression, gesture, body movement, and costume are crucial to the development of how we present ourselves. Finally, in non-mediated contexts, presenting oneself to others involves both the use of language and a broad range of nonverbal cues.

However, when messages are exchanged in mediated environments, the range of symbolic information narrows; for instance, telephones only communicate language, tone of voice, and auditory cues. Physical appearance, facial expressions, and body gestures are missing from the virtual exchange. A limitation of the virtual world technology is the body gestures of avatars are programmed by the virtual world. The people communicating the message do not always control these gestures. Thus, the building of self-identity is only partially in the control of the people who communicate in a virtual world.

Avatars are also used on commercial shopping sites. Attractive-looking avatars can persuade people and expert shoppers are even more persuaded by expert avatars (Holzwarth, Janiszewski, & Neumann, 2006). In general, avatars positively affect an online shopping experience. Although, these avatars may be software programs, they do have a positive influence on shoppers, just like an actual person.

Self-Identity

Theories about self-identity can be placed in two large categories. The first views the individual as having an integrated or self-actualized identity. Howard Gardner

(1983) describes this integrated view as: "A self that is highly developed and fully differentiated from others . . . individuals who appear to have understood much about themselves and about their societies and who have come to terms successfully with the frailties of the human condition" (p. 252).

In contrast to the idea of an integrated self, is the view that an individual is comprised of a set of selves. "Rather than a central 'core self' which organizes one's thoughts, behavior, and goals, the person is better thought of as a collection of relatively diverse masks, none of which takes precedence over the others, and each of which is simply called into service as needed" (p. 252). Because physical presence is separated from the communication process, Internet communication tends to foster the second notion of a set of selves. People can present themselves in a variety of different ways through textual correspondence and assume any number of identities. This is especially true about the idealized avatar. Students want to look good.

> Basically they say how there are not that many studies done since second life only opened in 2003 but there have been a few where the results stated that when people have more attractive/taller avatars this gives them more confidence in the real world..I know my avatar looks like she didn't get hit with the ugly stick but instead the whole tree and because of that I really don't like going and talking to people in the Second Life worlds. (student, Internet marketing class)

Presently, scholars have conflicting opinions about the influence of the Internet on self-identity. When examining the impact of the Internet on identity formation, a central issue is the replacement of physical presence with textual or symbolic representations of self. Internet environments create new methods of interaction that are no longer grounded in a shared physical reality. As a result, each communicator has an opportunity to create his or her own idealized self that presents a new version of the individual to others.

> I spent alot of time editing my characters apperence, I tried to make it somewhat resemble myself. I was really excited that we got to edit the make up and hair and clothes . . . I found it alot of fun. Everytime I log on I change my appearence a little. At first I made my own outfit and then I teleported around to different places where you can get some free clothing. (student, Internet marketing class)

> I will admit that it was kind of fun being able to personalize my avatar. I think it's great that the user is able to create an avatar that reflects what they want. It really gives a user the ability to look how they aspire to look, or to just be themselves. I suppose for some people it can be a way to be something they are not, if that's what they choose. (student, Internet marketing class)

Image Management

Students view Second Life to be a new type of media environment that provides similar social interactions as face-to-to face experiences. Scholars can review theories of face-to-face self-development and apply them to virtual worlds. Because people are treating virtual worlds in the same way they are treating the real world. Thus, virtual worlds can have an impact on identity formation. People need to manage the image they present in online spaces.

Impression management has been researched by Patrick O'Sullivan (2000). He states: "the diffusion of newer technologies, such as electronic mail, answering machines, and videoconferencing, into social uses supplements 'old' technologies, such as the telephone and letters, to provide people an increasingly broad array of channel options for conducting their interactions" (p. 407). However, the type of channel that we use to communicate influences the communication process. For instance, leaner channels (electronic mail, letters and chat) can be used in ways to obscure the unattractive qualities of a person. Digital representations of self can be edited and modulated to represent a person in a positive way. Physical and personality deficits can be edited out of texts, such as shyness. Teachers will find that one or two students in a class that never speak in public will be active in online discussions. Conversely, students who are active in a face-to-face setting may be reserved online. Providing different communication options for students will enable more students to participate in class discussions.

O'Sullivan (2000) discussed three primary factors guiding channel preferences when communicating with others: interactional controls, symbolism, and social skill. Interactional control involves the characteristics of the channel and how the channel is used to influence the communication exchange. For instance, when people are delivering bad news, they will use e-mail because they are not exposed to the emotional reaction of the other. Similarly, people have been known to break-off relationships through electronic mail for the same reason. According to McLuhan (1964), channels both have a symbolic message context and a symbolic meaning that is embodied by the medium. For example, while some people will break-up using e-mail, others think that the channel is too impersonal for this type of message. Some channels are viewed as appropriate or inappropriate for certain types of exchanges. Social skills contain the ability to maintain competent social interactions, along with the technical skills needed to use the channel. For instance, to use e-mail, a person must know how to write a language, type, and use a computer.

Theories about image management can help to explain how people present themselves online. First, the question "How do technologies influence communication?" is changed to "How do people use communication technologies." The simple answer is that they use them to connect with other people. The killer application on the Internet is e-mail, it is a computer program that is necessary and desirable for Internet usage. In the beginning of the Internet, people first started to identify themselves through e-mail addresses and signature lines.

With e-mail addresses, there can be a real world mapping of the user name to an actual person, for example JohnSmith at Wired.com. From this address, a name and organization can be identified. It is assumed that John Smith works for *Wired Magazine*. The name of the person and domain name are identity markers. The domain provides the account and "yields contextual cues about the writer—and about the reliability of the [message]" (Donath, 1999, p. 35). The contents of a posting will present more identity information about the person than the e-mail address. The content "provides a chance to get a sense of the writer's 'voice' and to see how he or she interacts with others in the online social environment" (p, 38).

Similar to e-mail addresses, the signature line at the end of an e-mail messages are deliberate identity signals. "Signatures can be used to anchor the virtual persona to the real-world person" (Donath, 1999, p. 40). Signature lines can show that you are a professional, similar to a business card, and not a teenager playing around on the Internet. Signature lines are in the total control of the user and allow the user to help define his or her identity. With the widespread use of the Internet for business and social purposes, it is advisable for individuals to manage their own identity or personal brand on the Internet.

Personal Branding

On the Internet, personal branding is the management of one's online image. Similar to branding a product or service, people can use marketing-like techniques to brand their own identity on the Internet. As a result, in the digital age, identity formation takes on the character of personal branding. A number of tactics were being pursued that the researchers have noted over the past few years, and these include personal websites, the use of social networks, online diaries or blogs, search engine representation, avatars, representation on commercial sites, and use of e-mail.

In social networks, Larson (2008) discovered that individuals brand themselves through a discourse of sincerity. Larson conducted an ethnographic study on a Danish social network called Arto and found that the participants did not like Fakers, people who posted fake profiles on the site. In contrast, the users liked sincerity and developed an identity by having friends post testimonials about an individual. These personal testimonials from friends added to the credibility of the individual. The personal branding and identity formation "are continuously constructed through their network and in different situations—they basically exist and become real through their network and those specific situations" (p. 212). In essence, the personal branding of the individual comes alive through the network connections and types of situations they present themselves in. Another type of presentational situation is the development of a personal website.

Personal Websites

Perhaps the most popular strategy available to users is the construction of a personal website. A website provides the user complete control over their identity presented online. Research on self and the World Wide Web include works by Nicola Doring (2002), Girish Gulati (2004), Hugh Miller and Jill Arnold (2003), Hope Jensen Schau and Mary Gilly (2003), Simine Vazire and Sammuel Gosling (2004), and Eleanor Wynn and James Katz (1997). Recently, there appears to have been a move away from html-style software packages and hand coded script for creating websites using user-friendly web based software programs. Programs, such as Word Press, enable users to easily create and edit blogs. The personal website can also be established in social communities, such as Facebook and MySpace. Similar to Word Press, Facebook and MySpace pages can be designed with a minimum of effort. Increasingly, people are representing themselves across multiple social network platforms where social circles are not necessarily exclusive to one particular platform or another. Some social networking sites are primarily social, while others are more business oriented, for instance, LinkedIn. Consequently, people are using more than one social networking site to present themselves online, one site for business and the other for pleasure.

The Social Network

A popular method for personally branding oneself electronically is the social network, discussed above (see Grossman, 2006/2007). People tend to have perceptions about favorability and or exclusivity toward particular platforms which can be explained through the popularity of a small number of social networking programs, such as MySpace or Facebook (Case, 2007). The social networking site in which one chooses to be a part of also speaks toward the type of digital citizen a person presents themselves to be. Facebook is based on a college metaphor, LinkedIn with that of working professionals, and MySpace started with musicians and then opened up to become a broader network representing a wider society. For instance, at one point in time, Facebook was college-aged students and teenagers used MySpace.

It is generally seen as acceptable to promote oneself in a social network—indeed this is one of the primary purposes for engaging with a social network in the first place. Self-promotion is also seen as a method of branding an individual, and this is very similar to marketing concepts. Often people use their pictures like a corporate logo. Another way to market in social networks is to leave comments on other people's pages. What one says to others is as important a reflection on one's brand as what one says about oneself in one's own space. One way to have one's own space is to start a blog, which enables an individual to present his or her own opinions and personal experiences.

Online Diary/Blogs

The year 2006, started the widespread use of consumer blogging. Blogging is an active method for promoting or branding oneself online (Hoppough, 2006). Bloggers build social communities where individuals regularly contribute to others as a means of increasing awareness and generating content. The spreading of your name through blogging is a way to gain identity recognition on the Internet (Melillo, 2007). For instance, the founder of the Lab for Social Computing at RIT has a blog called *mamamusings: elizabeth lane lawley's thoughts on technology, academia, family, and tangential topics*. The blog helps to build Elizabeth's reputation on the Internet as a specialist in social networking. However, blogs can also hurt the reputation of individuals and products. One such example was Nintendo's release of the new gaming platform the Wii. Within weeks of its launch blogs began to report problems with the hand held controllers causing physical damage to consumers (Melillo, 2007).

As more user-friendly web based software programs become available (such as Word Press), these programs enable users to easily create and edit blogs. "People from all over the world, all walks of life, or all faiths and backgrounds had recorded their most intimate thoughts and experiences in which they invite the rest of the world to view them (Wojtowicz, 2005, p. xxi). The following is a sample of a personal blog entry:

> We can only live life well to our own standards, with so many changes in life, so many conflicts, it is rather difficult to live with a stern set of ideals, and in which case is that really living? Do humans not desire freedom above all else? Do they not claim life is worthless without it? When living by these codes, you are restraining yourself, hindering your freedom, hence how can you truly live? (Davidmaski, January 28, 2005 @ 6:45 pm; cited in Wojtowicz, 2005, p. 72)

People will share their philosophical thoughts and recipes through blogs. Personal blogs are as varied as the people who create them. Blogs enable individual people to truly represent themselves online. Popular blogs are easily found through search engines. For example, when you type "Liz" into a search engine, the top spot can be mamamusing by Liz Lawley or Liz Claiborne's website. Now with the widespread use of YouTube videos Liz Taylor is also competing for the number one position. Search engine recognition is another way to personally brand someone.

Search Engine Representation

Search engine representation is another form of personal branding. For example, it has become popular for individuals to engage in the popular phenomena known as 'Googling oneself' or ego surfing. Where an individual's online representation (be it a blog or personal website) is categorized on search engines, it demonstrates that an individual has a presence on the Internet. "These days, it is rare for someone not to appear by name somewhere on the web, but appearance on a search engine seems to put a person on the global stage" (Halavais, 2009, p. 140). Where one's brand stands with regard to search engines is therefore critical. Managing your placement in Google searches is a form of image management and some individuals have paid to get their name at the top of the list. For example, Susan B. Barnes the freelance and magazine writer manages to get her name at the top of the Google and Yahoo searches. Although many of the sites in which my name is listed are heavily trafficked, the freelance writer needs to be on top because the website is her business tool.

In addition to business marketing, one's reputation in search engines is also important to those wishing to positively brand themselves online. Employers will google individual job applicants to find information about the candidate. Facebook pages that contain drunken party pictures or blogs with a strange sense of humor will turn-off future employers (see Barnes, 2006). What others say about oneself is also an important reflection of one's personal brand and image management on the Internet. Increasingly, people will monitor search engines to ensure consistency in their brand image. Companies have emerged that can manage an individual's personal branding. In many ways, our name listed in Google is out of our control. In face-to-face and computer-mediated conversations people gradually reveal themselves to others. "Search engines change those [communication] rituals, providing a way of finding out about someone without engaging in the ritual dance of conversation" (Halavais, 2009, p. 141). Thus, we do not have total control of our personal branding online. One method that enables an individual to control their impression management is the avatar, which represents a person online.

Avatars

Given the popularity of three-dimensional virtual worlds, an important key to personal branding is the avatar that one creates. Avatars are created in virtual worlds, such as Second Life and *World of Warcraft*, Increasingly the Web is becoming more visual with YouTube videos, flicker, visual blogs, Facebook, and the easy exchange of pictures through e-mail. Currently, people appear to be divided on the nature of their pictorial representation, some people will use real pictures, or images of other items, such as cartoon characters. For instance, "the vast majority of [Second Life] citizens opt to stay human in Second Life. But, some choose avatars based on fictional characters from real-life movies, comic strips, or books" (Rymaszewski, 2007, p. 12). The nature of an avatar says a great deal about one's depiction of self, whether it is choosing your favorite character or creating an avatar that actually resembles an individual.

Avatars are a branding strategy that allows an individual to totally control the way they are represented online. Unlike search engine representation, users decide how they want to be seen by others. Another personal branding strategy is the way in which an individualis represented on commercial Web sites.

Representation On Commercial Sites

Identity can also be established on commercial sites. For instance, the popularity of shopping online has caused some vendors to create the "personal wish list," which can be found on Amazon and other online stores. Individuals should also be mindful of the image they portray in the goods and services that they covet. Others can see this information and form an opinion about the shopper. Similarly, the messages people leave about their consumption habits of goods and services also needs examining. One increasingly popular feature of e-retail sites is the ability to leave comments on their consumption experience. This can present a great deal about one's personal brand.

The rise of Internet television has also influenced personal branding strategy. YouTube is an example of a site that has become extremely popular in the past few years (see Garfield, 2006). What an individual watches on these sites can become known to other by the comments or the ratings one confers about content in on these sites. What you say on the Internet can tell others a great deal about an individual's personal brand and the ability to represent oneself. People should be aware of everything that they post on the Internet.

Use of E-mail

New technology, such as social networking, has created new opportunities to brand oneself online. However, e-mail still represents one of the key vehicles for presenting and managing one's identity. As previously discussed, the e-mail address says a great deal about an individual's identity. The content of e-mail messages also provides an individual the opportunity to express more of their personality. E-mail messages can be carefully crafted and edited to show the positive aspects of an individual. However, some people find it easier to use Facebook for communication with friends rather than e-mail because in Facebook you don't have to remember an e-mail address. As a result, Facebook has replace e-mail as a method for keeping in contact with friends and family.

Summary

From avatars to e-mail, people can represent themselves in a number of symbolic forms, including words, photos, visual avatars, and personal blogs. All of these can be used in education to represent an individual. Some of the representations are in our total control, for instance, the e-mail messages that we write, while others are in the control of software programs, such as search engines. The idea of personal branding is trying to manage an individual's identity and representation on the Internet.

Theories of identity management (O'Sullivan, 2000) and theories developed from face-to-face communication can be applied to computer-mediated communication. For example, Mead's (1932, 1934) ideas on the formation of self can be applied to the awareness of others on the Internet. Goffman's (1959, 1974) concepts of front and back stage behavior help to describe different styles of communication and how one can give and give-off information about the self.

Additionally, media environments, such as the Internet, can be compared to face-to-face contexts. We symbolically interact with others online in similar ways as we interact in-person. But, in a mediated environment, people need to be aware of the limitations and symbolic influences of the software being used in the communication exchange.

Note

1. Spelling and grammatical errors are retained from the original student blog entries within all quotes

Chapter Three

Space Versus Place

with Christopher Egert

Individuals perceive each other on the Internet. But, why do we say that we are chatting and not writing online? This terminology probably occurs because we perceive ourselves to be in some kind of a perceptual space when we "talk" to others. Beginning with the introduction of personal computers and moving into virtual reality, this chapter discusses how people relate to their computers and online environments. Using concepts of cyberspace, space and place, it explains how spatial concepts relate to social networks and computer-mediated communication. Our concepts of space influence how we perceive communication in social networks and online learning systems. However, a larger question about space in contemporary culture is whether or not any space is unmediated?

Space has more physicality and space is more social. In the previous chapter, Meyrowitz stated: "Before electronic media, there was ample reason to overlook the difference between physical places and social situations. Places defined most social information-systems" (p. 116). Travel time was required to move from one place-situation to another. As a result, communication and transportation were concepts that used to be associated with each other). However, with the invention of the telegraph space no longer was a central condition for communication to occur. People no longer had to be face-to-face or use the Pony Express to communicate.

Changing concepts of space can be analyzed by using the media ecology perspective. A key media ecological concept revolves around the conditions of attendance in the communication process. A central question for conditions of attendance is: where do people have to be in space to engage in the communication process? Prior to the telegraph, people needed to be co-present for communication to occur. After the invention of the telegraph, telegraph operators in

New York City could get messages from London through a chain of operators located in various positions on the east coast of Canada and the United States. Thus, physical proximity was no longer a requirement for communication and the relationship between transportation and communication ended. Messages could be sent faster than a car, train, or pony express rider.

Moreover, as the world became electrified, communication media evolved from the telephone to the Internet and conditions of attendance changed. With the telephone, people could communicate across long distances. Later, the Internet introduced the idea of communicating on a global scale. Along with the change in conditions of attendance, came a transformation in our attitudes of space. Space no longer had to be a physical place, it could be the imagined space in which a telephone call exists or the imagined space of an Internet chat room. The geographic reach (physical space) and multidirectional (interactive) flow of messages across the Internet enabled people across distances and in geographic locations to communicate.

Concepts of the difference between space and place emerged. Although, people may have always sensed the difference, for instance, when we speak about a place of worship rather than a space of worship. The space is the physical building or church in which the congregation meets. The actual meeting is a place for the people to worship together. If the group meets in different spaces, they are still meeting each week in a place of worship. The people and ceremony are the same, even if the space is different.

Another clearer example is a cemetery. The cemetery is a space where we bury people. But it is a place that we come to remember lost relatives and people that were close to us. In the digital age, differences between space and place become more than a semantic difference.

Computers first presented the idea of electronic space through text-based interaction. Early computer games, such as space wars or pong, provided a sense of space through simple graphics or emoticons made up of alphabet letters to create the object to be moved around in the game. Later, the graphical interface was developed at Xerox Parc and pixilated images of computer functions began to appear in the space of the computer screen. Apple Computer then popularized the idea of graphical interfaces with the introduction of the Macintosh. Microsoft shortly followed with the Windows program. Using graphical interfaces, looking at the computer screen became similar to seeing a window of data and information customized for the individual user. As computer technology was developed, the idea of virtual reality eventually became popular and companies began designing helmets and interfaces that would immerse the user in cyberspace. Gradually, the computer screen became a place where one could watch movies, make phone calls, and interact on social networks or one could be in a place called cyberspace to view data. The notification systems (chapter 5) in Facebook, made it a place where students wanted to go. For example, reading newsfeeds about friends and the poking people made the place interesting. It is a place where students can communicate with someone next door or thousands of miles away.

Cyberspace

Today, cyberspace is a synonym for the Internet. William Gibson (1984) coined the term cyberspace in his science fiction novel *Neuromancer* to describe futuristic computer networks. Characters in the book entered a virtual world of data representations using neurological computer interfaces that connected the brain to the computer network. Once joined to the network, the characters could visualize digital information. Gibson contended that he assembled the word as an "act of pop poetics" to describe current computer culture. "Cyber" comes from the term cybernetics, created by Norbert Weiner (1954). Weiner created the term form the Greek word Kubernetes or "steersman"—to describe the science of feedback and control. Originally, cybernetics was applied to machine systems and later it was used to describe human social systems. In Gibson's book, the term cyberspace uses the idea of steering to create the notion of people navigating through a matrix of digital data.

Gibson's science fiction books are about an imagined future where computers are used to connect the global community. However, Gibson's inspiration for the idea of cyberspace came from watching kids playing video arcade games. In an interview, Gibson described these games as "a feedback loop with photons coming off the screen into the kids' eyes, neurons moving through their bodies, and electrons moving through the video game. These kids clearly *believed* in the space games projected" (McCaffery, 1992, p. 272). He observed how video games and computer users seem "to develop a belief that there's some kind of *actual space* behind the screen, someplace you can't see but you know is there" (p. 272). It is a concept of space that is created by people when they look at the computer and video screen. Cyberspace is a space that is also "a container, it is measurable, and it is specifiable, though these measurements and specifications are more fluid than in three-dimensional space" (Coyne, 1995, p. 155). We can specify number of nodes and addresses of computers and measure how many people visit a website. However, we think of cyberspace as a space that contains information rather than measurements.

In contrast, Lévy (2001) argues:

> Cyberspace refers less to the new media of information transmission than to original modes of creation and navigation within knowledge, and the social relations they bring about. These would include, in no particular order: hypertext, the World Wide Web, interactive multimedia, video games, simulations, virtual reality, telepresence, augmented reality (whereby our physical

> environment is enhanced with networks of sensors and intelligent modules), groupware (for collaborative activities), neuromimetic programs, artifical life, expert systems, etc. All of these tools are combined in exploiting the molecular character of digitized information. (p. 372)

Exploiting the character of digitized information also involves programs, such as YouTube, blogs, and photo sharing Web sites, where people can express their creativity. For Lévy (2001), cyberspace is more about the social interaction that digitalization does to information than the idea of space itself. The ability for students to express themselves through digital tools is another aspect of cyberspace. For instance, many young people are involved with making video remixes (chapter 10).

Strate (1999) describes cyberspace as "the diverse experiences of space associated with computing and related technologies" (p. 383). He argues that three different concepts of space are embedded in the concept of cyberspace—physical space, conceptual space, and perceptual space. Physical space is an aesthetic space because computers exist in an actual place. Computers are objects that are aesthetically designed and they exist in real spaces such as bedrooms, dens, offices, and kitchens. For instance, the early Macintosh was considered to be an excellent industrial design, Moreover, "Media now come in a lot of *different* sizes from the laptop, to the desktop, to the countertop, to the home theater, to the movie theater" (Reeves & Nash, 1996, pp. 194-195). In addition to the physical shape of the machine, the actual computer screen creates the illusion of three-dimensional space, just like three-dimensions are formed in paintings and photographs. Illusions of images on computers can be as realistic as movies or as primitive as cave drawings. This type of Cartesian space can be represented with three-dimensional coordinates. As a result, the "information can be stored, manipulated, and transformed by the computer and displayed" (Coyne, 1995, p. 156). An example of how this works is the flight simulator that trains pilots. Simulators are so realistic that people actually get ill when the simulated plane starts to spin in a crash.

Conceptual space is the information space that we imagine when we use computer networks. All of the digital information that we find on the Web, must be stored in some physical place. People conceive of web pages as places of location where information resides. Perceptual space is social or relational space. When people talk to other people through the Internet it is often in a chat room, on a discussion list, through e-mail, or in Facebook. All of these online places are perceived to be digital versions of physical phenomena. The chat room metaphor has a direct relationship to a physical room. Discussion lists are places that one goes to meet other people to talk about topics of interest and e-mail is analogous to physical mail that we send through the post office. People perceive digital data to be placed in space. For instance,

Stone (1991) has observed that people interact in cyberspace as if they are in actual physical rooms. Although cyberspace does not exist in a physical space, individuals believe it is an actual place.

Perceptual space has two dimensions—visual and relational. As a visual space, we can see images on the computer screen. People interact with images, icons, and words presented through the interface and web pages. The purpose of designing graphical user interfaces was to enable users to operate computers through visual rather than verbal commands. In addition to our visual sense, people can perceive others through computer networks, which is relational.

The term *telepresence* was developed to describe people participating from remote locations in a teleconference. Before the widespread use of computers, telepresence referred to the remote control of robots and equipment in outer space. Today, the term can be used to describe the perception of remotely interacting with another person in cyberspace. When interacting with others, "cyberspace enables and constrains human interaction in ways similar to physical space" (Coyne, 1995, p. 155). We can see the words and pictures created by others in cyberspace, which fosters the perception of the presence of another individual. But, the ways in which we interact together can be influenced by the media environment of cyberspace itself. Telepresence is an awareness of others across geographic space. This idea has been transformed into presence theory discussed in chapter 1. Establishing a sense of presence is important in Internet communication because people are not physically together. The sense of presence replaces the visual "first impression" and helps to compensate for the lack to visual information. Presence is perceived in a place not a space.

Space Versus Place

Can you rape someone in Cyberspace? This is a question that has been asked several times. First by Jullian Dibbell (1998) in *My Tinylife* and later by Alan Sipress (2007) in *Does Virtual Reality Need a Sheriff?* Both authors grappled with the idea of virtual rape and its impact on people. Dibbell noted the psychological damage that a virtual rape in a game called LambdaMoo had on the real life participants. In contrast, Sipress describes how police are now getting involved with Second Life simulated attacks. Second Life is a social place and a virtual space. However, it is the notion of place not space that involves law enforcement agencies.

Many computer-mediated environments use notions of space and spatial organization to make possible human interaction. However, there is a difference between "space" and "place." Although software designers use spatial metaphors to encourage human interaction, it is really the notion of "place" that organizes interactive behaviors. Understanding the difference between space and place helps to recognize the types of interactions that occur in social networks and any other form of computer-mediated communication.

Space is a three-dimensional world. It is the environment in which activities occur. Space is socially constructed and our experience with space references the external world around us. Software designers use spatial metaphors because they are a way to make virtual interactions more understandable. If exchanging written text with another online is called a "chat room," then the name indicates the type of behavior that occurs in this place on the Internet. Our concepts of social practices in actual space influence our behaviors in virtual places.

Spatiality is a mathematical notion and mathematics is how we measure space. Social disciplines, such as mathematics, are products of particular types of social practices. For instance, the forms of mathematical reasoning and abstraction are embodied through encounters and experiences in the living world (see Dourish, 2006). Geometry and algebra are studies with formal structures and patterns that have been developed through the centuries by individual mathematicians. Mathematics is a notion used by software designers and it is the underpinnings of computing, for instance, the use of binary math.

Geographic Space

Additionally, scientific researchers use mathematics to measure geographic areas and compare the topographies of different regions in space. Thus, mathematics is intertwined with spatial concepts. "Where topography is concerned with the unique aspects of particular and individual places, geography is concerned with the ways in which they are connected and can be fitted into a uniform whole" (Dourish, 2006, p. 301). The idea of the geography or space often refers to the earth and its different continents. The terms "virtual geography" and "electronic landscapes" are used to describe types of digital interaction and communication. Thus, the spatial metaphors of geography are applied to computer-based interactions.

For example, social media can be used as a tool to bring people together in geographic space. Smart mobs, discussed in chapter 1, are an example of what happens when people use smart phones to converge at a geographic location. For instance, it was reported that the Egyptian government blocked the usage of social media during their riots (Kang, 2011, Jan. 27). Why? Social networking tools can be used to make the riots even bigger, than they are now. For instance, the Syrians used Facebook and Twitter to call for a "day of rage" (Kennedy, 2011). Despite the Egyptian government's request, Vodafone Egypt and Franc Telecom restored some of the cell phone access to enable people to tweet (Pegoraro, 2011). "Google and Twitter teamed up to create a service for people send tweets from the nation through a phone call" (Kang, 2011, Jan. 31). However, Internet service was restored in several days. Unrest in the Middle East has been fueled by the use of social media. One demonstrator even mentioned Facebook on his protest sign.

Software programs attempt to bridge networking places with geographic spaces. For instance, the program Dodgeball enables groups of friends to find an engage with each other through mobile phones. "Dodgeball use can influence the way that informants experience public space and social relations therein" (Humphreys, 2008, p. 341). Dodgeball differs from other social networks because it involves real-world interactions. However, phones and portable devices need to locate where you are for these devices to work. Apple computer has come under attack from researchers and the press for creating data logs that store a person's different locations and this data could be collected (see Tsukayama, 2011). Location devices could introduce privacy issues into urban computing.

Another way to think about urban computing, is from a cultural perspective. "Mobility is also a crucial aspect of the modern city, from Baron Haussmann's redesign of Paris's thoroughfares in the 1860s, to the more recent availability of location based mobile services, to the flows of information and capital that connect physically and culturally distinct metropolitan areas" (Willaims & Dourish, 2006). A device called Jabberwocky detects people as an individual travels through a city. The device lights up when it encounters a person the user has met before. Many urban mobility experiments focus on discretionary mobility. People have the freedom to move around different cities and locate friends and colleagues.

How is this done? Mathematical models of space and the use of grid systems can be imposed over physical spaces and computerized spaces. For example, drawing a grid over a photograph and on a piece of paper to create an image; The grid enables a budding artist to reproduce a drawing of the subject in the photo. Photographs and artwork use perspective to create the illusion of three-dimensional space on a two-dimensional surface. The computer uses the same mathematical principles to create the illusion of space on the computer screen.

Similar to mathematics, perspective, used to create the illusion of three-dimensional space on a two-dimensional surface, is culturally learned. Different types of perspective have been used in different historical periods, for instance, Egyptian perspective is very different from the perspective that we use today. Current perspective has a vanishing point and horizon line, while Egyptian perspective twists the torso into positions that are not humanly possible. The twisting is to better show a process or activity being visually explained. An easier example in ancient art, is the depiction of big or large drawings of people to denote power, and smaller images of individuals to show those who are powerless. Ancient drawings are not about a giant human among pigmies. Instead, the winner of a battle appears as a large drawing and the people conquered are drawn small.

Place and Space

Place, like the place a battle occurred, comes before the notion of space. Space is socially constructed after the idea of place and it is created through our notions of mathematics, geography, and perspective. Both space and place are the products of social practice; however the social practices of space differ from the practices of place. For instance, Second Life is a place where people interact online and within the place, spaces can be created. Williams and Dourish (2006) argue that place is a process rather than an objector container" (p. 42).

In Second Life, organizations purchase islands and bounded areas that are considered to be spaces owned by the individual, college, or business. Moreover, people sell virtual items that are placed in the virtual spaces of Second Life. Dourish (2006) contends: "the predominant interpretation of the relationship between place and space has looked at space as pre-given and place as a social product" (p. 301). A question for software designers is what features of space are conducive for creating places for social interaction? What cues from real world interaction can be used to shape the behavior in virtual worlds? In Second Life, the virtual space parallels actual space in the world. For instance, the Rochester Institute of Technology has created a virtual campus with many objects that resemble locations on the actual campus. These virtual objects refer back to the physical items in the real world. The objects attempt to create the feeling of being on the actual campus. Consequently, one would expect people visiting the virtual campus to behave as they would when they visit the actual campus.

We live in a three-dimensional world that can be simulated on the computer. Physical spaces are organized for the needs of interaction in the space. For example, doors are designed to close in or out depending on the traffic flow in a space. People are familiar with the social conventions of physical spaces. Therefore, duplicating real world spaces in the virtual world means that people will understand how to use the illusionary space because it mirrors actual places.

Physical and Virtual Space

A number of features from the real world can be mapped onto the computer-mediated experience (see Harrison & Dourish, 1996). *Relational orientation and reciprocity* are understood in actual space and they influence how we behave toward others. People understand the spatial organization of the world and it is the same for everyone. We know that the earth is round and not flat. The concepts of down on the ground and up in the sky are ideas that we teach children. Children point to objects and adults identify them. Our shared experience of space lets us understand the sentence: "John is standing next to the bookshelf." Our movements in physical space reinforce mutual spatial orientations. Therefore, space is a shared and reciprocal concept.

Proximity and action enables people to understand the activities of others. When we see a group of individuals sitting around a table in real or virtual space, we understand something about the activity occurring—a meeting. For example, instead of standing around a ribbon being cut in physical space, a group of students and professors stood around a ribbon in Second Life to launch the Rochester Institute of Technology Island. The group behaved as they were at a real-world ribbon cutting, a speech was given and everyone applauded. Space can influence the ways in which we behave toward others on and offline because it often helps us to define a situation. For instance, if someone walks up to us in Second Life, we would expect them to start a conversation and not ignore our avatar.

Similar to *partitioning* in real life, virtual worlds use the concept of partitioning to separate activities. For instance, early text-based multi-user games (MUDs) enabled users to create rooms for socializing and interacting with others. People would chat with others in the same room and then move to a different room for another conversation. If an individual moves to a different room, he or she would then talk with the people in the second place. Second Life uses the idea of Islands to partition the areas used by different organizations. Some Islands are open to everyone and other Islands are restricted to members only.

To chat with people online, we need to be cognizant of their *presence and awareness*. As we move around the world, we are aware of other people and their actions, a topic discussed in the previous chapter. In the real world we can encounter others and seamlessly engage in conversation and interaction. In virtual places like Second Life, the same types of encounters can occur. When we see friends, we respond in a different way than walking up to strangers for the first time. The ways in which we behave toward people in physical space can be transferred to virtual place.

The four topics above provide critical cues on how to organize our behavior in different situations. "If we design collaborative systems around the notions of space which mimic the spatial organization of the real world, then we can support the emergent patterns of human behaviour and interaction which our everyday actions in the physical world exhibit" (Harrison & Dourish, 1996, p. 68). Therefore, software designers use concepts of space to help manage behavior in cyberspace.

Place

"We are *located* in 'space,' but we *act* in 'place'" (Harrison & Dourish, 1996, p. 69). For example, people act differently in a house and at home. Both are building spaces, however the home is where we live and we can be relaxed (backstage behavior from the previous chapter). When visiting the house of a friend, we would be more formal (front stage behavior). Place helps to frame the appropriate behavior in social situations. For instance, a professor's behavior is very formal at an academic conference and very informal at a rock concert. We would also dress differently because of the places we attend. The same places can hold very different events. The same hotel ballroom can be used for a high school prom, a wedding, and a psychic fair. All three events are associated with specific types of behavior.

The sense of place can transform a space into a number of different events. "A place is generally a space with something added—social meaning, convention, cultural understandings about role, function and nature and so on" (Harrison & Dourish, 1996, p. 69). Cultural understandings also contribute to our concepts of place. For example, Goffman's (1959) ideas of "frontstage" and "backstage" behavior are associated with different spaces. The way people behave in a bedroom is backstage private behavior. However, showing bedroom behavior on a Soap Opera television program brings the backstage behavior into a frontstage space, the living room of millions of people. The presence of people in a space can change the behavior of people in place. For instance, one would not gossip about a person who is standing next to them.

Moreover, people act differently at sporting events than they do at a musical concert. We learn behavior for different situations and place helps to convey the appropriate behavior for the circumstances. The agenda for architects and urban planners is established by the concept of place and the reason for using the space. For instance, designing a school is very different from designing a house. Our behavior is influenced by the notion of how people are using the place. In other words, placeness defines the context of behavior.

Making Place in Media Environments

Media Ecologists view media as information environments and people interact in and through these environments. Postman (1979) said: "Media ecology transcends several subjects of wider acceptance, including, for example, psychology and sociology, since it assumes that the psychology of people and their methods of social organization, are in a large measure, a product of a culture's characteristic information patterns" (p. 167). The social organization of media environments, mirrors culturally learned organization in physical spaces.

Media environments are places rather than spaces. While media are located in physical space, such as placing a television in the living room or kitchen, the activity of engaging with a medium is engaging in a social activity. For instance, we say that we are going to a chat room because it is a place where we meet our friends online. By all logic, it is not a physical space. A well-known MUD game in the 1990s, was called LambdaMoo. Physically, LambdaMoo was a computer under the desk of a researcher at Xerox Parc. However, people who participated in the game, perceived it as a place to go and see friends. It was a place where people from around the world could meet and greet each other. People create places in media environments and this place "consists of both that which subjects manipulate physically (Technology) and that which they manipulate incorporeally (Language)" (Wise, 1997, p. 70). Places are created as we share symbol systems (such as, language, symbols, images) with other people through the aid of technology.

Social Place

The term social space has been used in books previously published, the term should really be social place because place is where social meaning is added to space (see Wise, 1997). According to Postman (1985), although "a technology . . . is merely a machine," it "becomes a medium as it employs a symbolic code, as it finds its place in a particular social setting" (p. 86). As a result, "a medium is the social and intellectual environment a machine creates" (p. 86). When we are communicating online, we are in a place that creates a social environment. Postman (1979) explained media environments:

> Every society is held together by certain modes and patterns of communication, which control the kind of society it is. One may call them information systems, codes, message networks or media of communication. Taken together they set and maintain the parameters of thought and learning within a culture. Just as the physical environment determines what the source of food and exertions of labor shall be, the information environment gives specific direction to the kinds of ideas, social attitudes, definitions of knowledge, and intellectual capacities that will emerge. (p. 33)

For example, *World of Warcraft* is designed to be a game environment; it is a social place for play. In contrast, Second Life is an open environment. Although people's avatars may be similar to gaming avatars, the place is a combination of business and pleasure. There are a variety of different types of social places that are created through computer-mediated communication. As previously stated, human behavior in these social places is often shaped by behaviors from the real world. Two concepts that are important to the emergence of a sense of place and appropriate behavior are *adaption* and *appropriation*. These concepts apply to both physical and virtual space. For instance, people in apartment buildings will rent a unit in which the space is the same as many other units. However, the individual tenant will decorate the unit their own way.

As a result, the walls of the space will remain the same, but the inside of each apartment will look extremely different. People appropriate or adapt the space for themselves and it becomes a place to live.

The same idea can be applied to online spaces. Personal web pages are very different because the individual designs them and they are adapted for each personality. Every discussion list is slightly different because the members of the list set the tone for the discussion topic and behavior. When a person spends time and energy participating in a discussion list or online game, they are appropriating the list and game for themselves. People need to feel as if the technology is theirs. "It is only over time, and with active participation and appropriation, that a sense of place begins to permeate these systems. The sense of place must be forged by the users; it cannot be inherent in the system" (Harrison & Dourish, 1996, p. 70). For instance Facebook was originally designed for Harvard students. As students from other colleges began to appropriate the tool, it gradually became adapted as an international phenomenon. Users, the people who invest time and energy to maintain the place, drive the popularity of social networking sites.

Hybrid Space

Space and place can also create hybrid forms, such as space-less places. Harrison and Dourish (1996) state:

> The distinction between "space" and "place" is perhaps most strongly demonstrated by examples of the emergence of place *without* notions of space. Earlier, we introduced the concept of place as space invested with social meaning. The spaces can be computational, as well as physical. What remains is the tension between connectedness and distinction, which leads to placefulness. (p. 72)

The concept is the opposite of programs, such as DodgeBall that combine mediated and geographic space. There are examples of places that do not have physical spaces to use as a model for behavior. For example discussion lists and hypertext on the web. The term discussion list provides the idea that people should be discussing a topic. However, the nature of these lists is widely varied. Some lists will try to disrupt other groups, while others want to share intimate secrets. The group of people participating on the list creates the culture of the discussion list itself. Academic lists want people to cite the quotations from the list in published articles and support groups want their conversations to remain private.

Public information on the World Wide Web does not have a physical spatial comparison. Hypertextual linking, which people use every time they log on to the

Web, is a computer based concept. There is no physical space that is a hypertextual space. However, people tend to respond to hypertext links as places on the Internet. In fact grade school students will say they went to India, if they visited an Indian website. The World Wide Web, links people to numerous global places on the Internet.

These space-less places are considered to be hybrid spaces. "A hybrid space is one which is [sic] comprises both physical and virtual space, and in action is framed simultaneously by the physical space, the virtual place and the relationship between the two" (Harrison & Dourish, 1996, p. 72). For example when a course is taught in Second Life and in a real classroom, a hybrid space can be created. Guest lectures can be in Second Life along with the avatars of students; meanwhile the real students are all sitting in a physical classroom and engaging with the virtual world. This hybrid space includes both the real and virtual person. Moreover, the context of the actual classroom will help to shape the behavior of students in the virtual classroom. But, this is not always the case. The fact that people are separated from their words and actions can foster misbehavior.

The hybrid nature of media environments enables two people to imagine that they are in the same place while being physically distant. When interacting in Second Life, the visual space is not physically shared, but made available on computer screens. "Each of us is in a separate space; linked, but not shared" (Harrison & Dourish, 1996, p. 73). However, people perceive media environments to be actual places. Whether, meeting on a discussion list or interacting in Second Life, virtual worlds are filled with actual people. It is the connection between people that make people act and think they are in a place.

Architecture of Social Networks

Just like the architecture of a building; virtual spaces have system designs that enable particular types of behavior. Social networking sites tend to foster personal types of communication. However, the architecture of different sites tends to attract people from different socio-economic groups. Postman (1995) contends: "Because of the conditions in which we attend to them, different technologies have different *social* biases" (p. 193). The social bias of the computer is connecting people, which is why e-mail and social networks are popular programs. The architecture of a site also imposes conditions on how we can attend to a medium.

Papacharissi (2009) examined the architecture of three different social networking environments, Facebook, LinkedIn, and SmallWorld, and their impact on social interaction. She states: "social networking sites reinforce the social character of online environments by fostering interaction that is primarily interpersonal and founded upon norms of everyday interaction adapted to the online" (p. 202). Papacharissi describes the differences in architecture as tight and loose networks.

Loose networks, such as Facebook, are open to everyone and they attempt to create social unity on the site. However, there is "a built-in demographic bias, as not only is Internet access and literacy required to enjoy its privileges, but its initial user base was structured around privileged educational institutions" (p. 204).

LinkedIn is not open to everyone; membership is based on building a professional network of personal references and contacts. Thus, the social bias of this site is the limitation to business professionals or students from privileged schools who want to become professionals. The site has a "gated-access approach," which "means that connecting with others requires either a pre-existing relationship or the intervention of a mutual contact, which is a mechanism designed to facilitate trust among members" (Papacharissi, 2009, p. 204), the subject of chapter 9.

A SmallWorld is a private social network that is an example of a tight network. Existing members of the site, with inviting privileges, must invite new members; "members with inviting privileges tend to be individuals with large networks, frequent travel and higher levels of social activity, who have been members for at least a year" (pp. 204-205). The list has a celebrity clientele, including European royalty, actors, directors, and prominent people. This is an exclusive network based on social status.

None of the three networks are truly open to everyone, with the possible exception of Facebook, which has become more open over the years. Each of the three networks adopted different criteria for selecting new members and follow different protocols for the display of information, and the ability to customize one's own surroundings. Facebook and LinkedIn have virtual doors that can be easily unlocked, but the same is not true for A SmallWorld. Access to user profiles is open on Facebook, in LinkedIn the network is designed like a rolodex, and restricted on A SmallWorld.

There are advantages and disadvantages in these tight and loose networks. Extreme tightness provides more of a situational orientation for the users, they allow the "individual to adapt behaviorally, leaving the mind" to wander freely (Papacharissi, 2009, p. 214). In contrast, loose networks require users to be alert for behavior cues. For example, the idea of poking on Facebook was originally a playful idea, later on as people used the tool, it began to take on sexual connotations. Loose networks place the burden of structuring social norms on the individual as he or she becomes more socially engaged and interactive with other members.

Is the Internet Public or Private Space?

This is an interesting question. In "A Privacy Paradox: Social Networking in the United States" (Barnes, 2006), the topic of privacy in social networks was explored. Young people voluntarily place personal information into social networking sites, without realizing who can see their private material. While governments try to protect our privacy, social networks place information on the Internet that all can see. Lack of privacy was an idea that Mark Zuckerberg had when he developed Facebook, although he referred to it as transparency in the world (Kirkpatrick, 2010). He realized that transparency in the world would transform culture and how institutions work. It is the idea that everyone will know everything about everyone else.

Part of the problem with the Internet is that people don't always think of it as public rather than private space. Sitting home in your pajamas typing into a computer does not feel public. However, once information is placed on the Internet, we loose control over it. Individuals have no idea how the information will be read, shared, or reposted. So, you should think about the Internet as if it were a postcard, where anyone who sees it can read it. Vogt (2006) states: "The trouble with the Internet—or with much of it—is that it's inherently public. Unless someone erects barriers around the content they place on the Web, the material is accessible to all comers" (p. 1).

Misunderstandings about the public nature of the Internet can lead to social issues. For instance, the personal information revealed by teenagers can attract sexual predators. News stories about teens being lured by predators into child pornography (Garvin, 2006) and college students having problems with their universities for posting drinking and hazing photos (Wolverton, 2006), have been under discussion in main stream media. Social networks can reveal bad or poor behaviors demonstrated by students. Understanding that the Internet is not a private space for teens and students to express themselves is important for safe social networking.

Teaching Environments and Spatial Concepts

Much of this chapter has described the power of space and place to influence behavior. Behavior is also an issue in teaching environments; one would assume that behavior from a face-to-face classroom setting would influence the behavior of students online. Meloncon (2007) used metaphors from cultural geography to explore online learning environments. For instance, cultural geography relies on "spatial metaphors to describe teaching and writing because, in our everyday lives, we are involved in an endless, subconscious stream of spatial behaviors" (p. 33). It should be noted "spatial metaphors give us a sense of place and direction" (p. 33).

For instance, in *Writing Space*, Jay David Bolter (1991) uses the metaphor of space to describe texts and written documents. Bolter (1991) states: "The organization of writing, the style of writing, the expectations of the reader—all these are affected by the physical space that the text occupies" (p. 85). Electronic books use the conceptual space of the computer screen to define the text, which can be an unending series of hyperlinks. Spatial metaphors permeate our lives on and offline.

Moreover, Bolter (1991) contends: "A written text is a structure in space that implies a structure in time: writing turns time into space" (p. 107). He goes on to say: "In medieval codex the spatial structure is the pattern of rubrication and various sizes of letters; in a printed book it is the arrangement into paragraphed pages; in the computer it is the pattern of textual windows and images on the screen" (p. 107). Bolter is referring to the space of the computer screen in which images and text are displayed. Professors and students need to be able to adapt from the writing space used in a classroom to the writing space of the computer. In online learning, we have the space that text occupies and the social space of interaction between teachers and students.

The type of online environment the class is using influences interaction between students and teachers. Is the architecture a tight or loose network? Using courseware systems that are designed for class is usually a tight system that is only open to the registered course members. These systems are generally asynchronous with the possibility of chat features. In contrast, Second Life is open and synchronous, meaning that participants must be logged in at the same time. The features of the software will influence both the course content and student behavior. Additionally, our research has found that the design of social networking software spaces has influenced student attitudes toward courseware spaces. Students tend to compare their experiences with social networking to interactions with courseware. At times the student behavior does not follow the behavior in traditional classroom spaces. For example, instead of sitting in chairs during a Second Life lecture, students were running around and getting their heads caught in tables. This type of behavior would not be tolerated in a physical classroom. Moreover, getting one's head trapped in a table would hurt.

Mediated Physical Space

Our physical space today is embedded with all types of mediated devices, from cell phones to iPods. Like spiders, new technologies lure people into a web of messages. Media that form invisible webs through television, radio, digital signals, and cellular telephones surround people. Wires hidden in walls, halls, floors, and streets are intertwined into a global knot that connects us together. Negroponte (1995) predicted that these invisible strands will become even more transparent with the increase use of digital technology. Undetectable or unseen chips will be hidden within our physical spaces and people will be connected to computer networks as they move from one place to another. No longer will we need to carry a notebook computer because our physical environment will become one large digital system. Space will become one large network that connects us to the world of information. With the increased use of e-mail, instant messenger and mobile phones, Wellman (2001) has called this "perpetual contact." Wherever you are in physical space, you are always connected through perceptual place. "For example, when users get to a bar or cafe, they can 'check in' by sending a text message to Dodgeball such as '@ Irish Pub.' Dodgeball then broadcasts their location via text message to people in their Dodgeball network" (Humphreys, 2008, p. 343).

We live in a world filled with millions of sources of global information that travel through a variety of channels, including light waves, airwaves, computer networks, telephone wires, cable television, and satellites. Many authors have written about information overload and "data smog." Information overload refers to both the quantity and quality of information. According to Strate (1996), "decontextualized information is irrelevant, leaving us only with information overload" (p. 366). Similarly, Shenk (1997) coins the term data smog to describe both the unwelcome messages distributed through catalogs, spam, and junk mail, as well as, quick-cut television and twenty-four hour news updates:

> The blank spaces and silent moments in life are fast disappearing . . . Media is everywhere. Televisions, telephones, radios, message beepers, and an assortment of other modern communication and navigational aids are now as ubiquitous as roads and tennis shoes—anywhere humans can go, all forms of media now follow: onto trains, planes, automobiles, into hotel bathrooms, along jogging paths and mountain trails, on bikes and boats. (p. 31)

People are constantly connected to the world of information. Ultimately, mediation could become our physical environment, if it hasn't already. An example is when people walk around the streets with their iPods playing; they are listening to the world with their own individual soundtrack. Moreover, mediated communication has replaced face-to-face correspondence and many physical spaces play music or display television screens. Times Square in New York City is a perfect example of our mediated physical environment.

Modern technology alters communication space constraints because it distributes global messages. Postman (1992) states, "prior to the telegraph, information could be moved only as fast as a train could travel: about thirty-five miles per hour" (p. 67). After the telegraph, information and transportation were separated because space was removed as a constraint from the spread of news and events. Postman (1992) asserted that eliminating the barrier of space in information flows contributed to the following social changes: state lines were erased; the idea of context-free information was created (information was no longer connected to the social and political decision-making process); and information was turned into a commodity that could be bought and sold. In virtual worlds, the constraint of space takes on a new a new perspective because the virtual parallels the real world.

Interview with Chris Egert

Sue: Talk about space and place.

Chris: The problem of space and place is that there are a couple of levels. There is the conceptual level of the difference between the reality, physicality of the environment that you work in, such as the representation of space and the contextual appropriateness of place, which is what Harrison and Dourish (1996) talk about. But, then there is this practicality in computing terms of how do we do that? How do we limit appropriateness? Is there a way of constraining it? How do we deal with that? Space is actually the easy one. We have the ability to create planes, surfaces, and geometry, all these things that constrain the physicality of the world. I can build a room where you can't walk through the wall. I can compartmentalize the space into islands and regions and buildings.

Another analogy is one of walking. If I walk in a virtual world into a different room it is similar to going from one web page to another. The appropriateness is one of the issues that always become an issue. In games we can do things with appropriateness because the narrative of the game allows us to make certain choices and constraints that might affect the appropriateness of behavior. There are not too many open world games that are out there. In virtual worlds it is a little harder to do that and there are plenty of examples of all sorts of misbehavior in virtual worlds.

Web presence has the same problem, there are things a designer of a site wants to say are contextually appropriate for a certain section, but how do you enforce that? It is hard to say that this is an area where the constraint is family values. We see all types of people go online and violate those types of appropriateness rules and norms. How can we create that type of appropriateness? Lots of times it comes back to community self-policing, just like the real world. Someone does something contextually inappropriate and there are ways that we can handle it. For example, a student does something that is not right in the classroom, who is around that can regulate that behavior? Of course, there is the instructor in the classroom that can do it. However, we are more apt to misbehave in the virtual world because it isn't real.

Sue: The other part of space is the computer screen itself.

Chris: The part we forget about in space is our work environment itself. We are going through multiple mirrors of projection when we start talking about physical space. I am sitting in a chair, interacting with my computer, which is interacting with the keyboard, screen, and mouse. There is the digital image that is being projected onto the screen, the constraints of that. We can get a different idea of what space is by looking at the difference between playing on my laptop, playing on my home machine, or playing with VR goggles and gloves or any other devices that are there, so even our perception of space can change.

Summary

Today, information is no longer tied to space. From mediated physical space to the virtual spaces created by computer networks, concepts of space and place have changed since the invention of the telegraph. Separating physical places from communication exchanges creates a perceptual space/place where communication occurs. Although, computers and electronic media alter the concept of space, human behavior continues to be shaped by our notions of place. It is the social concept of place that gets law enforcement officials involved with actions that take place in virtual space.

However, concepts about human behavior are also shaped by physical spaces, which influence the ways we behave online. For instance, we know that we walk through doors to get form one room to the next. Software designers use spatial cues to help orient people in cyberspace. People also believe there is some type of perceptual space they enter when they use computer-mediated communication. Spatial metaphors are important in online learning environments because the space of the classroom is replaced by the space of the computer screen. Tight networks will structure the behavior patterns more than loose networks, which require the student or user to be more alert about social norms. Spatial cues and behavior are important in using social networks in online learning and for communication on the Internet.

Chapter Four

Structure of Networking Communities

with Stephen Jacobs

Place is a concept that helps to form communities. Without the sense of place, we would not have the virtual concept of community because people need to feel as if they meet somewhere. Computer programs such as discussion lists, social networks, and e-mail groups, can be used to build and maintain an online community. Moving from e-mail to social computing tools, this chapter discusses how people build online communities and social networks. Without the sense of community, there would be no social networks. Community is the glue that holds these networks together and helps to create a sense of place.

Building community is not automatic. Software has no emotion and community is built by sharing experiences, such as births, deaths, and personal achievements. Just because a software program brings people together does not mean the group will form a community. Community development must be nurtured and many factors can influence how a community evolves. As discussed in the previous chapter, the architecture of a social networking site can influence the behavior of individuals and how communities are built. In online learning, the formation of community is not inevitable; professors must provide the opportunity for it to happen. It is commonly known, that the Internet enables people to gather and form communities through cyberspace. Members of these groups meet in a perceived place created by computer networks, and people behave as if they are in an actual physical place.

Two types of virtual communities exist, one that is centered on a geographic space, such as the WELL and Echo, and the other that is formed through the sharing of mutual interests, including Usenet. There are various types of Internet communities, including: gaming communities, support communities, audience communities, academic communities, learning communities, and communities of interest. When people engage in an Internet community, they have the potential to form bonds similar to individuals who interact in face-to-face communities. The interesting fact about virtual communities is that they can provide a stable relationship environment for people who move around a lot. Wherever a person's physical location, members of online groups can stay connected. This is the point of online communities, they connect people.

History of Virtual Communities

As early as 1968, it was predicted that computers would be used as communication device to connect people. In their seminal article, *The Computer as a Communication Device,* Licklider and Taylor (1968) described how the computer could be used to support the formation of interactive communities. Unlike traditional communities, interactive ones would bring people together from geographically dispersed locations. Proving the prediction to be correct, computer scientists employed the early Internet called ARPAnet (Advanced Research Projects Agency Network) to form electronic research communities to share e-mail messages and working papers. Early Internet use of sharing information and expertise, greatly contributed to the rapid development of computer technology in the United States.

However, the ARPAnet was only open to universities and researchers working on government research. Students from universities without funding could not use the network. As a result, students working with the Unix operating system formed a network called Usenet to share information between colleges across America. "Unix-based news groups first appeared after 1979, somewhat independently of the mainstream ARPANET-Internet activities and under the general name of Usenet" (Ceruzzi, 1998, p. 298). The City University of New York, Yale University, and IBM developed another independent system called BITNET. BITNET, Usenet, and bulletin board systems operated in parallel to the ARPAnet. "After about a decade and a half of parallel operations, all three of these streams blended into a community of news, discussions, real-time chat and other venues for exchanging information, now found on the World Wide Web" (Ceruzzi, 1998, p. 299).

As the Internet grew, scientists, technologists, educators, and students became connected and more communities were formed. Valauskas (1996) defines Internet communities in the following way; they are "a collection of individuals who use computers, software, and other means to discuss common interests transcendentally, outside of time and space (p. 2).

Howard Rheingold (1993) wrote his book, *The Virtual Community*, twenty-five years after the first scientists started using the ARPAnet to form research communities. Rheingold was writing about the Whole Earth 'Lectronic Link or the WELL, a bulletin board system located in San Francisco. He states: "My direct observations of online behavior around the world over the past ten years have led me to conclude that whenever CMC [computer-mediated communications] technology becomes available to people anywhere, they inevitablyt build virtual communities with it, just as microorganisms inevitable create colonies" (p. 6). His often quoted definition of virtual communities states: virtual communities are "social aggregations that emerge from the Net when enough people carry on those public discussions long enough and with sufficient human feeling, to form webs of personal relationships in cyberspace" (p. 5). Rheingold (1998) describes virtual communities as:

> . . . a group of people who may or may not meet one another face to face, and who exchange words and ideas through the mediation of computer bulletin boards, and networks. When these exchanges begin to involve interwoven friendships and rivalries and give rise to the real-life marriages, births, and deaths that bond people in any other kind of community, they begin to affect these people's lives in the real world. Like any other community, a virtual community is also a collection of people who adhere to a certain (loose) social contract and who share certain (eclectic) interests. It usually has a geographically local focus and often has a connection to a much wider domain. (p. 116)

Although virtual communities have formed around the geographic locations of San Francisco and New York, such as The WELL (Rheingold, 1993) and Echo (Horn, 1998), other online communities are geographically dispersed. Earlier research (Barnes, 2001) on virtual communities revealed that people who are geographically disturbed could form communities that enable people who move around a lot to maintain constant friendships. "Rather than being seen as disconnected from a group or locale, these communities transcend these constraints, shifting from door-to-door relations to person-to-person and role-to-role interactions" (Katz & Rice, 2002, p. 122). A key idea to remember about virtual communities is the fact that people need to have sufficient human feeling to bond the group together. The Internet may be an indicator that people want a more connected lifestyle, the rise of social networking definitely illustrates this point.

Moreover, online communities can be made up of two different types of relationships—primary and secondary. Primary relationships are ones in which people know each other in multiple dimensions. In contrast, secondary relationships people only know each other in a single or a couple of dimensions (see Katz & Rice, 2002). It has been argued that the Internet communities are basically made up of secondary relationships because people come together based on a single topic of interest. Additionally, the lack of primary relationships may foster carelessness and misbehavior because individuals can feel less of a connection with others. A semester in an online course may not be enough time for a group to form a community. A community can only be developed if the students become emotionally involved with the subject matter and class. Although, online courseware can facilitate the formation of community, however, it does not mean that community will form. Moreover, the idea of virtual communities changes the concept of community.

Changing Concepts of Community

The separation of communication from physical space separated information from contexts and turned information into a commodity. Moreover, this aspect of computer-mediated communication removes the geographic space from community formation. Instead of forming groups based on the mutual needs of a physical community, people now form communities based on mutual interests. Moreover, the rise of new communication technologies provides new ways for people to socially interact and bond.

Traditionally notions of community were seen as groups of people who follow the same behavior rules and live in the same geographic area. These individuals have physical access to each other and share similar interests, mostly around the well being of the community. People in physical communities can hold face-to-face meetings and interact in-person. In contrast, people online share interests. These interests can range from playing online games to being in a support group for depression or illness. As a result, there is a shift in the notion of community from physical location to communities of interest.

The terms *Gesellschaft* and *Gemeinschaft* have been used by Jones (1995) to discuss the idea of community in the information age. Gesellschaft, also related to the idea of society, refers to individuals who have political, economic, and social relationships. Individuals come together into a Gesellschaft because of their common concerns and behavior. Instead of coming together, groups emerge from Gemeinschaft because individuals live together because of a commitment. For example, people living in the same co-op apartment building will form a community because of their commitment to maintain the dwelling. Individuals who live in Gemeinshafts know where they belong in society, people fit in as a son, daughter, farmer, businessperson, etc., and the confirmation of social roles is a reinforcement of concepts of self.

When society became more industrialized, Gesellschaft became a more powerful socializing force than local communities. The increased use of mass media created a shift from acquiring information from interpersonal communication to obtaining information from the media. Today, media act as the primary source of information about politics, natural disasters, and social norms. Beniger

(1987) contends that there has been a dramatic shift in interpersonal control over people's behavior by traditional communal relationships or Gemeinschaft, to impersonal, restricted, and mediated control or Gesellschaft. Thus, the introduction of mass media changed the ways in which people received information about social norms, the topic of chapter 7. Instead of learning behavior patterns from people around us in our physical locations, individuals turned to mass media as a method for learning their social behavior.

In contrast to learning behavior, developing virtual communities requires individual involvement. Involvement on the Internet "means participation in a jointly produced social, civic, or community activity. Involvement requires a person to participate and interact with others" (Katz & Rice, 2002, p. 5). A definition of "social interaction includes both the exchange of information among individuals and groups online and the influences of online interaction on offline communication, both face to face and through other media (such as the telephone)" (p. 5). One must be socially active in virtual communities and have those interactions influence other's offline behavior.

Types of Virtual Communities

Media companies have considered audience participation on a website to be a virtual community. This type of thinking confuses consumer content creation with the emotional bonds needed to form a true virtual community. Creating content on the Internet is not the same thing as bonding with a group of individuals. For instance, responding to a question asked by CNN News through e-mail is not forming a community. Although the medium may consider these messages to be part of the online community, they are not bonding people together. Additionally, these media "communities" are created by Web designers by providing an area on a website for users to add content by responding to a question or article created by the media company.

In contrast, groups of audience members or fans will share their interpretations of media texts through e-mail lists. Audience members, rather than the media, will form these groups. Some of the television programs that have attracted fans are *All My Children*, and the various versions of *Star Trek*. This has been called an audience community in earlier texts (Barnes, 2003). Audience communities establish their own practices and social norms, such as not flaming other people online. Baym (2000) argues that some researchers don't consider these groups to be a community. However, participating in these groups builds personal relationships. Baym (2000) says, "Being a member of an audience community is not just about reading a text in a particular way; rather, it is about having a group of friends, a set of activities one does with those friends" (p. 207). Through the exchange of ideas and sharing of personal information, members of audience communities form a bond with each other through the sharing of experiences online and off.

Morris (2009) defines a Twitter community as people who are:

- Asking questions that provoke thought, be they reflective or trival (but not rhetorical), and *responding* to them;
- Asking directly of me an opinion on something;
- Making a statement or observation that is uniquely your own. (p. 200)

Twitter's short messages may make it a more difficult medium to form a true virtual community. Many people may be fans of the people they follow on twitter, but the individuals are not emotionally bonded to each other. For instance, when an online group shares the death of a member together, they become more emotionally connected.

Two other types of virtual communities that create bonds are support communities and gaming communities. Online support groups can become virtual communities. Emotionally charged messages are generally exchanged in support groups and this type of message exchange can easily turn into a virtual community. Electronic support groups enable people to share common experiences, create stories to normalize their experiences, and meet people with similar issues. Moreover, a shift from speech to text can be beneficial in the support process because people can write thoughtful replies and carefully craft their messages. "For example, online communities of patients with various kinds of terminal or serious illness can supply both the anonymity and objectivity that patients cannot or may not receive from family or friends" (Katz & Rice, 2002, p. 121). The sharing of emotionally charged experiences can lead to the feeling that one belongs to a community.

Gaming communities bond because of the time people spend playing the game. Currently, one of the largest gaming communities revolves around the game, *World of Warcraft*. For example, a female player died in real life and her guild members decided to have a funeral for her in the game (type WoW Funeral into YouTube). Unfortunately, a competing guild decided to use the funeral as an opportunity to attack the mourners and the incident was spread through a YouTube video. A controversy was started over whether or not it was socially acceptable to attack a guild during a funeral.

Gaming communities are not new; they started with the game *Spacewar,* in the 1960s. "Spacewar, a computer program itself, helped to show how all games—and maybe everything else—worked like computer programs. When you went a bit astray, you modified your parameters and fixed it. You put in new instructions" (Levy, 1984, p. 61). The game used the combination of new methods of programming with computer-generated display screens. Players had to be co-present to compete with each other.

With the widespread use of the Internet, people could now play games interactively through the network. A number of researchers at the Stanford Artificial Intelligence Lab were avid fantasy game players and they developed a program called ADVENT. ADVENT was a text-based game where a player assumed the role of a traveler in a *Lord of the Rings* setting who would fight off enemies to discover a treasure. This game was one of the first MUDs (Multi-User Dungeons or Dimensions). Text-based MUDS enabled people to role-play and build interpersonal relationships. In addition to adventure MUDs, social MUDs emerged, such as LambdaMOO, a social MUD that paralleled the real world. It was a text-base game that is similar to today's Second Life social media environment because people came together to interact and play.

The final type of virtual community is based on geographic locations, and is called a community network. Participants in community networks share a common city or neighborhood. "Furthermore, as community networks demonstrate, on-line communities can be used to enhance geographically local communities" (Baym, 1998, pp. 37-38). The online participants generally know each other in real life or have real world connections. An example of a community network is the Blacksburg Electronic Village established for residents in Blacksburg, Virginia. Members of the Blacksburg Electronic Village state: "This communication system, in particular, highlights the fact that in a community, being informed about what happens, and being able to send and receive messages on any subject, helps its members feel part of the [physical and virtual] community" (Cohill & Kavanaugh, 2000, p. 114). Additionally, members stated that because of the network, they felt more committed to the community.

Finally, social media applications, such as Facebook and MySpace can be viewed as communities. When Facebook was first developed it was based on the idea of a face book that would show students faces to other new students in a college. It was meant to be an activity that fostered face-to-face relationships. Consequently, many of the people in a person's network on Facebook are people that the individual knows in other contexts. Moreover, family members who stay in touch and share photos can use the program. As a result, Facebook and other social networking sites have a relationship to the real world. Community is built from people known in the physical environment and the commitment to communicate may be fueled by real world influences.

Building Virtual Communities

Commitment to the community is a major factor in developing a virtual community. People must communicate and send messages to each other or the community will cease to exist. Virtual communities have been destroyed because leadership in the group is lost or individuals have misbehaved. Forming a true community "is a collective (evolving and dynamic) in which the public and private lives of its members are moving toward interdependency regardless of the significant differences among those members" (Doheny-Farina, 1996, p. 50). In our current society, people move, go to college, change jobs, and generally do not stay in the same physical location. Moreover, family members often live in different state, such as New York, Georgia, and Kansas. As a result, Hampton and Wellman (2001) state: "Community is best seen as a network—not just a local group. . . . Social ties vary in intensity and are maintained through multiple communication media; direct in-person contact, telephone, postal mail, and more recently fax, e-mail, chats and discussion groups" (p. 477). Social networks should be added to this list because they connect networks of friends together.

The popularity of social networks is based on the fact that when people are in a different location, they can easily stay in touch with family and friends. For instance, many college students stay in touch with their high school friends through Facebook. Similarly, parents can keep track of their children by looking at their Facebook pages.

Building Online Learning Communities

Both socially and educationally, students use the Internet. As online education expands, educators are being challenged to build online communities in addition to delivering information. Cassell and Tversky (2005) examined the formation of an intercultural community of young people from around the world. The young people were selected to join the group because of their motivation to discuss global issues. Moreover, they were told to think of themselves as a community. To build a community people need to make rules for themselves, elect leaders, and sanction misbehaviors. Additionally, "they identify as members of the group, and restrict membership to those who do belong" (p. 5). As discussed in chapter 1, social presence is also a necessary feature for building a successful online learning community. People must have a sense that they are communicating with other people, not just software.

Other characteristics include: 1) a minimum level of interactivity; 2) a diverse group of communicators; 3) a common public place where interaction occurs; and 4) a minimum level of continuous membership (see Jones, 1997). Community begins with interaction, which leads to commitment to a group. The Internet is an interactive medium that supports the interactivity between individuals. For a virtual community to form, there must be more than two communicators. By making this a requirement, database queries and database interactions are eliminated from the category of virtual community. As stated in chapter 3, interactions occur in a place online. Virtual communities are socially produced places that are created by people forming social relationships in cyberspace. These relationships are built through repeated contact with the group. Finally, a virtual community must have a minimum level of continuous membership. An online community needs people to participate and exchange messages or the group will cease to function.

Baym (1998) contends that influences on virtual communities are: 1) external contexts; 2) temporal structure; 3) system infrastructure; 4) group purposes; and 5) participant characteristics. Computer-mediated communication (CMC) is situated in a national or international culture. "In short, participants' communicative styles are oriented around common social practices before they even enter into CMC, practices that are unlikely to be supplanted by computer mediation" (p. 40). Moreover, people engage in CMC through different access points, such as work, home, or school. These contexts could influence the participants' participation in the group.

The temporal structure of an online community is either synchronous or asynchronous. With synchronous communication all of the participants are online at the same time. Examples are chat rooms, *World of Warcraft*, and Second Life. In contrast, communicators post messages at their convenience to asynchronous groups. The nature of the conversation will change between synchronous and asynchronous. For instance, chat conversations are generally short messages, while asynchronous communication can be much more reflective because people have time to craft their messages.

"As the differences in possible temporal structures suggest, computer network infrastructures shape interaction in many ways" (Baym, 1998, p. 44). Different types of software tools have different features. Facebook is designed to be a social network. It has many features, such as poking, and writing walls, to support social interaction. In contrast, online learning systems have places for students to drop off homework, discuss topics, and download reading assignments. As a result of the system infrastructure, Facebook and online courseware have different objectives and goals that support different types of activities. Using Facebook as a course management system requires creative thinking because Facebook was designed for social connections, not homework assignments.

Moreover, the purpose of Facebook is to form social networks of friends. It is not designed for a semester course where people come together for twelve weeks and leave. Friendships are not based on time factors in the Facebook software. The constraints of the software support social rather than educational uses. Courseware is used for just one class and then it is no longer available to the students. The goals of a group and why it forms influence the communication and behavior patterns of the participants. For example, if the group is a task oriented group, such as an online learning course, or the group is a recreational group discussing a topic of interest. Courseware management systems are designed for the dissemination and acceptance of college projects. In contrast, MySpace is designed for the dissemination of entertainment information and social interaction. For people who engage in personal talk over a long period of time, "maintaining friendships and acquaintances becomes another purpose of the interaction" (Baym, 1998, p. 47). This is also true for social networks.

Finally, the characteristics of group and member participants will influence computer-mediated interactions. A central issue is the size of the group, which varies from three to three thousand on the Internet. Another issue is the composition of members. Are all the members from the same country? Do members have inaction histories in real life? How participants perceive the group and how it is organized influence the group dynamic.

The gender balance can also influence group norms and behaviors. For instance, groups dominated by women can be more congenial than groups with many male members, where flaming or rude behavior is accepted. The National Science Foundation Grant researchers conducted preliminary research on gender styles of communication. This analysis conducted through ethnographic research and content analysis examined whether or not males or females used positive, negative, neutral or profane language in their messages. Both research methods found that females do not tend to express negativity in their messages. In the ethnographic research, it was discovered that males used profanity several times, while the women did not. In one learning environment the female posts were much more positive than the males. In the other two learning environments the ratio of male to female positive responses was 2:1. In addition, the content analysis revealed the following information:

- *Male positive responses:* 58 percent were directed at females, while 42 percent were directed at males
- *Male negative responses*: 14 percent were directed at females, while 86 percent were directed at males
- *Female positive responses*: 39 percent were directed at females, while 61 percent were directed at males
- Females gave no negative responses for either males or females.

When we examine all of the gender research together, we found that men and women will equally share messages. However, the styles of their messages differ. These differences in styles could have an impact on online class discussions, especially in discussion lists that have an uneven number of males and females. The gender imbalance can create a discussion imbalance. Members of the opposite sex seem to send more positive messages to each other and this could help the positive tone of a class discussion. Thus, these different message styles could influence online classes.

Learning Communities

Students who do engage in learning communities receive a number of positive outcomes. These include "The strong interpersonal ties shared by community members increase the willingness to share information and resources, setting the stage for collaborative learning" (Haythornthwaite, Kazmer, Robins, & Shoemaker, 2000, p. 1). Members of the groups must socially construct rules and norms of behavior. The questions to ask are:

> Do members recognize their environment as a "community"? Do they feel they belong to it? Then, to determine what characterizes community in that environment: What does "community" mean for members of this environment? What is its membership and boundaries? What are members' common goals? What history do they share? What rules of behavior have they evolved? Finally, if we find community to be a positive construct, we then ask: How can we promote community in this context and gain its benefits for individual members? (para. 8)

These questions have been used in research to identify community. But, not all online classes bond into communities. The goals of a learning community needs to be clearly articulated and people need to be encouraged to interact.

Communities and Social Networks: An Interview with Steve Jacobs

Sue: What are your experiences teaching online classes? How many years have you been doing this?

Steve: I started as an adjunct in the early 1990s. I was student teaching, guest lecturing in online classes back in the New School with Paul Levinson in 1985 or 1986 and I was a student in the classes in Connect Ed, if you want to go back that far (see Levinson, 1992). RIT was a "leader" in distance education, when distance education was primarily asynchronous bulletin boards, discussion groups, and occasionally an online text chat. I've taught online courses in that form, since the early 1990s.

Sue: You've been teaching online since the beginning of using computers for distance education, in your opinion, how often do educational groups form online communities?

Steve: Well, it is usual for them to form some kind of online collaboration during the time that the course runs. I have rarely, if ever had a class that continues to meet online as a group or a subset beyond the time the class ran. Unless the student is in a "fully" distance student course, here at RIT most of the time there is either a distance component to a class that meets face- to-face or there is a student taking an online course as an option to a face-to-face course where they can't fit it into their schedule. So, unless there is more than one class where people get together, you don't see much of a community forming that lasts beyond the ten weeks of the class.

Sue: How do you sense that people form communities?

Steve: It all depends on what your definition of community is. If you are talking about a group that meets regularly, formally to discuss projects and get work done, yes. If you are talking about a group that hangs out online together outside of the constraints of getting a project done, or attending a distance lecture, no. You will find an ongoing online community in a social or game space, one that has been formed within both the tool sets and constraints of the class. If you took the class away, if you took the assignments away, if you took the requirement of the class and the students to meet at a given time, do these people just get online to shoot the breeze, talk to each other, and play a game, no. You will find if students are taking a sequence of classes together that has an online component or is fully online, they will team up together on a regular basis, just as students who take several face-to-face courses will.

Sue: Do you think forming a community in education is important?

Steve: A community of practice within the confines of the course is worth while, people sharing ideas, people sharing expertise, people working together aided by online on collaboration for assignments, or peer writing or peer critique of writing, is very valuable. The online medium does, with some of the shyer students, offer them an opportunity to participate more because it is not physically face-to-face or physically in the same space. There is research for days that document the fact that some kids are more able to contribute in a non-face-to-face environment.

Sue: What did you find in your research?

Steve: We went to a group of different human-computer interaction classes and had them fill out a form about what features they would want in an online educational community, if we gave them all of the features that were available in MySpace and Facebook. If you could have a friending system, if you could have a Karma point system, if you could have this or that, rank what you would want in your educational space.

We also had them rank what communities they participated in online. Surprisingly, we gave them a choice of friends, family, work, school, and school came in as the second, not the third or fourth context in which they spent most of their time online, which we didn't expect. But, the other thing we found is that when we gave them a whole menu list of what they could have in a workspace, all of them picked all of the very most basic things—chat, real-time discussion, asynchronous discussion, those kinds of things. All of the wiz-bang sexy applications they did not want in their educational space.

Our instrument was not clear enough on a couple of items to allow us to get more of a focus on why, though it was clear from some comments that there was a kind of mind set that school space should not be a kind of fun space. The school space is for work only and gives us what we need to get our work done and leave us alone. There were also some people who were concerned as to whether or not we were suggesting we use their existing MySpace profiles for school-work as well. They didn't want their teachers friending them in their MySpace pages.

Sue: It's kind of ironic because when we were doing the National Science Foundation grant, students automatically related the online course tools that we were showing them to Facebook, MySpace and all of the social networking tools.

Steve: On the one hand, they all said that the course management system tools were inferior in terms of technology capability and application to the ones they use on their own. Then you go ahead and ask them, don't you want that stuff in the educational space? And, they said, no. My take on the data we got from the survey is that we kind of assume as educators that the teachers need to be educated on the use of the tools and the students because they use tools like this all the time, know what to do.

It seems to me that there needs to be some education to the students on the fact something between a school can be fun, the tools you use for school can be fun also. But, there are real applications for this stuff within the academic environment, like the I think some of the reasons the students did not indicate that they wanted those more powerful tools in their course management system spaces, is they need to be taught how they might use them in the educational space.

Sue: What I think is that students can't make the cognitive leap between using the tools for educational courseware and using them for socially oriented networking. What do you think?

Steve: Right, that is my belief as well. It is not only that we have to educate educators or train educators to use the tools at all. We have to educate the students on how to use them within an educational environment. Students don't make the jump automatically; oh I can use this for this and apply it to this part of my educational experience (Personal Correspondence, September, 22, 2009).

Influence of Social Media on Building Community

Our concept of community influences whether or not virtual communities are formed in online courses. The criteria for forming virtual communities listed above do not deal with the software criteria for supporting the formation of virtual groups. Or take into account the social media tools used by students. Today's teens are eager participants in the technology of social media. They use social media applications as an expressive medium for writing through blogs, journals, web pages, and other forms of written expression (Lenhart, Arafeh, Smith, & Macgill, 2008). In addition, creative expression through the creation or manipulation of digital media has become, for many, a central practice for social media. Over the last few years, the growth of teen social media access has exploded. According to the Pew Internet and American Life Project report on teens and social media, teen use of blog technology doubled from 2004 through 2006. In addition, the report stated that there are gender differences between the way girls and boys handle creativity and expression—girls contribute to blogs and boys participate in content sharing (Lenhart, Madden, Macgill, & Smith, 2007). Social media is highly collaborative for teens because content provides a focus for discourse and critique.

While social media is popular with teenagers, a shift occurs when students reach college. The familiarity of social media tools is transformed with the introduction of collaborative software to support the academic mission. As colleges make an effort to provide augmentation to the traditional classroom setting and improve distance education, social media tools are incorporated into classroom activities. These activities include: web access to coursework, e-mail, forums, and chats. However, in the academy much of this is done by the integration of social media capabilities into course management systems, rather than using the social media tools that college students are familiar with.

Despite the potential of course management systems to benefit from social media, there has been inadequate progress in the actual adoption of social media technologies by the students themselves. Many reasons could explain why: the lack of flexibility in the technology to support the types of interactions the students desire, the constraint that community only exists among registered students in the class and does not persist beyond the duration of the course, usability issues with course management systems that incorporate social media features, or lack of the social cues and features students expect as part of their educational and social systems.

As students were exposed to different social media systems, courseware, and course management systems in the NSF grant, a particular phenomena began to occur. A random sampling of 500 messages across both Forums and Administrator Feedback sections showed a 9.2 percent incident of system dissatisfaction with the different applications they were exposed to. Messages classified into user interface problems (52.1 percent), feature identification problems (34.6 percent), adminsitration problems (10.9percent), and personal issues with another student (12.9 percent). A follow-up survey in the last week of the course showed that 72 percent of the students did not think that the courseware and course management systems created a social network equal to or better than their preferred popular social media systems.

As a result of the disconnect between the social media software they used for day-to-day interactions and the course software, a survey was conducted to determine what features need to be added to courseware and course management systems; in order to bring them on par with social software students use on a social level. Twenty-five of the course's students responded to the survey. As the results were free-form response, three independent evaluators classified the textual responses into categories. The resultant responses were averaged to come up with the following list of needs for courseware and course management systems.

The most frequent responses indicated a need for courseware and course management systems to improve user interfaces, user-to-user messaging,

Table 4.1 Courseware and course management system needs (N=25 students)

Need	**Frequency of Response**
Better/More Intuitive User Interface	10
User-to-user messaging	7
Better Notification and Awareness Mechanisms	7
Better Thread Organization and Presentation	6
User Customization of Interface / Experience	6
Better User Profile Systems	5
Integrated Games and Fun Activities	3
Customizable Groups for and by students	2
Better Search Tools	2

notification and awareness mechanisms, thread organization and management, as well as customization systems. Students also indicated in their written responses that they wanted better ways to configure their systems, wider ranges of identity and avatar use, as well as better ways to manage group and individual messages.

Results of the analysis show that that student attitudes and concerns about social software and course management systems fall into the three areas of technical, social, and usability concerns. As discussed in the introduction and utilized by the National Science Foundation grant, these three dimensions can be used as a scale to analyze how students use social media tools. In terms of building communities, students do not automatically transfer their knowledge skills from using social networking to the educational context. Similarly, the idea of building communities in online classrooms is a combination of technical, social and usability issues. Students do not automatically form communities by using software. The idea of community must also be stressed through the social use of media. Students need to feel a commitment to the other students and interact accordingly.

Summary

The idea of a social classroom and the use of computers to introduce a more social environment into education, was recognized by educators. Educators such as Barrett (1992) and Shneiderman (1992) realized that networking was essentially social in the early 1990s. With the rise of social networks the social nature of the Internet became more obvious. Before social networking, Rheingold (1998) and Horn (1998) wrote about how the Internet can be used to build virtual communities. Their networks, the WELL and Echo, along with social media applications, were built on real-world connections. The WELL and Echo were geographically based to enable people to meet face-to-face after they met online. In contrast, people often know each other in-person before they become friends on Facebook. The connection to the real world context makes virtual community stronger in social networking applications.

Virtual communities based on common interests require a different type of commitment from its users. To form a virtual community, there must be: 1) a minimum level of interactivity; 2) a diverse group of communicators; 3) a common public place where interaction occurs; and 4) a minimum level of continuous membership. This type of commitment is not often found in educational classrooms. Students do not often form an online community during a quarter or semester period of time. One reason is because students do not transfer their knowledge of social networking from a social context to the educational one. An additional effort needs to be made to train both teachers and students how to use computer tools to build community. However, the idea of building a class community could be a powerful tool for helping students to learn because they will be supporting each other through the learning process.

Chapter Five

Awareness and Notification

with Chris Egert

Community Building is based on the software and social features of awareness and notification. Awareness is defined by Dourish and Bellotti (1992, p. 107), as "an understanding of the activity of others, which provides a context for your own activity." Awareness refers to indicators that are available while *using the system. Awareness and notification are important technical and social elements for maintaining online learning environments and social networks. Awareness techniques include: size, proximity, color, transparency and change. Notification is the external process of providing awareness to a user. The technological and social issues for maintaining awareness and notification will be discussed for online learning platforms and social networking systems.*

Notification and awareness are part of the technological side of social networking organizations. However, notification and awareness systems are found in a number of technologies that we use every day. The car's dashboard is a perfect example. Lights will come on when there is a problem with the car to tell you to go to the dealer or car repair shop. Speedometers tell us how fast or slow we are driving the car. Gas gauges report on how much gas is left in the car so we know when to refuel. Odometers count the miles the car has been driven and geographic positioning systems (GPS) guide us on the road to our destination.

Notification and awareness systems are important tools that we need to operate cars and devices effectively. Research from the National Science Grant indicated that students thought there was a greater need for better notification and awareness systems in social media tools. "Notification systems are typically lightweight, event-triggered displays of information peripheral to a person's current task-oriented concern, for example, system status updates, e-mail alerts, stock tickers and chat messaging" (Carroll, Neale, Isenhour, Rosson & McCrickard, 2003 p. 605). In the car scenario, the systems don't operate the car, but they notify us to events related to our driving. On computers, these messages notify users about events occurring on the computer, with other people, and of interest to the user. Additionally, they support awareness of the presence, tasks, and actions of collaborators. The following is a comment made by a student participating in the National Science Foundation grant.

> Student comment 15: PHPBB
>
> When I use the Rasputina PHPBB one of the great things about the forum is that it informs me when I have received a PM [Personal Message]. It does this by sending me an e-mail. This is opposed to the obnoxious PM system that Mycourses has. I'd rather get an e-mail that tells me exactly what the notification is than get some random beeping that doesn't tell me exactly what it is for.
>
> As for awareness factors, the one I like for the PHPBB is the little icon that informs me that there are unread posts. This icon looks like a piece of paper that is either white or yellow depending on whether it has been read or not, respectively. This is great because otherwise I'd be constantly clicking each thread to see if anything new has been written. The only time that it is slightly irritating is when it says that there are new posts but those posts have actually been written by me. It only happens occasionally, but for some reason the system recognizes the posts written by me as new posts that I haven't read.

The student appreciates the fact that the system will notify him or her of the messages that have not been read and when they receive an e-mail message from someone else. These notifications tell people about the actions of others and helps individuals to follow an online course discussion. Recognizing messages the user sends and unread messages, is something that would never happen when communicating in-person because all discussions are in real time. Notification systems make us aware of asynchronous messages that arrive at any time. Additionally, in face-to-face communication people work to create a common background or *common ground.* Common ground is easier to maintain in person-to-person communication because the space and place situational elements contribute to our understanding of the circumstances. The notifications help us to keep track of the messages of others to help form a common ground online.

Moreover, our social habits and conventions are integrated into our understanding of common ground. When people work online many of these cues are disrupted because our field of view does not show us where the other participants are located, or their emotional cues, such as tone of voice, gestures, and eye contact. Shared tools are not as easy to access when people are not co-present. This makes awareness and notification more important online because these reminders help to build a common ground between participants.

The birthday context is one in which common ground is clear in online communication. People like to be reminded of birthdays because we often forget the dates. All of the student comments in this chapter are from the National Science Foundation Grant.

> Student comment 42: Facebook
>
> Ok so like many of the members of the class I also am a slight Facebook addict. In my opinion its just one of the easiest way to keep connected and network with both old friends that you may not see often and new friends that you see everyday.
>
> One awareness indicator that I feel is very helpful is the constant birthday reminders. Sad to say, but many of us have a hard time keeping up with all of our friend's birthdays. For this reason I love the fact that as soon as I log into Facebook, the homepage automatically makes me aware of any birthdays on that day and also the ones coming up, making it almost impossible for me to forget to say Happy Birthday! Another awareness indicator is the minifeed. Unlike the birthday reminder, I feel this indicator is very annoying and unnecessary. As soon as you log on to Facebook you're immediately presented with God knows how many quick facts about everything that has been going on since you logged on. I feel this is stupid and gives me a lot more information that I really care to know about.
>
> An important notification indicator, that I think can be either negative or positive depending on the user, is the e-mails sent to personal accounts. These e-mails notify members of things ranging from messages sent to your Facebook account to invitations to different events. In my personal opinion I kind of like the e-mails because it gives me a brief overview of what's happening with my Facebook account and presents me with the option of deciding whether I need to log in and check everything or not.

In this quotation, the student mentions notification tools that she or he likes and dislikes. The birthday notification tool is a popular one because it lets people know when their friends' birthday is coming up so they can give a birthday greeting. Again this tool helps to create a social common ground. E-mail messages that notify users of changes to their Facebook account are also helpful for this student because it tells him or her when to log onto the program and add a friend or join a group. These systems provide information about what has changed since the user last logged into the system. However, the student does not like the mini-feed that appears when they log on to Facebook because it contains much irrelevant information for the user. While Facebook designers think that posting all type of information about friends is useful, this user does not agree. Finding the balance between information overload and distributing meaningful messages is an issue for the software designers of notification systems.

For instance there are only three commands that a person can use when they are notified that someone is following them on Twitter:

- Follow
- Not Follow
- Block. (Morris, 2010, p. 22)

These options limit the choices one can make for followers of their messages and are very straightforward in the software. Additionally, Twitter limits the number of characters that can be used in one message—140, which is a relatively short space. This program controls its notification and awareness systems more than other types of Internet software.

In addition to common ground and setting parameters for software use, another term associated with notification is *activity awareness*. "*Activity awareness is* project work that supports group performance in complex tasks. Activities are long-term endeavors directed at major goals like planning the layout of a town park" (Carroll, et al., 2003, p. 606). It involves assigning roles to people and carrying out different types of tasks to complete a project through online tools. In social networking, activity awareness enables users to know who is online and who is not. Moreover, activity awareness is central for organizing groups online and helping people to work together.

> Student comment 56: AOL instant Messenger
>
> The social software that I have chosen to discuss is AOL Instant Messenger. For this software, one awareness indicator is the "Buddy List." This is a window that shows all of the people that you are friends with on AIM who are currently online. You can also have it show who is not online. For further awareness of information about your friends, you can right click on one of their names in the Buddy List and choose "Get Info" to see what they have put in their personal profile, as well as their "away message." Away messages are also another awareness indicator that tell you what friends are currently doing. These awareness indicators both work very well because I always need to know who is online so I know who I can talk to. Also when people are "away," I like to know what it is they're doing.
>
> A notification indicator that the system provides is a small popup, as well as a noise, that indicate when your friends come online and go offline. You can also have notifications of when they become "away" or "idle" (haven't

typed a message in at least 20 minutes). These notifications work well for me because I like to know who comes online when they do so I know that I can talk to that person, and I like to know who goes offline so I know I can't talk to them anymore. Further, sometimes I'm waiting for someone to come online so I can tell them or ask them something, and this notification allows me to know when I can do that. The part about it that doesn't work very well is the noises, which become very annoying. Luckily you can turn them off.

Instant Messenger has a number of notification tools that enable users to see when others are online and who is currently using the program. These notifications make it easier for people to know the common ground of who is online and who is not. The activities of others are easy to ascertain. Additionally, the tools make it easier for people to communicate with others and see what is happening with the program. Although students may not know the terms awareness and notification, they depend on these tools to help them better understand online environments.

More important, these tools help to build a social presence because these notification tools make us aware of the presence of others. Even while away from the computer, an individual can leave an awareness message that states he or she will return shortly. These cues act as reminders to tell other users the person is involved with the discussion, although not at the present moment. It is evidence that a person is attending the discussion, which is a critical feature in creating socially meaningful interaction. These tools can act as markers to keep one's presence involved with a conversation while the person is not physically present.

The following are additional student comments about awareness and notification in the online systems used by students participating in the National Science Foundation grant:

Student comment 4: I use the social software AIM.

One awareness indicator provided by the system is on the buddy list. If you are looking at the buddy list, and one of your friends goes idle, it shows their name italicized grayed out to show that they have not touched their computer for fifteen minutes.

This awareness indicator is very helpful because you can tell if the person is actually there or not. Sometimes they put up away messages but are still there. Other times, people forget to put up away messages but you can tell they are not there because of the awareness indicator.

One notification indicator is when someone who is not on your buddy list messages you. A message box pops up and says, "xxxx screenname has sent you a message and is not on your buddy list. Do you want to accept?"

This notification is helpful because I don't want to start conversations with random people. Sometimes if someone I don't know messages me, I will ignore the message. Usually if the screenname is childish or has too many numbers, I will not accept the message. They seem like fake screennames to me.

The buddy list enables users to see the status of their friends online. This type of notification lets the user know when a person who is on their buddy list is available online and when a stranger is trying to contact them. In this case, the student uses screen names as a way to identify whether or not he or she wants to respond to the stranger. The next student message describes bulletin posts and e-mail messages as forms of notification.

Student comment 10: MySpace

One awareness indicator would be the bulletins posted it works for me because it allows me to see who is doing what in their lives. What events are taking place too. Often surveys are posted and they sometimes give me the opportunity to get to know friends better. I can't think of what doesn't work for me. I really enjoy the bulletins. I think they really "keep me in the loop."

Notifications are really convenient. I especially like it when MySpace sends me an e-mail letting me know I have gotten a message. I often communicate though MySpace to set up recording sessions and I need to respond in a timely manner. I also like that that the site tells me when someone's birthday is. I forget a lot, so that feature is appreciated.

Notification and awareness systems are an integral part of social networking systems and the users appreciate their reminders for birthdays and e-mail messages. However, it should be noted that these messages are between the system and user, not between person and person. Thus, it is an automated process. The system can send notifications immediately or store them to send once a week.

False Notifications

However, notification systems can be used to trick users into joining social networking sites. From personal experience, there are two sites that have used notification techniques to trick users into joining their sites. The first is the WAYN site for lifestyle and travel. An e-mail message appeared to be generated from a person that this researcher wanted to get in contact with. Instead of reaching the person named in the e-mail message, people began contacting the researcher because they were coming to visit New York City and the original name used was no where to be found. The researcher lives in Rochester, which is 360 miles away from New York City. People just saw New York and assumed it was near the city and they wanted a place to stay. To date e-mails sent from WAYN have not been answered, the notifications were ignored.

Another false notification came from a site called MyLife.com. The following e-mail message was received:

Mary Smith added you as a friend on MyLife™.

Please confirm you know Mary so we can connect you.

Do you know Mary?

Yes

When the yes button is pushed. The program takes all of the names in your address book and sends the message to all of your friends with your name in it. In both cases the person named in the e-mail message was never contacted. MyLife wanted a fee to join their site and every other day messages are still arriving from them saying that people want to get in contact. Additionally, a number of e-mail messages were received from the reserarcher's friends asking why they should join the site. The researcher told them to ignore the messages.

Similarly, the false phishing messages that are disguised as an official e-mail from banks or online services are examples of notification outside the environment. Phishing refers to bait that is used to catch personal information. The purpose of phishing is to acquire names, passwords, and sensitive data from users. These e-mail messages often link to false websites that may look almost identical to the official site. Phishing is illegal and it is trying to be stopped by Internet security companies and law enforcement agencies. By now Internet savvy users know not to respond to these messages. Some notifications are just plain ignored. But, other notifications are ones that we want, for instance the e-mail messages that we receive from MySpace or Facebook.

Chris Egert on Notification and Awareness Systems

Chris: Talking about MySpace, I log in and the first thing I get is an overview page with all of the things I should know about, how many friend requests I have, and events. The question with awareness is how do I organize that information, how am I presenting it as something reasonable, and how am I presenting that to the user? Is it textual? Is it iconic? What are the processes? What am I using to convey that information?

Think for a minute about MySpace, when I get my friends request, I get a banner that says you have four new friends' requests and then you can click on each one of the friends and get more information. So, there are two parts to awareness, what is concise and then there is the whole visual awareness problem. Ben Schneiderman (1998) talks about the visualization mantra, so it is basically this process where you have an overview and you investigate deeper into the details and it is a cyclical thing to be able to go in and dive deeper and to extract exactly what you need. Awareness is that top level of that visualization process, I need to know what is out there first before I can go in and get the appropriate level of detail that I would care about.

Sue: What is notification?

Chris: Notification, the purest form of notification is I am outside of the environment, so when I get an e-mail from MySpace that says you have a new friend request, I'm not actually in the actual environment. So, there are two levels of notification. Notification means, I'm not active or going out to seek it. I'm not logging into the site. I'm not the one going out to grab it. What's happening is a background process brings me that data.

Sue: Another example of being outside the actual environment is scam social networking sites because I am saying "Yes" I know somebody and that action is triggering a whole series of notification events or messages to my friends saying do you know this person? When they reply "Yes," that is going to trigger another series of notification events to their friends.

Chris: So, the easiest form of notification in the digital world is through e-mail. We see that all the time, MySpace mails us when an event approaches. We have newsletters that are automatically triggered that say here is something in a society that is going on. We have various reminders, such as prescriptions. I get a notification that my prescriptions are due and do I want to renew them. The problem with notification becomes the same problem as awareness, which is filtering. My in box may not be the best way to give me the information that I care about.

There are plenty of times when I missed automatic responses from these systems with things that I care about because it is just information overload. I get hundreds of junk e-mail every day and it is very easy for me to miss things. So, what other ways can we notify people? Instant messenger (IM) is becoming a popular way. Can I make a box that sits out there and I IM and I'm a receiver of certain events that I care about. So instead of the prescription company sending me something through an e-mail, it sees that I am online with IM and sends me an IM reminder. Is that appropriate? It is certainly something that would catch my attention more than an e-mail message.

And then custom techniques, we see a lot of these little desktop buttons that you can put on your task bar that are ways for getting information. An example is the newsfeed ones that you can put on as a background service and it receives events from some larger system. Maybe this gives you news items that you care about that comes up in a pop-up window that stays up for a couple of seconds and then disappears. We even see that with Outlook and Entourage, we see with e-mail that a little desktop widget pops up a box that says here's the sender and here's the name. The problem is information overload there.

Most of those things are instant space, so I get a new e-mail and I get a pop up that says you got a new e-mail. Something new is happening at a certain site and you get a pop up. After I receive a hundred of those in a day, the significance decreases. It is information overload. So how can I aggregate those? So how can I say maybe it's not as important to receive an instantaneous update as a notification? But maybe twice a day I get something that is an aggregate that says: "here are five things that you might want to know about." That is certainly the big challenge right now, how can you make things not instant space but cumulative so I am getting the right chunk of information not more often or frequently but more substance each time I get it.

Classroom Use of Notification and Awareness

Important aspects of courseware systems are awareness and notification. Students need to be notified of events and changes in class schedules. They also need to keep track of online discussions and activities. From the student's perspective, the information that they most value form a courseware system is getting grades quickly. Not having to go searching for their grades is one of the notification features that student's appreciate. However, the purpose of courseware is much greater than a grade. It is the form of communication between class members in a computer-mediated environment. Macdonald (2003) states: "students still need to learn how to interact online with their peers, and inevitably the extent to which their interaction contributes to their learning and understanding will vary with their competency" (p. 378). While students may not know the terms notification and awareness, these are tools that they depend upon in their social networks and to participate in class discussions.

Awareness of other student's activities is often important in online classrooms. "The receiver usually does not actively request this information, i.e., being aware about the state of work happens rather passively. It is this property that makes the provision of awareness so important: the information is exchanged without much over head on either the sender's side or the receiver's side" (Sohlenkamp, Fuchs & Genau, 1997, p. 2). Moreover, courseware tools and artifacts often mediate communication between students indirectly. When a message is posted or unread, the student is notified by highlights and e-mail reminders. As a result, awareness and notification play an important role in the communication process of courseware systems.

Summary

Students have definite opinions about the notification and awareness systems that they like and dislike. Some find the minifeeds of information to be too much information, but they all seem to agree that the Birthday reminder is a helpful to receive. Notifications and awareness features are built into software programs are automatically triggered rather than personal forms of correspondence. These features help to keep a common ground in online discussions because they keep track of the messages we have and have not read. In chat sessions, these tools will tell us which of our friends are online, offline or on a break. As a result, these automated features play an important social role in the process of online communication because they can help keep track of messages and social presence.

Information overload is a problem in awareness and notification systems. Designers need to anticipate the needs of their users and provide the right type of information and reminder cues. Too many cues and the user will stop paying attention to the information or get annoyed. In some cases, this has happened with the minified notices in social software systems. We don't need all the information about everyone online, just the people we most care about, which is something that an automated system cannot distinguish. However, these tools do help us to understand the common ground of an online discussion to keep the communication ongoing.

Chapter Six

Second Life and Education

with Neil Hair and Lyle Wetsch

Many technical and social factors influence computer-mediated communication, such as the ability to sense place and space. Virtual worlds create the sense of being face-to-face because we see visual representations (avatars) of others that mimic real world interactions. Often, avatars are created to be idealized versions of the individual. In virtual environments, people interact in a simulated face-to-face situation, which can mimic a classroom, office, or shopping mall. This chapter discusses the advantages and disadvantages of incorporating Second Life into blended education courses through the evaluation of two independent marketing courses conducted at two midsized North American universities. A portion of this research was conduced with a Provost's Learning and Innovation Grant *from the Rochester Institute of Technology.*

A topic in online education is the introduction of Second Life into the classroom because the virtual world is more engaging for students than asynchronous discussion lists. As a result, Second Life is an environment that should appeal to the digitally savvy student. For many years, the use of technology in education has been a controversial issue and the use of Second Life is no exception. Building on past arguments, Susan Barnes and Lance Strate wrote an article in 1996 called "The Educational Implications of the Computer: A Media Ecology Analysis," which argued that it was necessary to understand the advantages and disadvantages of introducing computers into education. This chapter will revisit some of the arguments of the 1996 paper in light of the new virtual world of Second Life used in online advertising and marketing courses taught in this new environment.

When the 1996 article was written, there were no virtual worlds or social networks, the World Wide Web was becoming popular and the use of computers in schools was still a controversial topic. Neil Postman (1979, 1985) was viewed as an antagonist, who argued against using computers in the classroom. His basic premise was that print-based literacy developed the linear and logical thinking skills necessary for a democratic society (see introduction). Moreover, the media ecological perspective that Postman pioneered argued that different media have different cognitive and intellectual biases that influence an individual's world-view (see Barnes & Strate, 1996). Television introduced an entertainment and visual perspective to understanding the world. Similarly, using computers in the classroom could alter the ways in which people view the world, and we should better understand how and why this new technology will change us.

That same year, The New London Group (1996) argued that "the multiplicity of communications channels and increasing cultural and linguistic diversity in the world today call for a much broader view of literacy than portrayed by traditional language-based approaches" (p. 60). In 1996, social and technological changes were altering the concepts of literacy in education. The visual/verbalist debates subsided as visual media became more socially acceptable. Postman (1979) wanted to counterbalance the visual bias of television with the linear aspects of print. But, technology soon morphed into digital technologies and the issue was no longer one of print versus visual, now students were engaged with new media usage such as online searches, the World Wide Web, games, simulations, discussion us lists, e-mail, etc. New digital technologies began to alter the ways in which young people viewed the world. In this new world of instant information, library searches were replaced with the World Wide Web. Finding information was immediate and the new encyclopedia became Wikipedia, with all of its' good and bad points. A new virtual generation was born that grew up with cell phones, instant messaging, and computer games. Writing about this new virtual generation, Proserpio and Gioia (2007) identified three features associated with teaching this new type of student: 1) active involvement by students in learning (constructivist learning); 2) facilitative social settings; and 3) problem-solving.

These features follow the concepts of a constructionist educational philosophy described in chapter 1. Students now need to be more engaged with their education and using computer programs, like Second Life. Interactive virtual environments are one way to engage them. Today, changes have occurred so quickly in technology that educators may tend to forget to look at the advantages and disadvantages of using a new medium before they introduce it into the classroom. For example, in the desire to engage students with virtual worlds, are the advantages and disadvantages of the technology considered?

This point is made at the conclusion of the 1996 article, Barnes and Strate stated: "Before traditional educational media is replace with computers, it is necessary to better understand the advantages and disadvantages of computer-mediated environments" (p. 204). The position was skeptical about using computers in education. Furthermore, it was argued that people should ask the following three questions before they integrate computers into the classroom:

What problem is it going to solve?
Whose problem is it?
Will solving the problem create other problems that we can anticipate?
(Postman, cited in Lohr, 1995, p. E16)

Similarly, a number of articles written about Second Life question its value in the classroom (Gronstedt, 2007; Kelton, 2007). For instance, Kelton (2007) described the risk involved with higher education institutions becoming involved with for-profit companies. "Commercial ventures can make corporate decisions that have a profound impact on our educational environment" (p. 9). Additionally, Gronstedt (2007) described the barriers for the widespread adoption of Second Life for corporate training. These barriers include the fact Second Life is primarily a consumer application, as a result, scheduling meetings can be problematic when the software is not running due to upgrades. Despite these problems, both authors tend to think that Second Life is a good tool for education and training. The authors examined the advantages and disadvantages of using Second Life in education. In the advertising course, the professors[1] were able to turn a disadvantage, the commercial aspect of Second Life, into an advantage for studying online advertising. Students explored Second Life as a case study in advertising and marketing.

Today's Students

Second Life is an environment that can be used in training and college courses, this was the assumption used for the design of the course on online advertising in Second Life. The professors designing the course were aware of Postman's concerns about media and the use of computers in the classroom. But, the new generation of students is more digitally oriented. "Today's students—K through college—represent the first generations to grow up with this new technology. They have spent their entire lives surrounded by and using computers, videogames, digital music players, video cams, cell phones, and all the other toys and tools of the digital age" (Prensky, 2001a, p. 1). Prensky goes on to say that average college students have spent less than 5,000 hours reading and over 10,000 hours playing video games and 20,000 hours watching television. Unlike Postman, who was viewing television as an influence on education, Prensky is looking at the new digital technologies and the media environments that they create and how digital technologies affect the education of students.

According to today's students:

- They do not want to be lectured to.
- They want to be respected, to be trusted, and to have their opinions valued and counted.

- They want to follow their own interests and passions.
- They want to create using the tools of their time.
- They want to work with their peers on group work and projects (and prevent slackers from getting a free ride).
- They want to make decisions and share control.
- They want to connect with their peers to express and share their opinions, in class and around the world.
- They want an education that is not just relevant, but *real*. (Prensky, 2010, pp. 2-3)

In contrast to Prensky's list, the course taught as part of the National Science Foundation grant found that students were resistant to change in education. The social media course was designed to help students in the workplace and develop skills that would help them in a real world situation. However, the students protested against assignments that did not fall into the traditional type of liberal arts papers. While students say they want relevant education, they don't necessarily recognize it when they are presented with it. A change in the educational system will need training for both teachers and students.

A key difference between Prensky's (2001 & 2010) argument and Postman's (1985) is the voice of the student. Postman's authority resides with the teachers. Students may not understand what they are asking of education. A similarity between the authors is the fact that both are exploring the influence of popular media on education, although their conclusions about how to change the system differ greatly.

Postman contended that television in the United States is primarily a medium that is entertaining. Therefore, the worldview presented in television is one of everything being entertainment. The entertainment factor influences how people think and it needs to be counterbalanced by education, which is print-based (Postman, 1979). By counter balancing the influences of socially based media with print-based media, we will continue to develop students to be grounded in critical reasoning, which is necessary for a democratic nation. From his point of view, "education tries to conserve tradition when the rest of the environment is innovative" (Postman, 1979, p. 25). It is a thermostatic view that balances the environment of education against the one of popular culture. At this point, the question should be asked: What changes in society would occur if the educational environment is the same as the popular environment?

Postman passed away before social networks and digital technologies dominated our cultural landscape. He did not anticipate today's student who is surrounded by digital technologies. Postman's solution to the problem today would be to counterbalance social environments with educational ones. According to the media ecological view, digital technology change the worldview of students and teachers need to be aware of this change, which is what Prensky is bringing to our attention.

Instead of a thermostatic view, Prensky's solution for contemporary education is to create partnering relationships between students and teachers. His partnership pedagogy is explored in *Teaching Digital Natives* and it follows the logic of constructionist education. In this new digital landscape, teacher's roles are:

- Creating and asking the right questions
- Giving students guidance
- Putting material in context
- Explaining one-on-one
- Creating rigor
- Ensuring quality. (Prensky, 2010, p. 13)

Instead of changing the role of teachers, some scholars think that reading is a key issue in ensuring the quality of education (Anton, 2011, Postman, 1979). Anton (2011) states: "students should read assigned readings, participate in class discussion, and then read again" (p. 4). The argument is that students have a difficult time understanding reading and that reading is too difficult. But, reading is an intellectual exercise and a part of contemporary culture. Could American culture or even digital culture exist without reading? Digital culture itself is based on the reading and writing of software code. Reading and writing are a central characteristic of social and educational culture. They help to shape the logical mind in ways that visual and digital media cannot.

Today, the media ecological concept that digital technologies alter ways of thinking is supported by scientific data. Scientific research conducted by social psychologists reveals, "people who grow up in different cultures do not just think about different things, they actually *think differently*" (Prensky, 2001b, p. 3). As a result, today's student thinks differently than students who grew up in a television-dominated culture because digital media surrounds today's student with a different type of media environment than television did. Today's student does not like to read. Getting a student to transform into a print-based learner in today's media environment of cell phones, instant messaging, and social networks, is next to impossible.

It is assumed that by using some of the tools, such as social networks that students use in their social lives will generate more interest in learning environments. However, the National Science Foundation research found that this may not be the case. Students don't transfer their social skills to learning in an academic environment. The context of school is totally separate from the concept of social life. Students use computers for word processing, web searches, and communicating with friends, but they do not realize that social networks can be used to support the educational process and the building of professional relationships.

For instance, the Second Life course employed some of Prensky's strategies combined with intensive reading and writing assignments. A combination of

Postman's and Prensky's ideas were used in the development of the course. The assignments were advertising industry related and Internet branding strategies, thus they were real industry assignments. Students worked in groups to create a marketing plan for an actual client. After writing the advertising strategy, the students presented their work to the clients. A second assignment was to review a person's personal branding strategy.

A questionnaire was developed to help people understand whether or not they were using all of the Internet tools available for personal branding. Students were given the opportunity to test their newfound skills at the RIT Innovation Festival, an annual event at the university. A booth was set-up to demonstrate the use of Second Life in education and students with clipboards questioned the attendees about their personal branding and made suggestion on how to improve it. Control was given to the students and it was their evaluation skills that helped to make the booth a success, in fact the booth won an award at the event. The pedagogy for the course was a combination of what student's want and traditional literacy skills. The students who finished the course had marketable skills that could translate into jobs.

Blended Learning

Today, it is assumed that students will use computers for coursework and computers are an integral part of higher education through the use of blended and distance learning. Blended learning is described as teaching that combines several different delivery methods, such as collaboration software, Web-based courses, and knowledge management systems. "The aim of blended learning is, quite simply, to join the best of classroom face-to-face learning experiences with the best of outside-of-class online learning experiences" (Starenko, 2008, p. 2). This is a type of teaching and learning that mixes various learning styles, including face-to-face classroom, computer-mediated communication, live e-learning, and self-paced learning (see Valiathan, 2002).

To facilitate this type of new learning at the Rochester Institute of Technology (RIT) campus, several blended initiatives were started:

> Both the pilot and project were based largely on the expectation that asynchronous, Internet-based communication technologies and strategies that were developed in RIT's successful distance/online learning programs—could be adapted for traditional classroom courses. We wanted to show on-campus faculty how they could use online technologies and strategies to increase interaction and engagement outside and between classroom meetings. (Starenko, 2008, p. 3)

The instructional design model for the pilot at RIT was described by Starenko, Vignare, and Humbert (2007):

> During Spring and Summer of 2003, Online Learning developed an instructional design model for a Blended Learning Pilot Project that drew upon: (1) the department's long experience with and commitment to asynchronous Internet communication technology for distance education, and (2) interest in the relative opportunities and constraints of different educational media or environments.
>
> For the purposes of the pilot, a blended course was defined as any course in which approximately 25 percent to 50 percent of classroom lectures and other seat time is replaced by instructor-guided online learning activities or experiences—primarily asynchronous discussion (whole and/or small group)—but also synchronous chat sessions, as well as online quizzes, games, discovery labs, and simulations. Because it recognizes the relative opportunities and constraints of each media environment, the model encourages, for example online interaction that extends discussion beyond the four walls of the classroom. (pp. 163-164)

RIT professor, Susan Barnes, discussing the pilot, stated in *Reflections on Blended Learning: Rethinking the Classroom*:

> The greatest success that I have had with blended learning was the recent course I taught in Second Life. We used the fact that Second Life is a commercial site to examine advertising in a virtual world. We had residents from Second Life come into the class and give lectures—of course this was done in the virtual world itself. Students had meetings in Second Life and they explored the environment. It was an amazing blended experience. (Barnes, 2008, p. 78)

Blended learning can transform the classroom experience into a deep and meaningful learning experience. "A source of this transformation stems from the ability of online learners to be both together and apart—and to be connected to a community of learners anytime and anywhere, without being time, place, or situation bound" (Garrison & Kanuka, 2004, p. 96). Garrison and Kanuka (2004) continue and state: "The real test of blended learning is the effective integration of the two main components (face-to-face and Internet technology) such that we are not just adding on to the existing dominant approach or method" (p. 97). Blended learning must find unique ways in which to use the Internet technology, this was done through Second Life by using the world itself as the focus of our advertising case studies.

Today's professors want to engage learners in activities that are more experiential because they know a student will not easily synthesize information from textbooks or written material. "The developing pedagogical issues around technology suggest a renewed focus on student-centered, constructive work" (Paris, 2001, p. 100). The constructivist view of learning is rooted in the ideas of Lev Vygotsky (1978, 1986) and Jerome Bruner (1966, 1996). Active learners, interacting with the physical and social worlds, view learning as a building process. How the social world is built through interactions in online learning environments was a fundamental issue in the online advertising course. The case study in Second Life planned for the course was designed to actively engage students in learning the topic of advertising through interaction in Second Life by focusing on the advertising methods used in the virtual world.

The professors developing the online course in Second Life deliberately wanted to engage students in a constructionist experience. Additionally, they wanted to engage students in the new experience of virtual worlds by teaching a blended course using Second Life. Moreover, the professors wanted to use a digital environment that would be new to the students and peak their interest in digital technologies. The assumption students would be motivated to take the course because a new digital technology was being used, proved to be correct when the students in the course were surveyed. The majority of the students had never used Second Life, although several students had heard about it from friends. Half of the class had previous experience with virtual worlds because they played online video games. Moreover, many of the students were anxious to learn more about the virtual world. The students welcomed the opportunity for innovative learning and experiencing new challenging concepts.[2]

Blended Learning Experience

Following in the Postman tradition, the professors considered the reasons for using Second Life in the course about online advertising. What would Second Life add to the learning experience? How would the fact that Second Life is a commercial world influence the course? Would the learning curve for Second Life hinder students from participating in the course? These were very real questions that needed answers.

In terms of the learning experience, the professors realized that they wanted to use Second Life in the course as the place to study online advertising. Students would study how successful Second Life entrepreneurs advertise their products in the virtual world. Interacting in the virtual world would also create a constructionist-learning environment. Thus, it was decided to invite the top entrepreneurs from *Time Magazine* to lecture in the class. Of course, the lectures would take place in

Second Life and the professors would use a large projection screen to show the presentations. As a result, Second Life became a way to bring outside guest lecturers into the classroom. Unexpectedly during one of the classes, one professor was out-of town and he lectured in Second Life from Texas to students in New York. An added benefit of Second Life is the fact that people can be located anywhere with Internet access to be a part of the class. So, people could be invited from around the nation and professors can travel and still be able to teach a class.

Once it was determined that Second Life itself would be the focus of the online advertising, the professors had a specific reason for using it as a teaching and learning environment. The course in Second Life would use Second Life as the subject of investigation. Additionally, the approach to the topic of online advertising was resolved by examining Second Life. Instead of teaching all types of online advertising, such as banners and pop-ups, the course would focus on virtual worlds. Thus, Second Life was added to the learning experience because it was the subject of the advertising case study itself.

Student Reactions

Student reactions to the decision of using Second Life, were positive in the course. The following are excerpts from online discussions about advertising in Second Life.

> By entering Second Life, advertisers are entering a consumer's world, which unlike the real world is run, and built by the consumers themselves. When attempting to advertise in these communities, businesses must keep this in mind and be careful not to offend consumers. (Student One)

> Any messages that will be created must not be like traditional advertising. The messages in the real world on TV, radio, etc. might be considered spam on Second Life. This place is made to give an experience to the consumers, not to reiterate what real life ads are like. Give them the experience they want in real life but can't afford. Or present the brand in a new 'hip' light that resonates with the current real life campaign. (Student Two)

> Second Life "creates a whole new environment to develop new tool[s] and techniques for your business. We will have to take not only our knowledge of advertising and marketing, but also understand the intensions of SL users have (both RL [real life] people and their SL avatars). SL users are becoming a new demographic in the market, but pinning them down to one category will be difficult. Do you cater to the avatar's wishes, or to the RL person?" (Student Three)

From experiencing Second Life, the students were able to observe for themselves the consumer orientation of the virtual world. When looking at Second Life as an advertising environment, the students became conscious of the differences between traditional advertising and online advertising. Additionally, the use of avatars provided an interesting topic of discovery. Students had an opportunity to explore self-presentation and define their own identities. The fact that Second Life is a commercial environment with its own economy provided the students with a case study of an online advertising environment. As a result, the commercialization of Second Life was a benefit for the topic of the course and this disadvantage was turned into an advantage.

Advantages and Disadvantages

The fact Second Life is a commercial environment, raised some interesting issues for the professors. First, you need to be eighteen years or older to access the mature program. This meant that any freshmen that were only seventeen could not take the course. A second, however, larger issue, was the fact that Second Life contains adult content and x-rated material. There was no way to stop students from being exposed to this material as they wandered around Second Life. The professors were using the New Media Consortium Island as a central meeting place. But, once students left the island they were on their own. The university became concerned about the exposure to mature content and this became the most important topic of discussion before the course was taught.

It was decided to make the students sign a form that stated they were aware of the adult content they might encounter. Students were also given a lecture on misbehavior in virtual worlds the first day of class. Articles about behavior issues were distributed to the students. Moreover, links such as www.livingethics.org/SL.pdf were distributed to the students to prepare them for interacting in Second Life. With these measures in place, the professors wanted to prepare the students for issues they may encounter in the commercial world of Second Life. One of the additional issues was access to the environment and the learning curve needed to control a Second Life avatar.

To help with access issues, the Rochester Institute of Technology's Online Learning hired three students to work with the class to help students with their Second Life problems. Online Learning also created virtual RIT T-shirts to help build a community with the students in the class. The student aids held regular office hours and came to the first two classes to make students aware of the service and distribute the T-shirts. Additionally, the support hours were posted on the course management system used for the class. As a supplement to the student aids, technical questions could be posted on a course management system.

Research during and after the course revealed that access to using the Second Life program was not a problem. Three fourths of the class was problem free and the rest of the class suffered minor problems including performance. All of the students needed a computer with a graphics card that could run Second Life. For instance a student stated: "Second Life can be frustrating for some older machines because of the scale and the amount of graphic rendering that it needs. I know on my laptop you have to be very patient with having Second Life respond to your commands." While the professors were able to turn some of the commercial aspects of Second Life into an advantage, some disadvantages still remained, such as adult content and age restrictions. The first disadvantage was counter with education and course assignments.

Course Assignments

Assignments for the course included writing a weekly blog on their Second Life activities, writing an online identity paper, contemporary readings on marketing in virtual worlds (see DeHoff, 2006), weekly discussions, and working with a real client to write a marketing/advertising plan. The professors found six clients for the students to interact with. Three were located in Second Life and three were interested in incorporating Second Life into their promotional plans. Students met in Second Life to meet with their clients and plan their assignments. Of the three Second Life clients, one was a clothing store, one a furniture store, and the last one was a charity. The three off-line clients were a racecar company, a health care company, and RIT's online learning. The marketing articles helped the students to prepare their own advertising plans for these clients. One student stated:

> The SL program allows individuals to teleport from location to location, so traditional "poster" advertisements is not as effective as in "real world" constraints. In our tangible reality people cannot avoid advertising, but the metaverse allows for advertising avoidance. Different Marketing methods need to be explored—maybe the hosting of group events: SL picnics, SL dances, and other events that people can attend. (Student Six)

In addition to the marketing literature, students also had to read and discuss articles relating to behavior in online environments, such as *Does Virtual Reality Need a Sheriff* by Alan Sipress (2007). The following are student reactions to the article:

> The Virtual Reality Sheriff Article left me chuckling . . . virtual casinos complying with FBI laws. I have to wonder, as a NYS [New York State] resident and property owner, if my own purchase of the requisite RIT shirt

> will leave me subject to NYS sales tax? If I should someday decide to buy virtual property, will I pay virtual property tax? (Student Five)

> I feel that people are perverted and that it will show up in places like second life. However, the creativity and ability to connect with people and work on innovative projects is what comes with these freedoms and lack of restrictions, tax, etc. Therefore, I believe the state government and any other buerocratic [sic] affiliate should stay out of these systems. (Student Two)

The students were asked to write a weekly blog on their Second Life activities in an online course management system that was used to collect assignments and manage the course. These blog entries enabled the professors to find out what students were doing on social and business levels in Second Life. Students found jobs, lost their clothes, and bought new outfits. One student went to the "Best Practice for Charities in Second Life" presentation, which provided her with the experience of being at a live Second Life event and important information for her class assignment. At first, some students did not like Second Life, but by the end of the eleven weeks, their attitudes had changed.

Week one, the student did not like Second Life.

> So I'm not liking this second life very much. I went to the link that Owen [student aid] gave us to do the orientation of the nmc [New Media Consortium] and now when I try to fly it doesn't do anything but then when it does it goes on forever and then crashes. I can't seem to get out of this loop and might just give up on this class. I don't have patience for things like this. Give me a program that is stable and not full of bugs.

By the sixth week the student was pole dancing.

> Yes this coming [from] the person that was the most skeptic of Second Life. Well I figure if you are going to play the game you have to Play The Game. As most of you have figured out you do need money in this world. There aren't many jobs there. You have a camper, host, escort, model, designers, and dancers. I tend to search and hit different places based on the fact that i like to listen to music. Well i happen to land in a place that had good music and I liked the people there. They had jobs available a hostess and dancers. I wanted the hostess because you only have to hang on the dance floor and welcome people. I started chatting with everyone and they asked if I wanted the dance job. Well I never realized how hard it would really be. Not so much the dancing because that is just select the pole and dance. It was more of what they call emoting. It is a type of speaking to attract people that are on the dance floor to tip you. They offered classes to learn how to which i did attend one. They also give you a mentor. She gave me advice on what to

> say. I also had a man mentor that i danced with. the first day that I did it was ok because there wasn't that many people there and I was new. The next day I went back it was a lot busier and it was after the emoting class. I started but after a very short time I decided dancing wasn't in me. Although this is a game, you have to bring some of your rl [real life] parts in and talking the way they wanted me to, to complete strangers wasn't in me. I still go there and dance because I like the music and the people but I turned my pole over to someone else. (Student Seven)

These are the types of entries that people wrote on their blogs. In another blog, a male student made friends in Second Life, which he converted into a real life interaction:

> Besides that I have met some interesting people who I started to hang out with. We mostly just go to clubs and the cafe. Its a group of 4 guys (at least i assume because there avatars are guys) and we just talk about random stuff like politics, the stupid stuff we have seen so far, etc. . . . They are really helpful with answering my questions and getting me used to SL a bit more.

It turns out that these avatars lived near the student's hometown. So, he meet them on spring break face-to-face. Things went well, however the virtual encounters may have been better than the real life one.

Students were able to adapt to the virtual world of Second Life and online advertising. Through discovery, the students exhibited learning how to use advertising in this new environment on the Internet. An advantage of Second Life is the professors succeeded in using the virtual world as a learning experience, which made the students think about advertising in new and unique ways:

> The ideas and tools in business that work on real people need to be adapted or transformed to the avatars in Second Life. The channel of delivering an advertising message has changed considerable with the introduction of the avatars. As stated in the Metaverse article, the people who created the avatars are likely to think more emotionally in the instance of having an avatar. This allows businesspeople to tap the underlying desires of the avatars creators. (Student Two)

> In regards to Second Life, I believe the only way that consumers can and will be reached will be solely through emotional branding. Reasoning to support this assumption is that the people who are most likely to participate in a virtual world, are those who are looking to create a world for themselves based on dreams and desires. These desires could in fact come from a lack of fulfillment in real life, so they look to a virtual world like Second Life to experience their dreams. Hence the tactical idea of emotional branding would appeal to them. (Student Eight)

Generally the student reactions to the course were very positive and the professors received a very high evaluation from them. A student commented: "I liked having a class in Second Life the other day. Since, I am in the Online Learning group it was nice to experience a lecture in this setting. It helped me to have a better understanding of what our client is trying to do" (Student Four). Another student reported: "I learned a ton this quarter. What other class are you going to have [a] guest speaker on a weekly basis come in and speak frank about how they make lots of money in a new technology. Every week it was the same theme. Advertising will either make or break you depending on how you do it." Thus, the Second Life learning experience helped the students to actively learn about advertising and how it works in real life and virtual worlds.

Student Misbehavior

But, every course can be improved. We had a space on the course management system for students to make comments about improvements. One suggestion was to make in-world goals for the students. Setting benchmarks will motivate students to get in and explore the environment more. An example of an assignment would be to tell students to find a place or a person in Second Life.

In addition to improving the course, the behavior of the students needs to be evaluated. Most of the students were well behaved. Some did come in contact with adult content, which is a disadvantage of using Second Life. Consider the following story from one of the online blogs:

> Although this new experience wasn't fun at all. It was actually scary. I was off exploring different places and landed on an island that i shouldn't have been there. Some of the area looked nice so I figured that if I just stayed away from the "bad" things it would be ok. Well I have no idea what happened but someone im'ed me which I didn't mind because that is what is suppose to happen but what i didn't like was the fact that they knew where i was going without being with me. I didn't like that at all. It freaked me out and I couldn't have left fast enough. there should be PG, Mature, and XXX ratings of these islands.

Coming in contact with x-rated materials is a disadvantage of working in Second Life. This type of content may offend some students. Additionally, student behavior can be problematic. When students were asked to join speakers in the virtual world, their behavior was rude by face-to-to face standards. Instead of politely listening to the speaker, the students were running around in Second Life like children on a playground. This behavior repeated itself when one of the professors lectured in Second Life from Texas. Students were running around and getting their heads stuck in the middle of tables during the lecture.

Another, more disturbing event of misbehavior occurred when a student brought a gun to the final class party in Second Life. The student was attempting to play a prank with a friend and didn't think what implications a gun would have on the event. Fortunately, most people ignored him because they knew the student played many hours in video games, where the use of weapons was acceptable behavior. However, the university did not view the incident as casually as the students in the class. The student with the gun had to be told that his behavior was inappropriate (see chapter 8 for more details).

Advantages and Disadvantages in Second Life

There are positive and negative aspects for teaching in Second Life. The two most positive are lectures and remote teaching. With Second Life we can extend the classroom and open it up to outside lecturers that are located anywhere. This brings outside experts into the classroom. Additionally, professors can go away to conferences or out-of-town to lecture and still teach their classes in Second Life at their colleges. You just need someone to set-up the system for students to view on the large screen. This solves a problem for busy professors who sometime have conflicts between conferences and teaching.

The commercial aspect of Second life can be a negative factor for classes in Second Life. But, the commercialization of Second Life played an important role in the course content being discussed. The guest lecturers described how they advertised in Second Life, which was information the professors were not fully aware of. The professors had examined the history of Internet advertising (Barnes & Hair, 2009) and Barnes had worked in the traditional advertising industry. The material provided by the guest lecturers became the information that the students needed to execute their final projects for a virtual world. In fact, one of the guest speakers ran an x-rated business, but did not show any of his virtual products.

The x-rated aspect of Second Life is negative for classroom learning. This is a problem that cannot be avoided. In the blogs, the professors did discover that the students did come in contact with this material during their travels. X-rated material is something that we need to warn students about and it may deter some students from using this virtual world.

Student behavior is another issue that could be considered a disadvantage of Second Life. Students seem to view Second Life as a new playground rather than a traditional classroom. So it is better to project the guest speaker on a screen and have the students sit in traditional classroom seats. Otherwise, they may spend their time running around in Second Life rather than listening to the lecture.

Moreover, students do need guidelines on how to behave in virtual worlds. Misbehavior by students can also be a potential problem.

Postman's Questions

After looking at the advantages and disadvantages of Second Life, Postman's three questions should be examined: "What problem is it going to solve? Whose problem is it? Will solving the problem create other problems that we can anticipate?" (Postman, cited in Lohr, 1995, p. E16).

Second Life solves the problem of bringing lecturers into the classroom. We now can open up the classroom and make it more social as we invite experts into the class to share their knowledge. Additionally, professors can lecture to their students when they are out of town, So, Second Life can solve the problem of being in two places at the same time.

Moreover, Second Life solves the problem of bringing constructivist learning into the classroom. Today's students are not engaged with lectures and reading, Second Life is a method of engagement that can contribute to the experiential learning experience.

Who's problem is the introduction of experiential learning? As students change, professors also need to change. Professors need to find new methods of engagement for students and Second Life provided an educational environment in which the students could discover the concepts of the course for themselves.

Bringing in guest speakers is a professor's issue, it is not always easy to find people. But the students benefit from hearing a professional voice and it makes the classroom real. So it is also a classroom issue, and Second Life adds to the classroom experience. However, using Second Life as an educational environment does create problems because it is a commercial place.

X-rated material can come into the classroom and students can behave badly. The first problem was anticipated and the second was not. The changing behaviors of students is a topic that needs further exploration along with how to integrate digital tools into education.

Summary

In summary, Postman's questions are still relevant today. We need to think about how and why we use virtual environments in the classroom. How can these environments best be used for constructivist learning? Our new generation of students is surrounded by digital technologies and we need to learn how virtual worlds can engage them in meaningful learning experiences. At this point, our research reveals that students did use Second Life as a rich learning experience. However, we are continuing to explore how students react to Second Life as a learning experience and we will continue to question the use of virtual worlds in the classroom. Additionally, balancing virtual interaction with traditional reading and writing assignments is important.

The fact that Second Life itself was the focus of the course and not just the vehicle for teaching the material in the course, was an important factor. It helped to motivate students in the course through the use of the virtual world, which gained their interest. This type of teaching can help students to self-discover the material being presented in a course. Experiential learning is the style of learning that best works with today's digital students and using real world examples helps to capture a student's interest.

Notes

1. The professors teaching the advertising course were Susan B. Barnes and Neil Hair of the Rochester Institute of Technology. Lyle Wetsch taught a marketing course in Second Life.

2. Survey conducted in Online Advertising Course at the Rochester Institute of Technology (RIT), fall quarter 2007.

Chapter Seven

Social Norms

Social norms are the rules that a community considers to be appropriate and inappropriate values, beliefs, attitudes, and behaviors. These rules may be explicit or implicit. Norms are often transmitted by non-verbal behavior, for example with "dirty looks," when people act outside the norms. Social norms may also be transmitted through stories, rituals, role-model behavior, and the media. It is more difficult to understand social norms through online behavior because online environments separate people from their words. Social norms need to be established through both words and behaviors. Thus, a new set of online behavioral norms is emerging on the Internet along with a number of misbehaviors.

Every electronic group establishes its own norms and values and these values can be based on face-to-face interactions. "Social norms are also rooted within the behavioral contexts in which users live" (Baym, 2010, p. 81). Additionally the existence of social norms is directly related to the enforcement of ethical behavior. Enforcement is vital when individual and group interests' conflict, as it encourages people to act in a desired or appropriate way. Informal sanctioning by group members is the primary source of enforcement. How this happens is discussed in this chapter.

As previously stated in chapter 4, when society developed into a more industrialized culture, Gellselschaft became a more powerful socializing force than local communities. The increased use of mass media created a media shift from acquiring information from interpersonal communication to obtaining information from the media. Today, media act as the primary source of information about politics, natural disasters, and social norms. Beniger (1987) contends that there has been a dramatic shift in interpersonal control over people's behavior by traditional communal relationships (Gemeinschaft) to impersonal, restricted, and mediated control or Gesellschaft. Thus, the introduction of mass media changed the ways in which people received information about social norms. Instead of learning behavior patterns from people around us in our physical locations, individuals turned to mass media as a method for learning social behaviors.

Online social behavior is often called "netiquette" and it includes rules designed to prevent people from having to read useless information, to limit false or fictional identities, and to protect an individual's privacy. When members of a group create a set of behavioral norms, online groups can grow into communities. For example, some groups will not accept members that do not use their real names included in their e-mail addresses, whereas other groups will allow people to use pseudonyms. Rules for netiquette include being sensitive to other people's feelings, seeking help from others in the group, and to help new users (newbies) when they join the group (see Adams & Clark, 2001).

Each group establishes its own behavioral norms and new members of the group need to understand and conform to the rules of behavior. When first joining a new group, it is recommended that people lurk for while before they join the conversation. Lurking is reading messages without posting. By lurking, an individual can learn the proper behavior in the group. Typical responses to unusual behavior are confusion, pity/distain, or anger/hate. Hate messages can turn into flaming, a common Internet behavior. Flaming is to negatively and/or incessantly talk about someone or discuss a relatively uninteresting subject. Flaming is a part of Internet behavior that does not mirror real life activities.

General Internet Norms

There are a number of behavioral norms for the Internet. For example, do not write in all capital letters because capital letters indicate shouting. Additionally, people sending and receiving e-mail messages expect a reply to their message within a short period of time, for instance within twenty-four hours. Flaming is a type of behavior that is common on the Internet. Flaming is considered to be a form or rude behavior. Although it is rude, many people flame and flaming is a part of general Internet behavior.

Flaming behavior is considered to be caused by the lack of emotional cues in computer-mediated correspondence. Early researchers argued that the lack of emotional cues in computer-mediated communication would lead to antisocial and impersonal behavior online, such as flaming and uninhibited behavior.

But, in contrast to early research, it was discovered that when people are physically separated, stronger levels of affection and emotion can develop. In some cases this emotional bond can surpass or be equal to face-to-face relationships, which are called hyperpersonal computer-mediated communication (Walther, 1996). Hyperpersonal communication happens when the Internet correspondence "is more socially desirable than we tend to experience in parallel ftf [face-to-face] interaction" (p. 17). An example of hyperpersonal communication is when a couple meets online and then gets married. The number of people who have met their significant others online is growing with the popularity of online dating sites, such as match.com and e-harmony. Today the idea of meeting and developing a relationship through online methods is no longer a stigma, it is accepted as normal social behavior. Thus, Internet behavior influences face-to-face actions.

Basic Rules of Netiquette

Similar to off-line experiences the basic idea of "Do unto others as you would have them do unto you," applies to the Internet as well (See Wood & Smith, 2001). Wood and Smith state there are five basic rules of netiquette. First, people must realize that the Internet is not private. Although people may think that the messages they send are exclusively for another user, this is not the case. Information can be stored for later retrieval and forwarded on to others. Don't say anything on the Internet that you wouldn't put on a postcard, a postcard that is being sent to your grandmother. For instance, writing an e-mail message complaining about your boss or company could end up in the hands of someone you are criticizing. It happened to David B. Whittle (1997) and he lost his job.

Second, people think it is rude when others clutter their e-mail boxes with unwanted messages—spam. An individual should avoid spamming, especially the forwarding of chain messages, which demand participation and replies. Third, a flame is considered to be a hostile message. When you receive a flame think twice about responding with another flame because a flame war may break out and disrupt communication in the group. For example, a group was formed to flame other groups. The flamers joined a cat-loving group and then asked for a recipe for roast cat. The ensuing flame war caused such a commotion that the cat lovers list was destroyed, which was the goal of the flamers.

Fourth, write brief messages because long diatribes are generally considered to be bothersome. Finally, observe a good form of writing. Some e-mail writers fail to observe standards of grammar. They don't spell check their work or use capital letters. Netiquette requires the writer of an e-mail message to write in the same way they would for the reader of a printed message (see Wood & Smith, 2001). For instance, a number of people applying for a job in online learning at RIT did not use print-based standards. Instead people wrote with acronyms (BRB, LOL, CU, etc.) or used all lower case letters. These resumes were thrown in the circular file and they were not considered for the job because of their poor use of e-mail. The lesson to be learned here is that how you present yourself in e-mail is a representation of self (chapter two). Someone who will not take the time to write a proper cover letter is probably someone that you do not want to hire as an employee.

In contrast to Wood and Smith (2001), Whittle (1997) describes netiquette based on six personality traits: civility, respect, generosity, responsibility, focus, and discipline. Civility is being courteous to others. Many online services and colleges have Internet policies, which state that people should be civil when using the network. "A key ingredient in making the cyberspace experience worthwhile for ourselves and for others is civility—and the more we can learn about how others would like to be treated, the more we can make the experience an enjoyable one for ourselves and for others" (pp. 105-106). At the center of netiquette rules for behavior is a concern for the well being of others and us. If you are a considerate person in real life, conforming to this rule should be easy online.

Individuals should be respectful of others. The Golden Rule applies on the Internet as well as real life. To be deficient in respect is certain to result in a contentiousness, flaming, and difficulty in an online communication. "You may criticize ideas, but not individuals. This is not only good logic but common sense" (Whittle, 1997, pp. 106-107). Ideas can be discussed reasonably, however when a person is attacked, a flame war is likely to erupt. Also remember to be tolerant of the mistakes of others. We all made mistakes when we first used the Internet, be especially respectful to new users.

Be generous to others. Since the early days of the Internet, people have shared ideas and advice with individuals. "The sharing of your tidbit of information, your tip, or your program increases dramatically in value when it benefits several hundred people" (Whittle, 1997, p. 107). An example of being generous was the development of the Linux operating system by thousands of programmers around the world. By each person volunteering their time and skills to the project, an operating system was created that could rival the software produced by Microsoft. However, there is an ethic to this volunteer work online.

Be responsible for your own words and give credit to others for their ideas. "When you accept ownership for your words, you are concerned with the impact those words have and assume responsibility to avoid harm to others" (Whittle, 1997, p. 107). People need to accept the responsibility for the words they speak or type and deal with the negative and positive consequences of those words. Moreover, "the destruction or theft of another's data is unconscionable" (p. 108). Hackers leave the data untouched on a system; however, they may add their own information. Even the people who hack other people's computers consider destruction of someone else's data unethical. Real hackers, not crackers who steal information, respect the data created by individuals.

Keep messages online as brief and simple as possible. We have to remember that some people are paying to read messages. Internet providers, especially in countries outside the United States, charge different types of service fees. "The 'cost' of your message can be calculated by adding the average value of the time it takes each reader to read your message plus the bandwidth cost to download and/or read it online" (Whittle, 1997, p. 108). People's effort is worth at least $10.00 per hour. So, keep messages short and don't waste other people's time. For this reason, sending chain letters is considered an inconsiderate form of social behavior because these messages waste people's time and money.

Dealing with Bad Behavior

Whittle's final personality trait is to be disciplined. When people violate the rules of behavior on a discussion list, they can be removed or shut out of the list. Few people on a list will complain if an offender is blocked out because usually this person has been disrupting the normal flow of conversation. People who make worthwhile contributions to a list are rewarded with praise. "Those who contribute nothing, poison the well, flame, spam, curse and abuse, are often berated—which usually only serves to increase the level of contention and disharmony" (Whittle, 1997, p. 109). Discipline is needed to ignore these bad behaviors. People on a list that has become disharmonious will ignore the abusers or in the worst-case scenario, they will be asked to leave the list.

There are four basic forms of misbehavior, which include: harassment, silencing, capturing transmission, and interference with reception (see Wood & Smith, 2001). Harassment is the forced reception of unwanted messages, such as flaming. However, on college campuses harassment can be the unwanted messages from another person, especially a person of the opposite sex. Cyberbullying is a topic that is now being addressed on and off campus. This type of misbehavior often occurs in social networks.

Social networking has introduced cyberbullying into online transactions. An example of cyberbulling is the story of Phoebe Prince, who took her own life after a barrage of vicious taunts. The verbal abuse and physical threats may have driven the teen to death. Phoebe moved to the United States from Ireland and she was a very attractive girl. Classmates called her "Irish whore" and were jealous of her good looks. Social networks are places for all types of bullying experiences, another teen named Megan Meier killed herself after a fictional boyfriend dumped her and make rude remarks on the Internet. What started as a joke turned into suicide and an arrest for the woman posting the messages (Pokin, 2007).

Another less upsetting form of misbehavior is silencing. Silencing is the interference of current or future transmissions or the destruction of past archives of messages. An example of this occurred in the virtual community called the WELL (Whole Earth 'Lectronic Link). A member erased all of his messages from the archives and the action became known as mass-scribbling. He erased years of discussions on the WELL, creating holes in the conversations. "It seemed an act of intellectual suicide" (Rheingold, 1993, p. 34). Moreover, the programming tool for scribbling was posted on the WELL by a disgruntled member for anyone to use. Stopping people from receiving their messages and deleting messages from a list's archive, are considered forms of misbehavior.

A form of misbehavior is also capturing or controlling the transmission of another person's message. For instance, when someone posts an offensive message under the name of another user. A classic online example of this type of misbehavior is described in a book by Julian Dibbell (1998). It happened in the virtual game called LambdaMoo, a site designed to explore the formation of social relationships in computer-mediated communication. A character named Mr. Bungle appeared in the main living room of the game one evening using a software tool called a voodoo doll. A voodoo doll can control the actions of other characters in the game. Mr. Bungle controlled by a group of New York University students began to make the other characters perform perverse sexual acts. The voodoo doll was stopped by a Wizard (experienced programmer) on LambdaMoo. The player was removed from the game. Ejecting the offender is a typical response to this type of bad behavior.

The fourth form of misbehavior is interference or obstructing the ability to receive messages. This can occur through mail-bombs and mass flaming or in the case of Mr. Bungle, the character was thrown out of the game. Additionally, individual's using a bozo-filter that prevents the messages from a particular e-mail address to enter a mailbox, is also a way to obstruct messages.

Three additional types of online misbehaviors are trolling, provocateurs, and misrepresentation (see Barnes, 2003). Trolling is baiting people with outrageous messages and these messages are designed to start a flame war or disrupt the group. For example, sending a message asking about how to prepare a recipe for roast cat to a cat lover's list will start a flame war. Originally, trolls were designed to make new Internet users appear clueless when they read these messages. Experienced users would know not to respond to the outrageous post. However, some people found trolling to be a game that could be used to disrupt online groups. For instance, the cat lovers list was never the same after the post about roast cat.

Another similar form of misbehavior is the provocateur problem. Although, online discussion groups need people who will ask provocative questions to start online conversations, this technique becomes a problem when individuals use it to disrupt discussion groups. The problem was first encountered on public affairs discussion lists when anarchist groups tried to shut the lists down. However, "their technique was taken over by individuals with a more pointed purpose—to nullify the effectiveness of discussion lists that aim to increase public participation and decision making through the Internet" (Barnes, 2003, p. 251). Provocateurs can work in groups or as an individual. They can sign onto a list using several different names. Generally, they insist on sending off-topic messages to the group, which is what causes the disruption.

Misrepresentation is using someone else's identity or changing your identity to someone of the opposite sex. When a user changes sex, it is called gender-bending. The word was first described in 1985 to describe an event that occurred on CompuServe, an early conferencing system. A prominent New York male psychiatrist named Alex changed his identity to a female named Joan. As Joan, he became friends with a number of women on the network. When his female friends discovered that Joan was a man, they felt betrayed. Although, gender-bending is common in online games, people in discussion lists do not expect this type of behavior to occur. Remember that different types of online groups create diverse norms of behavior. For instance, gaming environments are different from support groups (see chapter 4).

Different types of online groups manage misbehavior in a variety of ways. For example, after the rape in cyberspace, LambdaMoo set up a legal system to handle inappropriate actions. In gaming environments, Wizards can eject people who behave badly. Similarly, systems managers and moderators of lists can have people thrown out of the group. Or an individual can take action by using a bozo-filter, a piece of software that buries e-mail messages from someone on the hard drive. In a worst-case scenario, users can leave the list where the offenses are taking place.

Software can be used to control misbehavior and it can be used to create it. For example Google Bombs use text linking practice in which the link does not actually describe the content to which it points. "So, if a group of people want to use a Google Bomb to attack you, they will point anchored text links to their website or blogs or social network profiles with your name as the words that are in the link. But the page linked to actually contains derogatory or defamatory content" (Dozier & Scheff, 2009, p. 101). Misbehavior is common on the Internet and people have developed various software and behavioral methods for dealing with it.

Building an Online Relationship

Individuals join discussion lists and to meet other people. People exchange e-mail messages and begin to form friendships. Most Internet relationships are based on shared interests. Interest replaces physical location as a reason for people to build friendships.

Another reason for building relationships is human attraction. People are attracted to others through the words they express and the types of behaviors that they exhibit online. First impressions, our initial feelings toward someone, work on the Internet as well as in face-to-face situations. However, when meeting online we don't have the physical appearance as an evaluation tool to decide whether or not we like someone. People get to know each other through their words rather than physical attractiveness. People can develop relationships regardless of the limitations of the medium.

To understand relationships through the Internet, the rhetorical framework for understanding interpersonal relations. developed by Phillips and Metzger (1976), can be applied. Phillips and Metzger contend that people have goals and these goals influence the formation of friendships. For instance, a person might want a new friend to discuss a hobby or they may be looking for a romantic relationship. The framework has six standards for identifying interpersonal behavior: sharing common experience, security and satisfaction, understanding the other, role-play, reciprocity, and benefit.

People spend time sharing information through the Internet. Over time, relationships are built through the sharing of common experiences. In fact, it takes more time to develop an online relationship than it does to form a face-to-face one. For instance, Walther, Anderson and Park (1994) state: "Interpersonal impressions [do] develop over extended time interaction in CMC, and they developed more slowly than in [face-to-face] interaction" (p. 477). Additionally, difference between face-to-face and computer-mediated relationships occur in the initial stage and then dissipate over time. However, one important consideration is whether or not people expect their online relationships to be ongoing and possibly lead to future contact. People who consider relationships to be ongoing, will work harder to continue the relationship.

Security and satisfaction combine the feeling that one fits into society with verification of one's identity by others. People need to feel secure in their online relationships and for relationship bonding to occur. We tend to believe the words of others, this is why misrepresentation is considered misbehavior. The social presence of others in computer-mediated relationships helps to support a feeling of satisfaction. Plus there is the flexibility of the medium. Twenty-four hours a day you can find someone to talk to on the Internet. As described earlier in this chapter, some people believe that their Internet relationships can be more satisfying than their face-to-face ones.

According to Phillips and Metzger (1976), "Each individual in a relationship is able to monitor his [or her] behavior as well as take the position of the other in order to perform an analysis of the situation in which he [or she] finds himself [or herself]" (p. 182). Understanding the other uses a dual perspective; a state of mind that takes into account that another person may see the world entirely differently than they do. Dual perspective enables individuals to organize their messages according to how they think another person will receive it. Moreover, on the Internet people can use the idea of negative spontaneity, not immediately responding to a message, to craft messages and spend more time carefully reading the messages of others.

Behaviors are projected as roles. People can play a variety of roles in computer-mediated communication. Role Play in different Internet sites could be being yourself on a social network, taking on the role of a character in *World of Warcraft*, or assuming a nickname in Instant Messenger. The Internet provides the ability for people to take on different roles in various online environments. Moreover, the roles we assume in online contexts can influence the development of online relationships.

Online and face-to-face relationships are developed through reciprocal exchanges. "Each person, consciously or unconsciously, conducts a review or his [or her] ongoing relationships and, following the pleasure principle, acts to maintain those that satisfy and diminish or extinguish those that do not" (Phillips & Metzger, 1976, p. 182). In the process of maintaining the relationship, something must be exchanged. For example, if you tell a person something personal, they expect the response to also contain some personal information. Responding to messages is the first step in building reciprocity in Internet relationships. Another way to develop the skill of reciprocity online is to engage in reflected listening and mirroring part of a person's message back to them. All of these behavioral factors contribute to a successful online friendship.

Teenage Behavior

Teenagers and college students use social networks to establish communication channels with their friends. News and reports have written about the use of teens and technology. "Reports in the press and surveys from parents find points of view that range from exuberant, discussing how socially-interactive technologies can save youth from social isolation and depression, to alarming, focusing on how constant use of these technologies fosters anti-social behavior" (Bryant, Sanders-Jackson & Smallwood, 2006). Studies by the Pew Internet and American Life Project, indicate the majority of today's youth are living an intensively connected lifestyle. The Pew/American Life studies show that 94 percent of pre-college youth ages twelve through seventeen use the Internet and/or e-mail (Lenhart, Arafeh, Smith, & Macgill, 2008). Approximately 89 percent of them access the Internet from home and 77 percent get access from their school. Many of them have their own computer at home that is separate and distinct from the "family's" personal computer, providing them individual access to the Internet and the online world (Lenhart, Arafeh, Smith, & Macgill, 2008).

Young people are using social networking to "enhance communication among friends and family, to made make plans with one another, and to maintain social contact outside of their day-to-day face-to-face conversations" (Bryant, et al., 2006). Added incentives for teens are the ability to time-shift and talk at non-traditional hours. Moreover, teens use social media platforms as a means for expressive written communication through web pages, blogs, and social networks (Lenhart, Madden, Macgill, & Smith; 2007). In addition to the written word, social media also provide a platform for teen expression in visual arts via art, photo, and video sharing sites and remix. Creating a sense of identity is a key reason why teens need to express themselves online.

According to Pew reports, teen use of blogs doubled from 2004 through 2006. In addition, the report showed usage differing across the genders; with girls most often contributing to blogs and boys most often participating in content sharing (Lenhart, Arafeh, Smith, & Macgill, 2008). For teens, "Blogs are personal journals or reversed-chronological commentaries written by individuals and made publically accessible on the web, and they have distinctive technological features that set them apart from other forms of CMC" (Huffaker & Calvert, 2005, para. 10). For instance, there is more flexibility and anonymity in the digital world, which makes teens feel more comfortable expressing their feelings and sexual orientation. Language is a method for expressing and exploring sexual identity. Moreover, social networking tools, such as Instant Messaging, can create intimacy between users and form a sense of connectedness. Social media strengthens the preexisting networks of an individual.

There is a gender difference in the styles of communication in males and females (also see chapter 4). Online groups dominated by females tend to "self-disclose" information and they try to reduce the tension in a discussion list. For example, females present themselves online as friendly and smiling. In contrast, males tend to use impersonal and fact-oriented language. Additionally, males are less concerned about politeness and sometimes violate the rules of netiquette (see Huffaker & Calvert, 2005).

Two social issues with teenage behavior using social media is the idea that teens will freely give up personal information in social networking sites and teens frequently will text messages while driving. Teens don't seem to understand when it is or is not appropriate to use the Internet. Teens do not seem to realize the Internet is a public not private space. When someone sits in their bedroom typing their intimate thoughts into the computer, those thoughts become public. The privacy of the physical room becomes overshadowed by the medium. However, as many times as teens are told the public nature of the Internet, the privacy of private physical space seems to negate the warnings of a public place (see Barnes, 2006). "Teenage bloggers are revealing a considerable amount of personal information, as well as multiple ways to contact them online, the danger of cyberstalking and communicating with strangers online is a serious issue" (Huffaker & Calvert, 2005, para. 63). Which, many teens do not seem to be aware of.

Another serious issue is texting while driving. "A graphic British public service video that portrays a fatal accident caused by a texting teenage driver has been the talk of Facebook and other places where young Americans congregate, but a study suggests that it hasn't done much to change their habits" (Halsey, 2009, para. 1). A quarter of teenagers with cell phones are texting while driving. Distracted driving led to over 5,000 deaths in the United States last year. "Teens told Pew researchers that they texted while driving to find friends, get directions and flirt. Some said they tried to restrict texting to when they were stopped at red lights" (Halsey, 2009, para 10; also see Madden & Lenhart, 2009).

No matter the reason, texting while driving leads to distracted driving and it is a danger. The number of people killed and injured because of texting is alarming. Many states are now making it illegal to text and drive. Social media can cause deaths and several writers have documented the ways in which people react online to a death of a friend.

Online Death

Several examples of online death have been described by Rheingold (1993) and Barnes (2001), in which the online behavior has been observed. Previously in this chapter the idea of deleting all of your e-mail messages from a virtual community was mentioned. However, there is more to the story. Rheingold referred to the act as "intellectual suicide" and that is exactly what happened. Blair, the man who committed the act, killed himself shortly after deleting all of his messages. A traditional funeral was held and most of the people were from the WELL Many of the members of the WELL lived in San Francisco, so it was possible for them to attend in person.

Other suicides have been reported as a result of messages posted on MySpace. For instance, a young man named Josh contacted a thirteen year old girl named Megan on MySpace. After months of sending positive messages to Megan, Josh sent a message that he no longer wanted to be friends. After his message, a number of people began to post negative messages about Megan and she became very upset. Shortly afterwards, Megan hung herself in a closet. As it turned out, there was no real Josh. He was a character made-up by adults.

> A mother constructed a profile of "good looking" male on "myspace" in order to find out what Megan (Meier's daughter) was saying on-line about her daughter. (She) explained the communication between the fake male profile and Megan was aimed at gaining Megan's confidence and finding out what Megan felt about her daughter and other people. (Pokin, 2007, para. 85)

Some of these behaviors by adults have lead to criminal actions. So pretending to be another person on Facebook or MySpace can have real-world consequences for the individuals involved. A difference between Facebook and MySpace is that Facebook requires people to use real names.

In contrast to suicide, Barnes (2001) writes about a natural death of a list member. The members of the list were dispersed and a virtual funeral was held online, where positive comments about the person were shared. Someone once said that a virtual community is not really a community until it shares in grieving for the death of a friend. A discussion list called Interpersonal Computing and Technology lost one of its prolific members due to natural causes. The list moderator only posted testimonials for the member for several days, so members of the group could share their thoughts and feelings. The following is one of the testimonials:

> Sad, sad . . . Are there no tears in cyberspace? How many times have I rehearsed what I might say if I had the chance to meet him? Let it be said that, even through this indirect modality, he has had a small but strong influence on a life on the other side of the Earth . . . (Hooper, 1995). (Cited in Barnes 2001, p. 244)

A norm that has formed in cyberspace is to hold virtual funerals for people who have passed or to spend time paying tributes to the person. All types of online environments hold virtual funerals. For instance a funeral held in *World of Warcraft* has become legendary on the Internet. A girl who was a *World of Warcraft* player died in real life. Her online friends planned a funeral in game to memorialize her death. They posted notices about the event on *World of Warcraft* message boards. What started out as a respectful affair turned into a battle when a group called Serenity Now decided to attack the mourners. The entire event has been captured in a YouTube video and can be found by typing in "*World of Warcraft*+funeral."

MySpace has formalized the process of funeral memorials by starting a web site called www.mydeath.com. The site is for members of MySpace who have passed. When the site was first encountered in 2006, the memorials were for members, most of whom died in car accidents between the ages or eighteen and twenty-four. Www.mydeath.com states it is "an archival site, containing news articles, online obituaries, and other publically available information." Today, the front page of the site shows memorials for celebrities. To find the real members, people have to click on "Latest Articles." Death behavior on the Internet has been formalized by posting tributes, creating virtual funerals, and posting information on www.mydeath.com. As people use social networking as a major communication tool, online behavior is developing norms that may be similar or different from face-to-face behaviors.

Norms for Online Classrooms

Norms for all types of behavior have been formalized on the Internet from death to classrooms. Online teaching can provide several benefits that are unavailable in face-to-face contexts. For instance, students have more time to reflect on their writing when they use asynchronous e-mail. Writers should be conscious of why they are creating the message. Different reasons for sharing e-mail in a class include: presenting an argument, information sharing, and asking or answering questions. When preparing a message, a student needs to consider the audience reading the message, for instance name dropping, using obscure or obscene language, techno-jargon, and overly long messages can alienate readers (see Barnes, 2003).

Rude behavior can disrupt the flow of conversation in a class using computer technologies. The following are rules that can be followed to avoid flames in educational environments:

1. Try to limit the length of your messages to make them easier for other people to read. Scrolling down too many screens of text can loose the reader.
2. When making references to people and ideas provide sources and if you introduce a new concept, it should be explained.
3. Carefully read the messages of other students. Try to respond to what is being said and give other students a fair chance to answer messages.
4. Avoid profanity and personal attacks on others. Arguments and debates should consider and respect other students. A personal confrontation should be done through private e-mail and not in public group discussions. (Barnes 2003, p. 219)
5. The posting of information or explanations, which display a shared interest in topic with the group. This shows a shared commitment to keep the list ongoing.
6. Emoting in text, using an emoticon or word in angle-brackets <sign> to illustrated verbalized pauses for thought of emotion. (Murphy & Collins, 1997)

Computer-mediated communication in the classroom is conducted between students and teachers, and students and students. "Discussion and dialog between instructor and students and among students is a key feature of computer conferencing and the foundation of constructivist learning techniques" (Murphy & Collins, 1997, para. 1). Rules of behavior need to be established to make sure that all voices can be heard in an orderly manner.

Adding computer discussions to a class can make it more engaging for students. Disclosing personal information and exchanging reciprocal messages can establish personal presence. However, these messages need to be exchanged in a turn-taking fashion and rules need to be established for the educational group. "Without any protocols other than [netiquette] . . . the students made off-task remarks, used acronyms and other text-based shortcuts, occasionally reprimanded each other, and turned what was an instruction event into conversation chaos" (Murphy & Collins, 1997, para. 45). Online instructors need to make their intentions clear on how a group will perform in cyberspace, for example, the use of proper English, no cursing, and turn-taking.

Students do not easily translate the difference between their personal use of the Internet and learning environments. In fact, some students have questioned professors when the students are asked to write proper English essays for online distribution. The students belived that if the material was online it should be written in the online jargon they were used to. Moreover, students have written rude and profane messages in online courses. Similar to teenagers, students don't seem to realize that teachers and online learning staff could be reading these messages.

When people are removed from their words, they tend to misbehave in ways that are not similar to face-to-face communication. People take more liberties online because there is a sense of anonymity. Today, there are a number of social networking sites for the purposes of business, common interests, dating, face-to-face facilitation, friends, pets, and photos. Using these environments for educational purposes has not been widely adopted. Therefore there is a gap between social networking sites and educational ones.

Social Networking Norms

The most common model for social networking "is based on the presentation of the participant's profile and the visualization of her network of relations to others" (Gross & Acquisti, 2005, p. 72). The use of real names in profiles is encouraged in many social networking sites, such as Facebook and LinkedIn. Moreover, researchers have found that offline identities carry over to online behaviors (Hargittai, 2007). Profiles are connected to a person's public identity. Other types of information generally presented are hobbies, interests, current and previous schools, and employment. Some sites have questions on drinking and drug habits and sexual preferences as a part of the public profile.

The definition of a "friend" varies on social networking sites. Some people invite everyone to be their friend, while others have a conservative definition of friendship. For instance, a person may have a dozen of intimate friendships and list hundreds of hundreds of acquaintances as "friends." In many cases, the quality of friendship on social networks is low, which indicates weak social ties between people. Thus, a paradox emerges, people must post intimate and private information on the social network to maintain close friends; however, this information is also revealed to acquaintances and strangers. Gross and Acquisti (2005) state: "The ability to meaningfully interact with others is mildly augmented, while the ability of others to access the person is significantly enlarged" (p. 73).

Although the ability to access a person is increased, social networking sites provide methods for communicating through online channels with an individual's previously established face-to-face social circles. Kim and Yun (2007) contend: "Empirical evidence has repeatedly indicated that communication technologies are used to maintain pre-existing relationships" (p. 299). Once people connect as friends on a social network, they can be removed. Removing a friend is easier than deleting a profile because some social software environments have mechanisms, such as links, for eliminating people. "However, the social implications of deleting friends can discourage users from doing so. Furthermore, little is gained by deleting friends; indeed, many people strive to get as many friends as possible" (Goldbeck, 2007, para. 44). As a result, people tend to add more friends than delete them.

Two additional norms associated with social networks are data collection and voyeurism. Social networks are a place where young people can pull together information. For instance, young people will share poems and ask for feedback; they will create polls about school issues; ask friends for help with problems and homework. "Unfortunately, many students are unable to effectively evaluate the information that they gather from these various social contacts" (Lamb & Johnson, 2006, p. 56).

By posting all this data on the Internet, social networks provide a venue for voyeurism. Bumgarner (2007) states: "People can pursue the profiles of various users, read about other users' interests, read their friends' comments on their walls or view their friends" (para. 14). Additionally, voyeurs can view a user's photo album and see all their pictures. Voyeurism and exhibitionism go together. Individuals need to self-disclose the information for voyeurs to see. People have to be willing to put their profiles and photos on Facebook and other social networking sites.

It should also be noted that not all students use social networks. Despite the reports that teens and students are heavily connected, Hargittai (2007) reports that some students are non-users of social networks. Despite knowing about social networks, 12 percent of the students in Hargittai's research did not use social networks. Groups that were less likely to use social networks were students who lived at home with their parents, and Hispanic students. Hargittai's results show a new type of digital divide forming in the information age. As a result, professors cannot assume that all of their students are members of a social network or know how to use social networking technology. Social networking skills is not always a social norm for young people.

Summary

In order for groups and communities to form in online environments, social norms need to be established, such as don't waste other people's time or resources. Different groups create different types of rules for behavior. For example, an academic discussion list is very different from an online game. In an educational online environment, the rules of turn-taking, and being respectful of others is critical to keep conversations from becoming chaotic.

Today our understanding of norms of behavior is transmitted through the media. In online contexts, it is recommended that a user lurk, or just watch before joining in the group. By watching, one can learn the norms of the group and avoid flames. Flame wars can destroy a group and in some groups are avoided because they disrupt the conversations, for instance, an educational group.

Although, many of the social bonds we make in social networks are weak ties, some people do tend to think that the online connections are more satisfying than their face-to-face friends—hyperpersonal communication. Teens and students are avid users of social networking and place their profiles online. This may be a form of exhibitionism, which results in creating a form of voyeurism on social networks. In contrast to exhibitionism, a small percentage of teens do not use social networks, which creates a new type of digital divide is forming and student experience with social networking cannot be assumed.

Chapter Eight

Ethical Issues in Online Communication

In Second Life and other online environments the separation of people from their words allows individuals to misbehave in online learning environments, without any accountability. Research on Internet behavior indicates that people misbehave because they are not physically associated with their actions. Moreover, the writers of this book have observed students themselves misbehaving in virtual spaces. This raises ethical issues for educators who want to teach in virtual environments because unknown events can occur during class time. For instance, rape, simulated violence, and virtual abuse have all been reported in Second Life. Online learning environments and social networks create new ethical challenges for educators, examples will be presented in this chapter.

Development of the Internet represents one of the fastest, changing, and adopted technologies in human history. The creation of the World Wide Web has brought together a wide variety of media including, text, images, video, and audio, into one single medium. The Web has changed the face of communication and ushered in a new world of electronic commerce. Internet success brings with it a new set of ethical issues, which are facing our culture today. These issues include: changes to personal, professional, and social values; equal entitlement; free speech; and control over personal information. Social networking has particularly challenged our notions of what is personal and private information and who has access to this data. Second Life confronts teaching in a commercial world that is filled with pornography. With the advent of social networks ethical issues need to be incorporated into Internet discussions.

Internet and Ethical Values

In Society, we stress the need for ethics and personal responsibility and this is also true for online interactions. Without rules for civic engagement, discussion lists would be chaos and cease to function. We would not be able to have blended education, where part of the course is holding conversations online. However, the Internet is a decentralized system with no single entity in control—academic, corporate, governmental or non-profit. Yet all of these various organizations must co-exist with millions of individuals who use the Internet for their own reasons and purposes. This new medium of worldwide communication has no sheriff. It is up to individuals to maintain law and order in the "electronic frontier."

Laws and regulations do not effectively control the Internet. Instead, correcting technology with technology has been more successful. For instance, the development of programs that enable parents to block pornography from home computers that children use. "This reflects the net's paradoxical nature—it empowers individuals and allows them to exercise their rights, including free speech, more vigorously, but it also makes possible effective technical controls that can undermine those rights" (Spinello, 2000, pp. 1-2). Whittle (1997) states: "The principles of ethical standards are surprisingly universal, including qualities such as propriety, fairness, honesty and treating others as we would like to be treated" (p. 110).

One way to control the Internet is through the behavior of individuals by teaching them ethical behavior. Ethics is a series of right principles defined by a group or community of individuals. For instance, the Institute of Electrical and Electronics Engineers (IEEE) have developed a code of ethics along with the Association of Computing Machinery (ACM) to regulate professional behavior when dealing with computers. These rules include: honor confidentiality; honor contracts, agreements, and assigned responsibilities; improve public understanding of computing and its consequences; accept responsibility; avoid real or perceived conflicts; and avoid injuring others. To counter unethical behavior in social networks, Facebook is developing a series on safety tips to educate parents and young people. Some of these tips are available on YouTube. On a more personal level, Willard (1997) incorporates many of the rules of netiquette described in the last chapter into her discussions of "cyber-ethics," such as respect resource limits, tread carefully, respect the privacy of others, credit the source, and speak responsibly. Personal responsibility is central to orderly communication online along with the "golden rule," do unto others as you would have them do unto you. These two concepts should guide your behavior on the Internet.

Brief History of Computer Ethics

Computer ethics is not a new topic. It was first developed in the 1940s with Norbert Wiener. Like many aspects of the development of the Internet, the creation of ethics and computers was related to the war effort. Wiener made some insightful conclusions about the social and ethical consequences of computer technology. In 1950, his seminal book, *The Human Use of Human Beings*, was published, which established him as the founder of Computer Ethics. More importantly, this work established the basis for computer ethics research and analysis.

In the 1960s, "Donn Parker of SRI [Stanford Research Institute] International in Menlo Park, California began to examine unethical and illegal uses of computers by computer professionals" (Bynum, 2001, p. 11). Parker contended that some computer professionals left their personal ethics "at the door" when they entered the computer center. As a result, he published, "Rules and Ethics in Information Processing" in a journal sponsored by the Association of Computing Machinery (ACM). After the publication of the article, Parker was asked to be in charge of a group that wrote the first Code of Professional Conduct for the Association of Computing Machinery, which is still in use today.

Another ethical work published in the 1970s was Joseph Weizenbaum's, *Computer Power and Human Reason*. Weizenbaum became concerned that a growing tendency at the time was to view humans as machines. He had written a computer program called Eliza that mimicked the questions asked to a patient by a Rogerian psychotherapist (see chapter 1). When people interacted with the program, they became emotionally involved with it and shared their most intimate thoughts. This led some practicing psychiatrists to believe that computers would be performing automated psychotherapy. The idea of replacing human therapists with machines outraged Weizenbaum and he wrote a book about it.

By the 1980s, social and ethical issues of computing were becoming public issues, such as computer crimes, invasion of privacy, and software ownership. A number of books were written, for instance Sherry Turkle's *Second Self* (1984). Sociology and philosophy books and articles began to appear (see Bynum, 2001). The issue of computer ethics began to be explored by a number of different disciplines, including philosophy, sociology, psychology, business, law, journalism, and information technology.

In 1991, Terrell Ward Bynum conducted the first international conference on computer ethics, which attracted participants from the United States and seven different countries (see Bynum, 2001). Interest in computer ethics was now on an international level, for instance Simon Rogerson established the Centre for Computing and Social Responsibility at DeMontfort University (UK). Rogerson wanted to develop a "second generation" of computer ethics codes (see Bynum,

2001). A first step in development is to define the term: "Computer ethics identifies and analyzes the impacts of information technology on social and human values like, health, wealth, work, opportunity, freedom, democracy, knowledge, privacy, security, self-fulfillment, etc." (Bynum, 2001, p. 16). Topics in computer ethics include: computers in the workplace, computer security, software ownership, and professional responsibility. For the purposes of this book, we are not discussing the illegal aspects of computer ethics, instead we are focusing on personal ethics because social media is a personal medium.

Personal Morality

Netiquette describes many of the rules for personal conduct on the Internet. Since the early days of the Internet there have been discussions about self-regulation online. As previously stated, self-regulation is important because the Internet is a decentralized network and no single entity controls it. Instead it is up to millions of individuals to keep order on the network. Previous attempts of self-regulation have dealt with limiting commercial use of academic networks, restrictions to the distribution of pornographic materials, and hate speech (see Hamelink, 2000). However, rules for sending and receiving e-mail have also been established. For instance, it is suggested that individuals do not immediately respond to flames. Instead, people should wait twenty-four hours and then communicate with the flamer through another channel, such as a private e-mail message when the flame is sent to a group.

Rules for individual use of e-mail can also be found in a university's "Network Use and Ethics Statement." Most colleges have these statements and users are made aware of them. These statements include rules that prohibit the fraudulent use of university computers, infringing on the rights of others, avoid language that is abusive or offensive to the average person, and theft of data. Different groups also have ethical standards for freedom of expression and the distribution of child pornography.

A central concept for personal ethics is to remember that e-mail on the Internet can often get into the hands of other people, beyond the recipient of the message. Confidential messages should never be sent via e-mail. Individuals need to take responsibility for their words and actions online to make sure the information does not get into the wrong hands. The Computer Ethics Institute has ten basic commandments for computer use:

1. Thou shalt not use a computer to harm other people.
2. Thou shalt not interfere with other people's computer work.
3. Thou shalt not snoop around in other people's files.

4. Thou shalt not use a computer to steal.
5. Thou shalt not use a computer to bear false witness.
6. Thou shalt not use or copy software for which you have not paid.
7. Thou shalt not use other people's computer resources without authorization.
8. Thou shalt not appropriate other people's intellectual output.
9. Thou shalt think about the social consequences of the program you write.
10. Thou shalt use a computer in ways that show consideration and respect. (www.tekmom.com/tencomman/index/html)

These commandments are reminiscent of types of laws proposed by Moses in the Bible (see Exodus 20: 1-17). Moreover, "they reflect the standards that apply to human communication in civilized societies" (Hamelink, 2000, p. 42). With the creation of many different ethical rules for individual behavior on the Internet, a question still remains: Can we follow the rule of society established in face-to-face interactions? Or do we need new types of rules for virtual spaces?

Social networks introduce new types of ethical issues for individuals. During the National Science Foundation Grant, students were surveyed about ethical behavior issues in social networks. For instance, they were asked: Is going through a person's friend list and "friending" those people without knowing who they are an appropriate form of behavior? The majority of the students disagreed with this statement, while a couple agreed with it. Twenty-six students answered the seven point Likert-scale survey with seven being strongly agree and one strongly disagree.

The survey asked students about appropriate behavior online. A summary of the results, show that students mildly disagreed that there should be spelling errors in e-mail messages, but they were neutral about using shortcuts such as r u there. They strongly disagreed that it was appropriate to place sexually explicit material on someone's wall and were neutral about obtaining information about others online. However, they mildly disagreed with employers using social networking sites to gain information about future employees. Moreover, the students were neutral about sharing MP3 and video files through the Internet, although this is often against the law. See Appendix A for the full survey.

The results are very interesting, in certain areas such as spamming and chain letters the students agree with the general rules of netiquette presented in the last chapter. However, they are neutral about the idea that spelling and grammar are important. Moreover they are neutral about adult language and cursing. These perceptions could have serious consequences for education, which prizes the importance of good grammar and where cursing has not been considered generally acceptable. For example, the quotes in this book from the students using Second Life are full of misspellings and grammatical errors. Moreover, there was a considerable amount of cursing in the class discussions.

New issues introduced by the Internet are spoiling and file sharing. Spoiling is the "active process of tracking down information that has not yet been aired on television" (Jenkins, 2006, p. 292). For instance, people would find out what happened in episodes of Survivor by checking satellite images and questioning hotel staff where the show would stay. Then they would post this information on the Internet before the network aired the program. The students did not think that spoiling was acceptable. In contrast, file sharing, which has serious copyright infringement issues was considered to be acceptable. Moreover, sharing these files with strangers was not seen as problematic. The students were neutral and mildly agreed with this type of behavior. Herein lies a difference in ethical concepts between young people and the music industries.

Professional Morality

One ethical issue that the students did not agree with is using social networking sites as a way for employers to search for information about possible employees. Information on social networks is not private and anyone can go and look-up a profile. Employers tend to think that looking at an individual's profile will provide them with more information about the individual and it is ethical to do so. In contrast, the students did not agree. Herein lies a professional ethical dilemma that has yet to be resolved.

Ethical issues for professionals occur in relationships with employers, colleagues, clients, competitions and the organizations in which computing professionals work. Unlike older professions, such as medicine or law, computing professions do not have as much of a history or organization for dealing with ethical issues. A typical issue relating to employers and employees occurs when an employee discovers something wrong with a product that is being produced by a manufacturer. If the employee wants to bring this problem to the public's attention, he or she will probably lose their job. However, if the problem is anonymously exposed, the employee can remain unknown to management. The dilemma to speak or to remain silent about the issue is an ethical one that people sometimes face.

The term for exposing a company for bad practices is called "whistle-blower." The Internet can provide a method for whistle-blowers to speak. Whistle blowers using anonymous re-mailers can strip their identity from their messages to remain anonymous. "Thus, the re-mailer acts as a filter that keeps the person receiving the mail from knowing who sent it" (Cavazos & Morin, 1994, p. 16). Although, whistle blowing is considered to be a positive use of re-mailers, there are concerns about criminals and terrorists using this technology for illegal purposes.

Another type of issue that commonly occurs is when a person moves from one job to another. What corporate secrets can they speak about and which are confidential? For this reason, many computer companies have people sign non-disclosure forms that states the person cannot speak about what they have seen.

An issue for social networks is whether or not a company sponsors a discussion group. For example, Apple computer sponsors the Apple discussion group on MySpace and they publically acknowledge their role on the list. However, an ethical issue can arise when a person who represents a company goes online and praises their product without informing the group of his or her affiliation with the company. Because of the viral nature of information on the Internet, negative news about a product can spread quickly through the network. As a result, Internet marketing specialists recommend that companies have a strategic plan in place to deal with negative messages about them.

Another example is medical school students who violate the privacy of their patients by posting detailed information on blogs. Historically, doctors have been held to a higher standard, but in the age of social networking these standards are not being upheld. "Medical students may be accustomed to being free with their thoughts and photos on the web, but the Internet is not a free-fly zone for future doctors" (Mann, 2009, para. 14). Many medical schools are putting in place a policy that describes proper and in-proper use of the Internet. Currently, students who violate patient confidentiality are informally reprimanded or expelled from school. While, other professions are having similar problems with information posted on social networks, medical students create more of an inappropriate issue because patients are directly affected.

Due to the new types of ethical issues that computer technology introduces into society, many professional computer organizations have established their own code of ethics. These organizations include the Association of Computing Machinery and the American Institute of Electrical and Electronics Engineering (IEEE). Around the world, computing organizations have established their own codes of ethics, including Canada, Singapore, and Sweden.

Additionally, businesses are establishing their own code of ethics for using Twitter. This technology enables employees to shoot off quick blasts of messages to the world. In addition to blogs and embarrassing pictures on Facebook, companies now have to worry about dubious postings to twitter. The basic rule that companies are telling their workforce is "Don't be stupid" (MacMillan, 2009, para. 3). Don't say anything on Twitter that you would not say to your mom. Again, the public nature of the Internet is being addressed.

Social Morality

While professional organizations prepare codes of ethics for their members, the age of the group advancing Internet technologies keeps getting younger. "For many of us baby boomers or older, we are not part of the groups advancing this technology and we most certainly are not in the majority of those developing the rules and shaping the culture of cyberspace" (Tuman, 1999, p. 159). One issue associated with Internet use is that young people have no senior role models to help them form their ethical values online. In the past, young people learned from their parents, but today parents are not as familiar with Internet technologies as their children.

Moral development requires interaction with the community. "When we take our communities for granted, or worse—take without giving to others—we pollute the moral atmosphere, lower the ethical standard of living, and create unhealthy habits, including elitist neighborhoods and bigoted hometown, dysfunctional families and uncivil workplaces" (Bugeja, 2005, pp. 50-51). Bugeja (2005) is concerned about the moral impact of technology on in-person communities. Just because we have technologies that can bring people together on a global scale does not mean the technologies will foster communities (see chapter 4). The role of communities needs to be examined in terms of digital technologies because there is disagreement on whether or not the Internet will improve geographically based communities and whether or not virtual communities are imaginary of not (Gross & Acquisti, 2005). In addition, not all people can access online communities because you need to be computer savvy. The Internet does not provide equal access to everyone.

Equal Entitlement

Equal entitlement relates to access to technology. Postman (1995) writes: "The advantages and disadvantages of new technologies are never distributed evenly among the population. This means that every new technology benefits some and harms others" (p. 192). When the Internet was first introduced, white males dominated it because it required expensive equipment and computer skills to access the Internet. Thus, there was a large digital divide between those who had access and those who did not. As more user-friendly methods, such as the World Wide Web, became available, access to the Internet was open to more people. By the year 2000 over half of the men and women in the United States were Internet users (Katz & Rice, 2002). The idea of a digital divide began to decline. By 2001, Internet use began to mirror the populations of men and women in the United States. Katz and Rice (2002) explored the differences between Internet users and nonusers. They examined the attitudes attitudinal influences upon each group. The nonusers found barriers such as "costs too much," "access," and "too complicated" to be obstacles to Internet use.

In her study on Internet users and nonusers, Hargittai (2007) examined the differences between people who use social networking sites and those who did not. She found that 12 percent of the student population she surveyed did not use social networks. The 12 percent of students in this group were Hispanic or they lived at home with their parents. Although, adults may assume that all young people use social networking, this is not always the case. This research is now being duplicated at RIT, to test the assumption that all students use social networks.

While the gap between young people who use social networks and those who do not is relatively small, this is not the case in worldwide Internet usage. On a global scale, the gap between countries that are wired and those who are not, is widening. Not all nations have equal access to the Global Information Society. "The present disparity is no new phenomenon. When new technologies are introduced into societies the chances to benefit from them is always unequally distributed" (Hamelink, 2000, p. 82). However, for people to participate in the Global Information Society, they must become digitally literate.

People need to be digitally literate to participate in today's wired culture. Public institutions can only function as people become more literate. For instance, many government agencies have put their forms online and make them available through websites. People need to know how to access the web to have access to the information. As a result, those who do not become digitally literate cannot participate in portions of society, especially, in the development of information capital.

Information capital is related to social capital. Social capital is the development of an individual's personal social network (Van Der Gaag & Snijders, 2004). According to Wellman, Haase, Witte & Hampton (2001), social capital is increased offline interpersonal contact, organizational and political participation, and commitment to community. Simply stated, social software is software that enables people to interact with each other and build social networks that increase their social connections.

Information capital "embraces the financial capacity to pay for network usage and information services, the technical ability to handle network infrastructures, the intellectual capacity to filter and evaluate information, and the ability to translate information into social practice" (Hamelink, 2000, p. 91). To gain social and information capital, one must participate in digital societies, equal entitlement deals with who does and does not have access to the network and digital tools.

Free Speech and Content Controls

Equal entitlement also has a relationship to who can and cannot participate in free speech on the Internet. The Internet has greatly expanded an individual's opportunity to exercise their First Amendment Rights. The medium is one of limitless expression for those who have access. Probably the biggest moral issue on the Internet is free speech versus content control. For instance, in the United States, there have been efforts to suppress pornography. The First Amendment protects pornography. However, parents and educators want to restrict this information from getting into the hands of children. Therefore, people want to eliminate pornography from school libraries and home environments with young children. To date, the best solution to this problem has been a software solution, the design of filtering programs that will enable educators and parents to block these sites from school and home computers.

France and Germany have tried to control hate speech on their web servers. "Many groups, such as white supremacists and anarchists, have Websites that advocate their particular point of view" (Spinello, 2000, p. 58). For example, one point of view is that the Holocaust never happened. France does not permit this information to be promoted on French websites. The logic for their argument is that the Holocaust did happen and saying it did not is historically incorrect. False historical information should not be placed on French servers.

Instead of false information, students may say negative statements about a teacher on their web page, blog, or social network page. For instance, Sean described one of his high school teachers as "over-weight with uncut hair" and included a photo of the teacher on his personal website (see Spinello, 2000). The high school suspended Sean and ordered him to take down the web page. This action raised the issue of whether or not the school infringed on the student's rights. A lawsuit followed and the student's rights were up held. As a result, websites such as www. ratemyprofessors.com have been created for students to evaluate their teachers. Schools and professors cannot censor this site because the First Amendment protects it.

Personal Information

The first Amendment protects an individual's free speech, it does not control what individuals say. Young people freely give up personal information about themselves when joining social networks on the Internet. Afterwards, they are surprised when their parents and others read their journals because they mistakenly thought that only their friends would be able to see their information. Communities are outraged by the personal information posted by young people online, such as the teacher comments previously described. Colleges are happy about the personal information posted on social networks because networks enable campus security to keep track of student activities on and off campus. The posting of this personal information by teens and students has social consequences (see Barnes, 2006).

Social networking sites flourish "on a sense of immediacy and community. The spirit is independent, even rebellious" (Howe, 2005, p. 218). Young people are using these sites by watching the behavior of their friends rather than observing parental use of social networks. Parents have no clue about the information teens are publicly revealing on the Internet (Sullivan, 2005). In the United States, we live in a paradoxical privacy environment. On one hand, teenagers reveal their intimate thoughts and behaviors online and, on the other hand, marketers are collecting personal data about people and storing it in databases. Thus, more personal information is becoming public information. This often occurs without the knowledge of the individual. Galkin (1996) said: "Much of the information that people would like to keep secret is already lawfully in the possession of some company or government entity, and what we want is to stop further disclosure without authorization" (para. 14). Social networks add to this problem because they create a central repository of personal information that people disclose often without knowing who could have access to the information.

The personal information revealed by teenagers on these sites also attracts sexual predators. For example, a thirteen-year-old boy as lured into a sexually coercive group of older men, who found him through a webcam (see Garvin, 2006). The boy had placed a single image of himself online with the hopes of attracting a girlfriend; instead, he was coerced into performing sex acts into the webcam. He was paid by over a 1,000 men to strip in front of the camera. The sexual predators also arranged trips with the young man to meet in-person. The personal information that young people have placed on the Internet had opened the door for sexual predators to abuse them. Match.com is being sued for allowing sex offenders to date people. As a result of the suit, Match is now checking the names of participants against lists of known sex offenders to try and keep them off the site (CNN News, April 18, 2011). Unethical behavior in social networks can also spill over into the classroom.

Classroom Ethics

Behavior exhibited on social networks by students has filtered into the classroom. For instance, teenagers misbehave online through cyber bulling and placing disparaging remarks on the Internet. Placing a disparaging remark about a classmate can influence the climate of the classroom. Moreover, teens engage in risky behavior to post videos on YouTube.

> Most suburban teenagers, it seems, can rattle off a litany of the latest teens-gon-wild offerings as though they were the local multiples listings: boys holding cellphones under the lunch table to photograph up girls' skirts; an

> innocent kiss at a party posted out of context on an ex-boyfriend's Web site; someone bursting in on friends who are in the bathroom or sleeping, drinking or smoking; students goading teachers into tantrums; assaulting homeless people. (Kilgannon, 2007, para. 10)

Goading teachers into tantrums has a direct impact on the classroom and its management because the authority of the teacher is undermined.

Several classroom incidents occurred during the grants described in this book. At the end of the Provost's Innovation and Learning grant, a student showed-up at the final party with a gun and proceeded to shoot his friend. Fortunately, there had been no incidents with guns at the university. As a result, the students at the party ignored the event. The faculty tried to raise the issue in the online discussion, but the students ignored the message too. Everyone in the class seemed to know that the student with the gun was an avid computer game player and the incident was an extension of his game playing. However, the university did not agree.

When the incident was disclosed to the university, they wanted to discipline the student and bring him before the committee on student misbehavior. The course teachers were able to convince the university that the incident caused no harm and they promised to speak to the student. When the student was confronted about the incident, he was shocked that it would be considered unethical behavior. He was only thinking about playing a game with his friend. But, understood how his behavior could be interpreted in a different fashion.

During the teaching of the Social Media Course, a young woman in the class verbally assaulted a male who had been in the military. Conversations went back and forth for about a week and the incident did create some bad feelings amongst students, which may have impacted their building of social networks. Of course, all of the messages could be seen by the professors and quite a bit of cursing was going on. The professors did not enter the flame war because they did not want to escalate the situation and it eventually died down.

Both examples generally never occur in a face-to-face classroom. As a result, teachers need to be aware that the Internet introduces new types of behaviors that can affect the classroom. Students don't think their teachers are reading the information or they don't care if they do. Classroom ethics is an issue for research and discussion in the digital age because life is not a game and everything is not entertaining.

Pornography and the Classroom

Second Life also introduced the ethical issue of pornography entering into constructivist learning experiences that use this environment. Second Life can spread pornography because people must be eighteen or older to join the site. This has implications for education, as some students are not eighteen yet when they start college. To make students aware of this situation, they had to sign release forms for our class and they were instructed that when traveling outside designated class space, they were at their own risk. Students were also asked to review the Second Life community standards at http://secondlife.com/corporate/cs.php. Precautions were taken to make students aware of what they may encounter.

Pornography has been an issue in Second Life. Rapes have been reported along with child pornography. German authorities investigated an avatar of a child that was having sex with an adult. Should this be considered child pornography? The participants are virtual. Linden Labs, the creators of Second Life, condemned the actions and cooperated with the authorities to locate the people behind the action. It turned out to be a fifty-two-year-old man and a twenty-seven-year-old woman; both were banned from Second Life (see Sipress, 2007)

Some students in the Second Life class did come into contact with pornography in Second Life. Most of them stayed away from these locations or existed very quickly. They knew that advances from a stranger could get them into trouble. It was necessary to make students aware of the appropriate ethical behaviors in Second Life. In fact some students who encounter pornography thought they would get into trouble in the course. However, pornography in Second Life is beyond the control of professors.

Summary

The Internet introduces new ethical issues into society. For instance, the idea of personal responsibility is often thought to be hidden behind the computer screen. But, just because people cannot see who is behind the actions on the Internet does not mean that we remain anonymous to our behavior. The Internet has no single organization that controls it; in contrast, control of the Internet is in the hands of individual users.

The idea of computer ethics is not a new one, but new applications, such as social networks, introduce new types of ethical dilemmas. Young people do not seem to be aware that the photos they place on Facebook or MySpace can be widely viewed. Moreover, they do not seem to think about how their actions can have an impact on others. But, unethical behavior on the Internet can affect real people. This is a lesson that is sometime hard to recognize because people are hidden behind their words.

Chapter Nine

Trust Online

People learn to trust by noticing the behavior of others; therefore the social behavior of an individual is important for establishing a feeling of trust. We need to be able to trust the people that we interact with on the Internet. Trust is the expectation that arises within a community of regular, honest, and cooperative behavior, based on commonly shared norms. Trust is emerging as a potentially central aspect leading to information technology acceptance. It is an important component of many social, business and educational relationships. This chapter will discuss building trust, the role of the media in creating trust, and the role of trust in online exchanges.

Trust encompasses the concept that people will fulfill their commitments to other people. The cognitive state of trust is a composite of benevolence and credibility. Benevolence is the belief in the good will of another person. Credibility is the belief in the character of a person and their integrity for doing no harm. For a large number of people the idea of trust is developed over a period of time and through experience. Most people have had experiences with the betrayal of trust. Individuals know they are trusted when they are asked to perform the same task over and over (see Phillips & Metzger, 1976). We trust others when they reciprocate with actions used in the exchange between people. For instance, a neighbor taking care of a pet or a co-worker helping on the job, or going to the movies on time with a friend.

Conversation and interaction rituals demonstrate trustworthiness and trust is generally built through the reciprocal exchange of small talk, and self-disclosure. In business it is establishing and maintaining collaborative relationships. On social networks trust is formed through the sharing of gossip and the politeness of users. The idea of trust in online settings may be assigned differently than face-to-face ones and have different meanings. For instance, we have many friends in social networks that can access our personal information, but how many of these people are close friends who we can trust? Although privacy is necessary for intimacy and personal trust, trust may decrease in online networks because of the weak social ties associated with online friends. A paradox is created here because more people can access our personal information without being trusted friends. Friendships in social networks are not as strong as face-to-face ones. As our information becomes more widespread, the number of friends we trust decreases. In contrast, as technology becomes more prevalent in our lives we are asked to trust it instead of people.

Technology and Trust

Every time that we purchase a book on Amazon with a credit card or book an electronic ticket for an airplane, we trust the technology to complete the transaction. As more companies move away from telephone operators to web-based services and automated telephone directories, people are increasingly being placed in a position of trusting technology for transactions and information.

While some may be skeptical of online commerce, the profits from online purchases keep rising. Similarly, people tend to trust millions of strangers that they encounter through the Internet. Online interactions are a combination of human actors and technology. The issue with trust and technology "is how to establish trust online in light of the enormous uncertainty about both the magnitude and frequency of potential harm" (Rosenbloom, 2000, p. 31). Because we do not see the people we are dealing with in online media, building trust can be more difficult. However, people behind the technology are a more important factor in trust through technology. Whether or not we trust someone shapes the nature of our interactions with others.

The media do encourage trustworthy behaviors through their transmission of social experience. For instance, presence theory described in chapter 1, is the sense of awareness of others. The stronger the transmission of personal presence through a medium, the stronger the sense of trust can be developed. In online exchanges, another method of instilling trust is through assurances, references, third-party certifications, and guarantees of privacy and security. An example is the Feedback Forum in eBay that rates an individual on how trustworthy they are to sell products. This type of third-party verification makes new users feel as if they can trust the eBay community.

Postman (1995) argues, "because of the symbolic forms in which information is encoded, different technologies have different *intellectual* and *emotional* biases" (p. 193). In the case of computers, the universality of the machine enables engineers and programmers to develop computers with different intellectual and emotional biases. For example, the computer interface can use design techniques to create a feeling of trust. There are a number of different issues that engineers follow to cultivate trust online, including security of the technology; knowledge about peoples actions; misleading language and images; disagreement about harm; informed consent; accountability; saliency of cues; insurance; and performance and reputation (see Friedman, Kahn & Howe, 2000).

Computer technology is not reliable or secure. The safety of code is unknown and the nefarious behavior of criminals has cracked code to manipulate end users. The users themselves must decide whether or not an online environment is safe. At present, the vulnerabilities of software are unknown and people must rely on the good will of others to create safety.

Knowing what people do online is helpful to ascertain how much risk there really is in online exchanges. The number of people who spread viruses, hack into computer systems, and steal identities should be compared to the number of average people, who use the network for work and play. To date, we do not have an accurate percentage of good to bad behavior online. The challenge for trust is how to develop trusting relationships in light of the enormous uncertainty about risk.

Adding to risk is the misleading use of language and images on the Internet. For instance, when designers tell us that their website has a "secure connection," what level of security should we expect? A visual example is the padlock-and-key icon in Netscape Navigator. What level of security does this icon represent? "Yet designers routinely use misleading language and images to convey to users greater reliability and security in the technology than is warranted" (Friedman, Kahn & Howe, 2000, p. 37).

Disagreements about an individual's understanding or harm can also impact trust. For example, we have hackers and crackers. Hackers were originally people who enjoyed playing tricks with computer code to find the most elegant solution to writing the program. In contrast, crackers are people who break into computer networks to access information. In between these two, are people who break into computer systems, but don't touch the data on the system. Which of the three are harmful? Would we all agree on the harm?

Harm can also come in the form of the software programs that corporations want to place on our computers. Several years ago, there was uproar about cookies being placed on user's machines. These are the small programs that enable Amazon to say your name when you access their website. In terms of trust, should companies be telling users when they place these programs on the user's computer? The idea of informed consent involves letting users know about potential harm and risks. Should companies inform people when they add software to an individual's machine?

What is the accountability of companies, especially advertisers who are using behavioral marketing, which involves using personal information about an individual to market products and services. Accountability applies to companies and individuals. We do not see whom we are communicating with on the Internet. Netiquette described in chapter 7, states that individuals should be accountable for their actions. People need to be responsible for what they say and do on the Internet to build trust into the network.

Insurance, or the "promise" to compensate an individual for future harm if it happens, is another way to establish trust. When evaluating insurance in a social arrangement, consider the adequacy of the coverage and the ease of obtaining the compensation. Insurance demonstrates that an individual or company wants to guarantee that it will meet its commitments.

Finally, how individuals perform and meet their commitments along with the reputation of the individual contribute to building trust. Performance histories, including past experiences with a person or company will establish trust. Additionally, third party endorsements, such as a recommendation from a friend, will develop a reputation for trust.

As described in chapter 1, the work of Reeves and Nash (1996) showed that people interact with technology in the same way that they would interact with people. Because computers are new technologies and we have no behavioral basis for their use, people tend to apply social behaviors between individuals to computers. This is illustrated by the development of software avatars that can carry on conversations in virtual reality environments.

Trust is dependent upon the social cues embedded in the online environment. Conversational behaviors build trust; therefore, creating a software agent or avatar that can converse with the user will create more trust in the interface. Cassell and Bickmore (2000) describe such a system, where software avatars are programmed to engage in conversations with users. Some of the techniques for trust that they are building into the interface are interaction rituals, such as building solidarity, transitions, establishing expertise, and acquiring information about the user.

The research is investigating interaction rituals to build trust in real estate sales encounters. It is easier to program a software agent for a limited context, such as real estate or medical information. From a visual perspective, the avatar's visual and verbal behavior must match. Avatars use conversational storytelling to establish their area of expertise by describing stories of past problem-solving behavior. Additionally, the avatars obtain information about the user that can be used to help achieve tasks.

There are four main goals associated with the small talk between the avatar and user. First, is to build solidarity. The program has predefined prerequisites to demonstrate solidarity. A rapport needs to be developed between the avatar and user before the individual will discuss personal information, such as income and other financial information.

Second, the transitional methods used by the avatar, create the feeling of natural language. The software will keep track of the current and past conversation topics. "Conversational bids that stay within a topic (main topic coherence) are given preference over those that do not" (Cassell & Bickmore, 2000, p. 54). Conversational topics can shift in a natural progression, for instance talk about weather can shift to the weather in Boston to the topic of Boston real estate.

Third, self-disclosing statements about the expertise and limitations of the avatar are necessary. The avatar does tell the user of some of the limiting features of the technology. This helps to build trust because it helps to define the nature of the relationship between user and avatar. Additionally, the software describes other people who the program has helped.

Finally, the software is programmed with a list of priorities to find out about the user. Because the context is limited, the information pertains to real estate and what type of real estate the user is interested in finding. "Results indicate that many users find the agent more competent, reliable, and knowledgeable when it uses small talk than when it engages only task talk" (Cassell & Bickmore, 2000, p. 55). These findings support Reeves and Nass's research that people treat technology like other people. The politeness factor that we look for in humans, when applied to technology, makes the technology more appealing and trustworthy.

Online Trust

In addition to technology, building trust between people is key to trusting online relationships. "The most important characteristic of a good networking group is trust among the membership" (Meshel, 2005, p. 105). If a member of a group cannot be trusted, he or she should be asked to leave the group. "In a virtual group, it can be hard to trust strangers who reveal little about themselves. For example, many rape survivor groups have to police their memberships to prevent people with prurient interests in the subject matter from interfering with therapeutic goals of such groups" (Crumlish, 2004, p. 128). For example, if Facebook decided to exert control and ownership over the materials posted to the site, users would no longer trust the company. They might exit en mass to another social network.

People have to trust each other and trust the companies they use online. Jarvenpaa and Leidner (1998) researched the concept of trust in teams that used computer-mediated communication. The research question was: Could people living in different countries interacting through computer-mediated communication develop a sense of trust with their other team members? After examining a dozen case studies, the researchers found that in the trust can be established in the early stages of online communication. "Communication that rallies around the project and tasks appears to be necessary to maintain trust" (p. 27). Agreeing to perform a task and completing the task creates trust. Additionally, complementary and cooperative behaviors also instill trust in oneself and others.

Interface designer, Ben Shneiderman (2000) contends that principles and guidelines can be used to design trust into online experiences. His definition of trust is "The positive expectation a person has for another person or an organization based on past performance and truthful guarantees" (p. 58). Trust is about expectations and how people and organizations will complete promises and their willingness to make good on failures. It can also be viewed from a contractual perspective.

Shneiderman (2000) proposes two principles and seven guidelines. The first principle is to "*Invite participation by ensuring trust*" (p. 58). Users need to receive strong assurances that the relationship they are engaging in is trustworthy. On the Internet, people may seek reliable sources about past performances of a person or organization. One way to gain trust is to place the logos of reliable companies on a website.

Guideline One under this principle is to disclose patterns of past performance. For example, airlines report on the on-schedule of their flights. Individuals and organizations should be open about performance and personnel to assure skeptical users. Guideline Two is to provide references from past and present users. A good example of this is the reputation manager that eBay uses of record comments on sellers. Guideline Three is to get certifications from third parties; getting approval from industry review boards or certifications from professional groups, such as the Association of Educational Journalism, Media, and Communication, or the Public Relations Student Society of America, which provide accreditation to colleges. Guideline Four is to make it easy to locate and enforce policies involving privacy and security. Privacy policies should be easy to find on the website and easy to read. The Chief Privacy Offer at Google stated: "privacy is about more than legal compliance, it's fundamentally about user trust. . . .If your users don't trust you, you're out of business" (cited in Fleischer, 2007, n.p.).

The second Shneiderman (2000) principle is "*Accelerate action by clarifying responsibility*" (p. 59). To make each participant's responsibilities clear is the first guideline. Well-designed websites should be orderly with easy navigation, meaningful product descriptions, and a user-friendly transaction process. Prompt apologies when something goes wrong and sincere efforts to solve problems can make customers become lifelong clients. Providing clear guarantees and compensation for problems can ease fears about credit card abuse and security risks. This is the second guideline; for instance, providing compensation for delayed deliveries. Finally, support dispute and mediation services. When a product or service disappoints a user, having a third party facilitator to handle the problem creates the feeling of trust in the user.

Trust is an important part of online interaction both for individuals and organizations. Trust can be developed between people. Organizations should pay attention to the guidelines described by Shneiderman to create business websites that promote elements of trust. In addition to these principles, the visual design of a website can also help to build trust. For instance, Korean Bank websites build the concept of trust by using three-dimensional clip art and cool pastel colors (see Boyd, 2003).

The Rhetoric of Trust

In addition to software, the rhetoric and metaphors imbedded in the English language can be used to promote the concept of trust. For example, metaphors we use in American culture can signify the idea of trust; such as, the expressions, "She looked me right in the eye" or "We worked together, shoulder-to-shoulder." Conversely, the phrase, "She went behind my back," illustrates the betrayal of trust (see Cassell & Bickmore, 2000). However, many of our relationships and negotiations are communicated online.

Today, we live in a "trust economy" because many of our daily transactions are conducted through the Internet. Where there is a certain amount of uncertainty in online transactions; however our sense of trust enables these transactions to occur. Boyd (2003) states: "Structural assurances attempt to demonstrate stability through messages that persuade users of the dependability of a site and its procedures" (p. 394). One reason why sites seem dependable is because of the reputation of their offline counterparts. For instance, if you shop at J.C. Penney's offline, it is reasonable to trust the site online. But, not all sites are connected to an offline counterpart: "Trust online is this kind of impersonal or thin trust because it often involves trusting the words and images on a screen rather than an identifiable person or even a familiar organization" (p. 395).

Trust online can be called "impersonal trust" because it is trust with people who are far removed from the user. We cannot see or hear the people we are asked to trust online. As a result, trust on the Internet involves both sellers and consumers. A seller must trust that the user will pay for the goods and services. Conversely, the consumer needs to trust that the seller will deliver the product or service. "Trust involves a belief in an agent's competence, predictability, integrity and benevolence" (Boyd, 2003, p. 398). With people and companies, trusters look for evidence of a history and reputation of trustworthiness. For example, websites of brick and mortar companies are more likely to create the feeling of trust than dot.coms. "As experience online accrues, however, trust becomes almost a given, able to withstand occasional violations that, had they occurred earlier in the user's experience, could have driven the person back to the 'safer' world offline" (p. 401).

Every rhetorical transaction that occurs through the Internet is an interaction that builds trust for future online encounters. Additionally, the problem-free interactions of others can also build trust in an individual. In building trust, companies should communicate messages that emphasize the reputation of the company. Building on the reputation, "online trust statements can include the names and titles of organizational representatives available to users, along with the links to information about exactly what those people can and cannot do to help users" (Boyd, 2003, p. 403). Developing messages that rhetorically instill the idea of trust is an important aspect of Internet communication.

"The language of trust is a rhetorical construction that can mitigate risk and promote participation in the form of trusting behavior on the Internet" (Boyd, 2003, p. 404). Boyd (2003) identifies four tenets for the rhetorical construction of trust:

- Initial trust is the most difficult to achieve.
- People trust what they already know, and trust becomes cumulative.
- Trust is in actors, not systems.
- Trusting behavior results from accepting a little more risk or extending a little more trust. (p. 407)

Finally, it is better to be specific when communicating messages to create trust. Provide detailed information on how the company will remedy mistakes or "make goods" on product or service problems. Creating messages that communicate trust is essential to online interactions.

Trust in Social Networks

Language maintains connections between people and it manages trust. Social networks are expanding social worlds, but what is the impact of this technology on trust and friendships. People need to know who and what Internet transactions to trust. Personal profiles can help to provide greater trust and reliability to the online presentation of self. Profiles include: self-descriptions, statements from others, a list of links to other members, pictures, lists of favorite books and music, affiliations, and career goals. Individuals have the opportunity to check profiles and find information about the person that would not be available in a face-to-face encounter.

The Internet can be a place to find reliable information about identity and affiliations. Using signaling theory, which seeks to explain what keeps communication honest, Donath (2007) describes the types of relationships in social networks. She states that research suggests that both strong and weak ties are formed on social networks. "Strong ties are close confidants, people relied upon in an emergency ad with whom one is likely to share multiple interests" (p. 7). People networks built on strong ties can supply extensive support for an individual; however, they also require a large commitment of time and attention.

In contrast, weak ties "are more distant acquaintances, people known in a specific context and towards whom one feels less responsibility" (Donath, 2007, p. 7). These types of friendship networks are easier to maintain on social networking sites. Looking at the interactions that people have on their social networking sites can help to discover which friends have strong ties and which are weak. For example, people who frequently post messages on a person's site are more likely to be a strong tie, than just a link to another friend. Donath (2007) contends: "By increasing the number of weak ties one can maintain, social supernet [an immense network of friends] have the potential to expand their users' range of information sources, while maintaining a socially local context of personal acquaintanceship" (p. 15). Receiving information from acquaintances helps to build an individual's social capital.

One would think that building weak tie friendships with people in a college class would also help to build social capital. However, the students in the Social Media class studied by Barnes, Eggert and Jacobs (National Science Foundation Award #0633401) did not take advantage of building social networks from their classmates. The concept of trust was one of the topic areas covered in the course. Twenty-three students in a class on Social Media responded to a series of questions about trust. Students are the primary group that uses social networks and their opinions on trust help to shed some light on young people's attitudes toward the topic. For instance, the "friending" question revealed that most students tend not to befriend people they do not know. This finding does not support the weak ties attitude toward making friendship connections in social networks.

Generally, the students were neutral about online activities. However, they do seem to agree that they would pay for online services. The fear of participation in online transactions does not seem to be present with this group of students. The purpose of this questionnaire was to ask students about their trusting behavior online. However, students also need trusting behavior in the classroom. See Appendix B for the complete survey.

Trust in the Online Classroom

Today's student seems neutral about trusting most Internet behavior, but trust is important for collaborative work in the classroom both on and offline. However, students do not always gain the trust of Professors in the wired-classroom. In the above survey, the question: "Would you share with someone your personal secrets online?" received a neutral response. This can be interpreted as the fact that students do not seem to be worried about sharing their private information on the public Internet. The cognitive disparity between what students do and say does not apply here. Often, students will put personal information on the Internet without realizing that the public can see it, they do not seem to be cognitively aware of the public nature of the Internet. The students just don't seem to care who sees their information.

However, in several of the online courses taught by the authors, students have written statements that attack other students, attack the teacher, and use profane language. These types of behaviors make professors wonder if the students know who is reading their online messages. As a result, it appears as if students are not clear about public and private space on the Internet and making the distinctions between the public and private do not seem to be important to them. In contrast, the question about the Nigerian e-mail seems to indicate that young people believe the stereotype that all mail from Nigeria is spam. It has been reported that Nigerian students have difficulty getting college staff to take them seriously because of the Nigerian spam problem, so people do not trust these messages. Nigerian e-mail is an example of how the idea of risk influences trust. If a person or website seems to be risky, people will not trust them.

Trust in the classroom is important for collaborative work. Hanlin-Rowney, et al. (2006) explored the concept of transformative learning in an online class. They developed a foundation of trust as well as the group norms of listening, speaking from their experiences, and questioning deeply. They learned to respect difference and each other's unique experiences and perspectives. A foundation of trust as well as the group norms of listening, speaking from their experiences, and questioning deeply, were essential to the collaboration. Students learned to respect differences and each other's unique experiences and perspectives. Additionally, working groups must perceive the people they work with to be trustworthy, or else the group will not function. Moreover, individuals in the group must trust in their own ability to get the job done. The cultivation of trust is a vital component in group cohesion. Cohesion of trust is shown in the respect that students display toward other students.

However, students do not always gain the trust of their professors in the classroom. The laptop computer, which was once viewed as a classroom innovation has become a classroom distraction. "Wireless Internet connections tempt students away from note-typing to e-mail, blogs, YouTube videos, sports scores, even online gaming—all the diversions of a home computer beamed into the classroom to compete with the professor for the student's attention" (De Vise, 2010, p. A01). Ninety-five percent of the Students from Georgetown University admitted that they had used their laptops for purposes other than taking notes. As a result, some professors have banned laptops from their classrooms. Additionally, some schools have developed switches for the faculty to turn off the Internet during class. As a result, teachers do not trust students to exhibit the proper behavior in the classroom.

Summary

Trust is the commitment that we make to others and the belief that others will meet their commitments to us. Trust is built through experiences with people and technology. We trust other people when the individual reciprocates with actions in exchange. Technology is trusted when the programmers and developers design trust elements into the interface. In general, we tend to trust people more than technology. Technology, such as avatars, can build trust by mirroring human behavior. Small talk can lead to the development of trust and the disclosure of personal information.

Language and rhetoric are central methods for creating trust. Rhetoric and metaphors can be used to signify trust in a relationship. In social networks, language and symbols enable people to develop both strong and weak friendships. Weak friendships can provide information to individuals that will increase their social capital, the topic of chapter 11. In contrast, students seem to be neutral about most of their online transactions. Adopting a baby through the Internet was one of the few questions that received a strong reaction from the subjects. This neutrality is also noticeable in the classroom. The trust between students and teachers is declining as students use their laptop computers in class for everything except class notes. However, developing trust is central for groups to work collaboratively on projects. In conclusion, trust is important for classroom cohesion.

Chapter Ten

Remix Culture

Social norms are changing as people utilize online environments to build trust in the new digital landscape. Additionally, personalization, remixed cultural artifacts, and social networks create a new type of "remix" culture that is centered on the use of digital technologies. Today there is no difference between talking to someone face-to-face and speaking to him or her through the Internet. Mediated and interpersonal communication is the same in the eyes of the young generation. Reality blends with media to form a larger mediated reality called Remix Culture. *These changes have profound influences on online education. Today's online learning experience is being influenced by social networking and remixed cultural artifacts. This chapter will explore remix culture and issues of education and literacy.*

The YouTube version of "We are the World" made with fifty-seven different artists from around the world is a perfect example of remix. Its creator combined videos from fifty-seven people into one remix of the song. One YouTube viewer commented: "This is so much better than the new [commercial] remix, you guys are amazing :):):):):):):)" (YouTube.com). Remix is the ability of computers to combine text, video, images and sounds together. It creates a new culture that is emerging on social networking sites such as Facebook, MySpace, and YouTube. However, most of all, remix is about you, the user, taking control of media content. Rishad Tobaccowala, the chief innovation officer at Publicis Groupe Media said: "We're in [a media] era where the human is God. Consumers are now in control of content: We're consuming it, retransmitting it, creating it" (Cited in O'Leary, 2005, p. 4). Consumers or users are in control of remix and the culture it creates.

Remix and Social Media

Do you post images of yourself on Facebook? Or, do you upload pictures taken on your cell phone and send them directly to your blog? People who engage in these types of activities are using media in new and unique social ways. They are using media as social tools to connect with friends and family. These new technologies are called: social computing, social software, and social media. Central to the rise of remix is the growing popularity of social media.

Remix Culture

While social media is an integral part of remix, *remix culture* is about using copyright material and other cultural artifacts to juxtapose fragments of contemporary culture in new and unique creative works. An example is the book *Reality Hunger* by David Shields. It uses fragments from hundreds of different authors to create a new project (see Kakutani, 2010). Kakutani states: "the contentious issues of copyright, intellectual property and plagiarism that have become prominent in a world in which the Internet makes copying and recycling as simple as pressing a couple of buttons" (para. 4). In a digital age, forget about copyrights everything is open to manipulation and interpretation. In digital media it is very easy to cut and paste, or forward information to others. Information is encoded into a symbolic form that supports copyright infringement. While we can cite from books and quote the author, we cannot do the same with films, television programs, or records. Thus, as cultural critics our reference media is limited.

The term *remix culture* was created by Lawrence Lessig (2008) to describe a culture in which copyright material and other cultural artifacts are remixed into new creative works. For example, Greg Gillis states:

> We're living in this remix culture. This appropriation time where any grade-school kid has a copy of Photoshop and can download a picture of George Bush and manipulate his face how they want and send it to their friends. And that's just what they do. . . .
>
> It's good because it is, in essence, just free culture. Ideas impact data manipulated and treated and passed along. I think it's just great on a creative level that everyone is so involved with the music that they like. . . . You don't have to be a traditional musician. (Cited in Lessig, 2008, p. 14)

The concept of remix is not a new idea. Artists have being remixing media for many years. Pop art remixes images from popular culture with fine art. For example, Roy Lichtenstein's use of comic art styles with paintings and Andy Warhol's use of soup cans or pictures of Marilyn Monroe (see Janson, 1995). Similarly, symbolists combine different mythological, symbolic, and iconic images together into a perceptual journey of remixed messages.

Comparing symbolism to the remix of today uncovers some interesting parallels. First, art historian Robert L. Delevoy (1982) contends that the symbolist movement is a "sudden awakening to the symbolic void produced by electronic civilization, and more particularly to the libidinal disinvestment brought about by the substitution of technical objects for the traditional acts of labor" (p. 9). If symbolism is remixed reactions against technological society, current remix is just the opposite. It embraces technology and all the features that digital programs can produce.

A second difference is in the nature of who is producing remixed images. Today, remix is taken out of the hands of elite artists and becomes a vehicle for individual expression. Anyone with a computer and some software tools can create a remixed video and post it on YouTube. Originally reactions against the social influences of technology, remixed images have become a symbol for personal expression and individual control over technology and social structures. "If old consumers were isolated individuals, the new consumers are more socially connected. If the work of media consumers was once silent and invisible, the new consumers are now noisy and public" (Jenkins, 2006, p. 19).

According to Postman (1995): "Because of the symbolic forms in which information is encoded, different technologies have different *intellectual* and *emotional* biases" (p. 193). One bias is the ability of digital media to make copies and replicate information. Another bias is the visual change that is occurring when media move from analog to digital forms of representation. Looking at the world through digital eyes is different than viewing it from an analog perspective because analog and digital technologies symbolically represent the world differently. This point is elaborated in William Mitchell's *The Reconfigured Eye*. Mitchell (1992) contends, "the visual discourses of recorded fact and imaginative construction were conveniently segregated [in analog media]" (p. 225).

Documentary and entertainment remained separate in the analog realm. Today, digital media disrupt this separation. For instance, digital photographs can be manipulated in ways that were unimaginable thirty years ago. As a result, the idea that a photograph is fact or truth no longer applies. Or, as Zettl (1996) points out, analog images interpret reality while digital ones manufacture it. With digital photography, it is difficult to tell an original from a copy of a photograph and identifying image manipulation is next to impossible, without special software. Although, analog and digital ways of seeing the world are different, users take advantage of the features of digital technology to create images.

Content Creators

Content creation often occurs in social media sites, such as YouTube and Facebook. A goal of social media is "the design of systems that supports groups with an underlying value proposition of building social capital" (Roland, 2004, para. 5). Social capital is the development of an individual's personal social network, and the topic of the next chapter (see Van Der Gaag & Snijders, 2004). According to Wellman, Haase, Witte & Hampton (2001), social capital is increased offline interpersonal contact, organizational and political participation, and commitment to community. Simply stated, social software is software that enables people to interact with each other and build social networks that increase their social capital. One way to develop social capital is to create a YouTube video. For example, Stevie Ryan created the character Loca on YouTube and achieved alternate-reality stardom (see McGrath, 2006). So many people watched her video that she became a celebrity on YouTube.

Stevie Ryan is an example of how an individual can become a media star in user-generated content circles. As users take control of media content, they personalize and recycle media. A PEW Internet and American Life study reports that 44 percent of people have contributed their thoughts, ideas, and files to the Internet (see Lenhart, Horrigan & Fallows, 2004). Content creators are likely to be students. But, the report places them into three categories: *power creators, older creators* and *content omnivores*. Power creators are the group that is most enthusiastic about creating content on the Internet. Older creators are titled for their age, which is an average of fifty-eight. Many of these people are retired or they work part-time. Content Omnivores are the group that has "tried more of all kinds of Internet activities—including content creating ones" (Lenhart, Horrigan & Fallows, 2004, p. 10). This last category is the group that is most likely to post videos on YouTube.

YouTube and Remix Culture

You can find an example of individual content creation when you look for the viral advertising campaign "Wassup" by Budweiser Beer on Google Photos. You will find people's interpretations of the concept. This advertising campaign generated all types of images that were a spoof of the commercial and individuals created all. The "Wassup" advertising campaign was also central to the beginning of *viral marketing*. Viral marketing is "using customer communication as a means of multiplying a brand's popularity through customers spreading the brand name" (Henning-Thurau, Gwinner, Walsh & Gremler, 2004, p. 39). It was established with the Anheuser-Bush "Wassup" campaign. "Although the ads were originally launched on TV, the campaign gained momentum on the Web with lightning speed" (Bannan, 2000, p. IQ20). People are now taking pieces of advertising culture and re-using the material for themselves. This also applies to YouTube videos.

YouTube is now at the center of many of our conversations. On January 1st, 2007, after a short AT&T commercial, the *New York Times* website video reported that much remained unknown about the death of Saddam Hussein. But, if you went to YouTube, there was a video of his entire execution. Instead of the stately videos shown on the TV networks, the YouTube video was shot with a cell phone. It was rowdy and you can hear the verbal confrontations during the incident. Although the amateur photographer was reportedly arrested, think of the global impact of his actions. Where should we now go for news? YouTube had more details than the *New York Times.* What happens when each of us with a cell phone can capture news events and post them on YouTube? Not only can we post the images, but we can also provide more information about events than traditional news media.

A major media shift has occurred as networks, news organizations, advertisers, and Hollywood no longer control the content of information available on the Internet. We the people now have control. The content is ours. We can place whatever we want on the Internet and it can go viral. Or, we can at least get our cable fixed and iPod batteries replaced for a reasonable price. These are two products that were the subject of YouTube activists.

Ben McConnell and Jackie Huba (2006) wrote about two publicized citizen activists in *Giving Up Control and Other Scary Lessons*. They described how Casey Neistat was dismayed when he discovered that the replacement battery for his iPod would cost the same amount of money as a new machine. The angry customer recorded an Apple support phone call that said "At that price, you may as well just go buy a new one." Neistat then mashed the audio with a video of iPod posters being spray painted with the slogan "iPods Unreplaceable Battery Only Lasts 18 Months." The video called "iPod's Dirty Secret" was then posted to the Neistat web site. Thirty friends were notified about the video and within six weeks the number grew to a million. This is an example how information can go viral. Apple Computer has since altered its policy on replacement batteries. Today's challenge for companies is how quickly to respond to negative information spread through the Internet. A company's reaction to negative videos now plays an important role in how the company is perceived.

Similarly, a disgruntled Comcast customer videotaped a Comcast technician, who fell asleep during a service call. The technician was waiting for his own company, which put him on hold. This sleeping beauty was juxtaposed with the song "I need some sleep." After posting the video on YouTube and mentioning it on a blog, the word was out. In two weeks the video was viewed over 200,000 times and a Comcast executive solved the frustrated customer's problems.

On the other hand, marketers are taking advantage of the remix landscape when they develop one-to-one viral sales appeals that are posted on YouTube. Consider the Smirnoff viral video that is a parody of rap music. A group of country club yuppies are rapping about living the preppie life in New England. In the middle of the rap are names of drinks made with Smirnoff products. What's different about this video is that this is "a real commercial made by a real agency, Bartle Bogle Hegarty" (Bannan, 2000, p. IQ20). Unlike many YouTube videos, it is not a video made by an individual. Advertisers have learned about the power of content creation and viral marketing.

Another viral example is the Diesel Underwear campaign with two gorgeous girls who kidnapped a Diesel sales manager and locked themselves in a hotel room for five days. This unconventional campaign was a marketing tool for Diesel's Intimate Collection. The stunt was a parody of TV shows like "Big Brother." This advertising strategy was taking a television concept and remixing it for the Web. Advertisers know that word-of-mouth communication is "deeply personal, exactly the opposite of the mass media message" (Downes, 1999, para. 81). Viral marketing is similar to word-of-mouth messages because the information spreads from one person to another. Additionally when you spread a message through word-of-mouth or viral marketing, the message seems to be much more personal than mass media messages.

Viral messages are also how information about remix is spread. Friends tell other friends about the videos. Remix is similar to advertising because both depend on cultural symbols and icons to communicate ideas. Many advertising campaigns incorporate some type of cultural symbol or icon. In some cases, like M&Ms, advertising remixes photos of people with iconic brands. If you don't know what M&Ms are, you won't go to the site to make your own "inner M." Therefore, cultural knowledge is important for remix culture to exist. This is also true because images depend on cultural knowledge to be understood and interpreted.

A key reason why remix is and would not be easily accepted in education is because of the subjective nature of the visual communication process. Currently, our educational systems are grounded in more concrete verbal message systems where words have a one-to-one relationship with definitions. However, much of what we encounter in the physical and virtual worlds are images and the messages are based in a certain amount of cultural awareness and subjectivity. Images are not clearly defined like words. Although, some have attempted to make visual dictionaries (see Cirlot, 1962), to date there is not one to define remix messages.

The role remix could play in education is unclear. The Internet provides an opportunity to bring together interactive experiences and a bricolage of diverse visual elements and ideas—remix. Bricolage is a French word that means "tinkerer" (see Papert, 1996). It reflects a different style of learning that is poking around until you get the right thing. It is the opposite of reading the manual. Incorporating remix into education will make us deal with different types of learning patterns and the area of visual communication along with the development of multimedia literacy skills. These are two topics that educators have shied away from. However, remix and its bricolage of images can be used for critical thinking assignments and political discussions. Remix could be used in education to promote discussion. Often YouTube videos are shown in various courses from Visual to Interpersonal Communication. Moreover, John Seely Brown argues that remix is a new form of social learning. He states:

> At some point it might be worth noting that the shift from linear logic to bricolage is actually a very subversive move away from the Cartesian Frame to much more of a situated, action frame. It also paves the way for considering the 'Remix Culture' as being a new form of social learning, social capital formation and becoming a more central member of a community of practice/interest. (Cited in Fischer, 2005, p. 2)

How remix could be incorporated into an education framework is yet to be explored. However, used logically, remix can create parody and topics for discussions and debates. Moreover, it is a creative form of visual and verbal expression.

Remix and Education

As computers are incorporated into education, they seem like a natural progression to let students express themselves in visual and verbal contexts. But, schools will have to incorporate some type of multimedia literacy and dual-coding concepts into the curriculum to take full advantage of the tools technology now offers us.

A fundamental change from mass media to interactive media is the use of multimedia as a form of expression. We no longer live in a print-based culture, instead we live in a multimedia one. Young people known as the Millennials or "Generation Y" have grown up using computer technology, such as instant messaging, Facebook, and blogs. Watching television is not as important to this generation (see Hirshberg, 2007). Regardless of their level of computer sophistication, using computers as a teaching medium is natural for Millennials. Today's culture is one in which students expect PowerPoint presentations and visual aids in the classroom.

As educators, should we jump on this cultural bandwagon? Remix could be considered a form of entertainment. Many of the videos placed on YouTube are for fun or to entertain us. Only a handful of videos could be considered a form of cultural criticism. For example, cultural criticism was typed into YouTube and the following videos appeared: bell hooks on cultural criticism, Christian missionaries destroying culture, BITCH magazine on cultural criticism, a documentary trailer, America the culture of celebrity, and Ingraham attacks O'Reilly. Politicians, such as Hillary Clinton, made none of these videos. Certainly this is entertainment, even if YouTube has entered the political realm. CNN's use of YouTube to ask questions of the democratic presidential candidates was a political use of the site. Although, some of the questions may have been entertaining, this approach opens up politics to user-generated videos. *New York Times* reporter, Katharine O. Seelye (2007) describes it the following way:

> Now imagine a kid in jeans and a T-shirt asking a question, less reverentially, more pointedly and using powerful images to underscore the point. Maybe he or she will ask about the war in Iraq—and show clips from a soldier's funeral. Or a mushroom cloud. If global warming is the issue, the videographer might photoshop himself or herself onto a melting glacier. The question might come in the form of a rap song or through spliced images of a candidate's contradictory statement. (para. 3)

In the political arena, the widespread use of YouTube is worthy of a classroom discussion. However, when we think of YouTube in the classroom, we need to think about its relationship to traditional literacy. Neil Postman (1979) pointed out that television literacy is different from printed literacy and we have now moved on to multimedia literacy. A central difference between the printed word and electronic media is the simulation of events. According to Hayles (2002), "Broadly speaking, representation assumes a referent in the real world. . . .In simulation, the referent has no counterpart in the real world" (p. 5). Digital media enable viewers to cycle back and forth between visual representation and simulation. In remix, creators can use both images of visual representation and animations that are totally simulated. Remix uses both representation and simulation to create messages.

Digital aesthetics put together many diverse visual elements. It is a practice of digital designers to juxtapose disparate visual elements in new ways. According to Bolter and Gromala (2003), "The French word *bricolage* has been used to describe this practice among postmodern artists and designers" (p. 104). The use of bricolage is commonly applied to digital art and design. This approach to design uses the type of learning styles describe earlier with Papert. Digital aesthetics weaves together diverse visual elements and the digital eye is an interactive eye that is constantly viewing an ever-changing media landscape, rather than a fixed page of print.

With the introduction of the Internet into culture, the new media landscape is now an interconnection of image-worlds. Burnett (2004) describes image-worlds as "physical and psychological infrastructures that are dependent upon images" (p. 6). Objects are taken out of their natural locations and placed into "more complex mediated space that is inscribed rather than natural" (p. 6). Today, "images represent a technological intelligence that shifts the ways humans see themselves, from individuals to hybrid personae, where identity no longer resides in one particular place, object or person" (p. 6). Relationships are now based on an individual's experience with image-worlds, such as YouTube videos. Our postmodern world is filled with more images than the past.

Images in mass media were introduced by the medium of television. In his book, *Amusing Ourselves to Death,* Neil Postman argues that because American television is primarily an entertainment medium, all information received from television tends to be entertaining. Kakutani (2010) contends:

> It's been twenty-five years since Neil Postman warned in "Amusing Ourselves to Death" that trivia and the entertainment values promoted by television were creating distractions that threatened to subvert public discourse, and more than a decade since writers like James Gleick ("Faster") and David Shenk ("Data Dmog") described a culture addicted to speed, drowning in data and over stimulated to the point where only sensationalism and willful hyperbole grab people's attention. (para. 12)

In addition to influencing attention, television has been cited as being responsible for a large educational issue—the decline of alphabet literacy. Postman (1997) was concerned about how the inability to read would influence a democratic society. However, Lessig (2008) argues, when you write in digital media, it "is to know that anything one writes is open to debate" (p. 67). Debate is a concept that is central to a democratic culture. Thus, some aspects of digital media promote the democratic skills that Postman was concerned about being destroying.

In addition, television and mass media in general represent a Read Only (RO) culture, where an audience passively views media content. "The business model of both [record and film companies] distributors of RO culture depend upon controlling the distribution of copies of culture" (Lessig, 2008, p. 37). In contrast Read/Write (RW) culture is reborn with digital media because audience members are now actively engaged with media content to create new media works (see Lessig, 2008). "The *code* of an LP record protected it from duplication, the *code* of a digital copy of that record does not" (p. 38). As a result, the literacy issues with television and digital media are similar. The Internet is an entertainment medium similar to television and the Internet contributes to a decline in reading.

Educators argue that the widespread use of television has eroded traditional literacy skills because students spend more time watching television (or today the Internet) than they do reading books, newspapers, or magazines. For instance, *U.S. Federal News* (2007) reports:

> Individuals age seventy-five and over averaged 1.4 hours of reading per weekend day and 0.2 hour (twelve minutes) playing games or using a computer for leisure. Conversely, individual's ages fifteen to nineteen read for an average of 0.1 (seven minutes) per weekend and spend 1.0 hour playing games or using a computer for leisure. (n.p.)

Because young people spend more time with entertainment media, than they do reading, there is a bias against the use of television and visual media, such as remix, for general educational instruction. However, this bias against visually-oriented media is not just a conflict between text and image, it is also based on how people perceive verbal versus visual information. Postman (1979) describes the difference as follows:

> Language is, by its nature, slow moving hierarchical, logical and continuous. Whether writing or speaking, one must maintain a fixed point of view and continuity of content, one must move to higher or lower levels of abstraction; one must follow to a greater or lesser degree rules of syntax and logic. . . . Imagery is fast moving, concrete, discontinuous, alogical, requiring emotional response, its imagery does not provide grounds for argument and contains little ambiguity. There are only feelings to be felt. (p. 72)

Lessig (2008) disagrees by arguing that remix is a new dominant form of "writing." The creativity required to make these works is a form of learning. However, remix culture is considered to be a type of entertainment and not a learning style. It is something that teenagers do in their social lives.

Access to this new writing style means access to a computer because most systems come bundled with the tools to mix images, or music, or video together. However, "Unlike text, where the quotes follow in a single line—such as here, where the sentence explains, 'and then a quote gets added'—remixed media may quote sounds over images, or video over text, or text over sounds" (p. 69). All of the different "quotes" or content elements get mixed all together, which creates a new work called a remix or mash-up. These works can have definite meanings, beyond the emotional appeal.

Cultural assumptions have been made to associate text with "logical" thinking and images with "emotional" thinking. Moreover, it is better to think logically than emotionally. Therefore text is considered better than images in educational settings. But advertising, which is more pervasive than television, uses *emotional appeal* to sell products and services. Often these advertisements use visual imagery to communicate an emotional message. In contrast, advertising that uses a *rational appeal* presents a logical reason why consumers should buy a product. Depending on the product, advertisers will have to select one of these approaches. But, complex products, such as computers and cars, may be sold using a dual approach. Television commercials will be designed to communicate an emotional message and print advertising will provide all of the detailed logical reasons why the product should be purchased. The widespread use of advertising in American culture can also influence the use of remix. Today, we live in an environment filled with media:

> When you turn around 360 degrees, how many different ads or logos will you see somewhere in your space? [O]n your car, on your wristwatch, on a billboard. If you walk into any grocery store or restaurant or anywhere to shop, there's always a soundtrack playing. There's always . . . media. There's ads. There's magazines everywhere. . . . [I]t's the world we live in. It's the landscape around us. (Hosler cited in Lessig, 2008, p. 71)

Advertising strategies support Postman's argument that the difference between visual and verbal messages is emotion and rationality. Advertisers understand the power of images and they know how to design messages that are both visually and verbally persuasive. More and more, however, print-based advertising is becoming almost exclusively visual with little or no text. Remix is closer to the visual strategies of advertising than it is to the printed word.

Because images are emotional and they do not have a one-to-one relationship to an idea like words, remix is more subjective. It is not as concretely logical as text. But, it is concrete enough to communicate the same or similar messages to large audiences. The popularity of YouTube proves this. According to Madden (2007), "57 percent of online adults have used the internet to watch or download video, and 19 percent do so on a typical day" (p.1).

Another difference between words and images is the fact that images are based on patterns. An understanding of messages based on the relationship of meaningful patterns is *Gestalt Theory*. Gestalt theory argues that visual perception is the result of organizing visual elements or shapes into groups. It is a concept that is more visual than verbal. Principles from Gestalt theory explain the nature of figure and ground relationships and how several figures can share a common ground. First, Gestalt psychologists developed the Law of Pragnaz as a basic principle, which regulates the segregation of the field of view into separate forms. The German word pragnanz is translated into English as "pregnant with meaning." The psychological implication of this concept is the notion that our mind seeks stable, regular figures in the environment. People feel uneasy when they are unable to find such objects.

When people see irregular and unstable figures and objects, they frequently feel uncomfortable and this can occur without a clear understanding about the source of the discomfort. Artists, filmmakers, and advertisers sometimes exploit this idea by creating unstable images and scenes in which people crave for stability (see Gombrich, 1984). Advertisers do this to grab the attention of consumers.

So, remix is grounded in a Gestalt understanding of messages, which is closer to advertising than print. In remix, the end product used Gestalt concepts to create meaning that is greater than the individual parts.

The literacy of remix, requires people to have a knowledge of visual and multimedia literacy skills because remix depends on the use of images and visual messages in the communication process. There are key cognitive differences between visual communication and print based communication, such as Gestalt learning. Gestalt learning is how advertisers communicate their messages because advertisers depend on a mixture of visual and verbal symbols to communicate an idea. It's not purely one symbol system or the other.

The Gestalt concept can also be associated with dual-coding, which argues that we perceive and comprehend information in both a text and non-text format (see Sadoski & Paivio, 2004). "A basic premise of DCT [Dual Coding Theory] is that all mental representations retain some of the concrete qualities of the external experiences from which they derive." (p. 1330). Thus, we can learn from verbal as well as visual messages because there are two codes. "The later is frequently referred to as the imagery system or code because its functions include the generation, analysis, and transformation of mental images." (p. 1330). Both systems are used in the process of reading and they are based in perception. Dual-coding explains how the messages in visual advertisements can be understood.

Personalized Media

Individuals generally create visual and verbal remixed messages and these messages are generally personalize in some way because individuals create the messages. In contrast to mass media, which is directed toward large audiences, media is personalized every time a person shares photos, music, and videos on a global scale. These messages are directed toward a small audience, but sometimes go viral and attract larger audiences. Similarly, citizen journalists are remixing and rewriting news content based on individual perspectives. Individuals can capture news events on cell phones better than the news agencies can cover them. Often these messages are sent to news stations and are then broadcast on television.

Advertisers have become aware of the personalization trend and they are getting consumers to become evangelists for their products. Additionally, they are personalizing advertising to include the consumer. "Chevy lets people upload photos of themselves and then watch an ad with their own faces pasted in" (Copeland, 2007, para. 4). M&M has launched a website for visitors to customize their own "inner M" and share the finished product with friends. "Brands express what we aspire to be and what we believe about ourselves, in a kind of commercial shorthand. Aspirations—for beauty and coolness and status and joy—are the stuff of brand loyalty" (para. 7). Brands have become our culture and this change is also part of remix culture because remix blurs news, entertainment and reality. All types of genres are mixed into YouTube videos.

Remixing people into advertisements is also an important part of the growing phenomena of remix culture. Remix is both the ways in which we use media and the ways we use media to create our own content. As previously stated, content creation is a central aspect of this new phenomenon. However, remix is also becoming a part of business. Individuals can now get paid for their online creations. YouTube now shares its ad revenues with top video creators, which is also contributing to the trend of personalization and *Me Media.*

Me Media is a term, which emphasizes the individualization and personalization of media. Me Media is "when consumers create media to fit their needs" (Kuchinskas, 2006, SR6). Me, I can choose which medium to watch, which YouTube video to play and which song to listen to on my iPod. I am the center of my own mediated universe. In a world filled with mediated encounters, it is easy to feel as if you are the center of everything, especially when you can create and personalize media content—remix.

Summary

Personalization and remixed elements of cultural artifacts create a new type of culture that is centered around digital technologies. Today there is no difference between talking to someone face-to-face and speaking to them through the Internet. How people are mixing, remixing, and mashing culture and cultural icons creates a new culture based on mediated images, sounds, and events. Reality blends with media events to form a larger mediated reality called *Remix Culture*. "Remix is an essential act of RW creativity. It is the expression of a freedom to take 'the songs of the day or the old songs' and create with them" (Lessig, 2008, p. 56). Remix culture always reminds us of mediated experiences, even in face-to-face contexts. Today the idea of reality is one huge mediated event. However, it is a media event that fosters debate and provides a wider variety of media for people to express their ideas and these ideas are often shared through social networks.

Some believe that remix is a new style of learning that it can be introduced into educational contexts. While others view it as a form of entertainment. Whether or not we are amusing ourselves to death with computers or not, is a question that needs to be debated by teachers and scholars. Currently, there is no clear answer on the issue of remix and education.

Chapter Eleven

Social Capital

The Goal of Social Networking

All of the previous chapters discuss the technical and social elements that contribute to the formation of social networks. These elements also contribute to the development of social capital. This chapter describes the goal of social networking—the building of social capital. Simply stated, social software is software that enables people to interact with each other and build social networks that increase their social capital. Building relationships is the goal of social networking and building social capital is a topic of interest in today's society.

Social capital is a concept mentioned throughout this book. In the introduction, social capital is defined as development of an individual's personal social network (Van Der Gaag & Snijders, 2004). This type of social network is increased offline interpersonal contact, organizational and political participation, and commitment to community. In addition to face-to-face interactions, computers used as a communication device can also be used to build social capital. Building social capital relates to social networks because networks help build personal relationships through the design of the software. As people exchange commitments to each other, they build social capital. For example, if one person agrees to send another person information and person one meets his or her commitment to person two, the first individual has improved their social standing because their word is trustworthy. At some future date, person two may reciprocate and return some other information.

In chapter 1, social capital is mentioned in terms of maintaining social networks to build social capital. However, several of the concepts described in the chapter contribute to the development of social capital. First, we perceive many digital technologies to be our personal media. The devices are extensions of ourselves, which is how McLuhan (1964) referred to communication and its technologies. The idea of personal media comes from both personal use and software designers. The term "personal computers" rhetorically confirms the concept of using computers on an individual level. Personal media enable people to communicate across time and space to enhance their ability to reach others.

A second concept is presence theory. Developing a sense of presence is required to communicate with people. We need to perceive another person communicating with us at the other end of the computer screen, so we are interacting with a person and not a machine. We can develop a sense of presence through social networks. Social networking reinforces presence because individuals can view profiles and photos of the actual person.

When individuals start to share user-generated content, they are using the third concept to start building social capital. They are contributing to the network community. Being an active part of an online group builds a sense of presence for the individual and adds to the building of social capital because a contribution has been made to the online world. For instance, placing a funny video on YouTube will make people laugh. The entertainment value of the video will make people think about the person who posted it. YouTube now has a policy to convert an individual's social capital into actual money through the sharing of advertising revenues.

Chapter 2 describes self-identity and how an individual makes him or herself known to others through the network. We need to recognize the other for the sharing of behaviors that lead to building social capital. We recognize others through symbolic interaction. Language, gestures, written words, music, and videos are all symbolic ways in which people express themselves. Through the sharing of these symbolic activities, we gain an understanding of others and ourselves. Once we are aware of other people, individuals can begin to manage their image or the impression they communicate to others. Social networks enable people to establish their image through personal profiles, pictures, and the ways they communicate to others. Because many of the systems used online are asynchronous, people have time to carefully craft what they say on the Internet.

However, people can communicate through media because they perceive the media to create a place for interaction, the topic of chapter 4. We perceive ourselves to be some place when we communicate through the Internet. It is a place where we meet and communicate with others. Without this sense of place there would not be the building of social capital online or virtual communities.

As argued in chapter 4, people can build communities and a sense of personal interaction. Social computing is developing software that enables people to interact with each other and build social networks that increase their social capital. Through the exchange of commitments and fulfillments people develop social capital and information online is exchanged through notification and awareness systems.

Notification and awareness are described in chapter 5. The designers of software often control these characteristics. Different types of software are created with different types of notification and awareness systems. For example, social networking software makes the activities of friends automatically know to other friends through news feeds. Poking in Facebook is also a method for making people aware of others. E-mail systems make recipients aware of new messages, for instance unopened mail is usually shown in a bold typeface. People need to be made aware of the communications from others. Without this feature, individuals would not know about messages being sent to them. As a result, notification and awareness are central technological features that support the exchange of social capital.

The building of social capital in Second Life has two dimensions. The first is to build social capital within the world itself. Because people use a pseudonym when communicating in the virtual world, they can interact with others as the virtual persona or as themselves in real life. The virtual world has its own economic systems and people can build social capital as they communicate online. For instance, the entrepreneur speakers in the Second Life advertising course have built social capital because they sell quality products and are involved with charity work. Their online social capital translated into the second dimension, the real world, when the speakers virtually came to the class. Students did get involved with the speakers in Second Life to further the development of social capital by exchanging favors. The speakers lived far away and it was not as easy to develop social capital in the real world. However, it was done in the virtual realm.

The exchange of services between people is established through social norms. Social norms are established in the online world of Second Life by observing the behavior of avatars. Following the behavior of others is one way to learn what to do. Looking at other people's behavior can also tell us what not to do. For instance, an annoying online behavior is repeating everything that someone says. The longer it goes on the more annoyed an individual can get. So, this is obviously a behavior that you do not want to imitate to gain online friends and build social capital.

While the above scenario is annoying, it does not present any ethical dilemmas. In contrast, an ethical issue is medical students discussing their patients in social networking software. Patient/doctor confidentiality is the key ethical issue here, doctors should not discuss their patients. Currently, there is a section of Facebook that is called "You and I Lost My Job Because of Social Media" and there are a series of posts from people who were considered unethical for one reason or another. Making derogatory comments about people or situations is a sure way to lose a job. People need to behave in an ethical manor to gain trust from others and ethics is central in building social capital.

In chapter 8, social capital is also related to information capital. Information capital is the finical capacity to pay for information services. Additionally, it is about transforming information into social practice. In contrast, social capital is the relationships that we build with people. Trust is needed for people to believe that you will live up to your social commitments. Many of these commitments can be translated into social capital.

Developers know the need for trust in software. Otherwise, we would not be able to buy products online. For this reason they need to find ways in which to program trusting features into programs. Rhetoric is a method for communicating trust. For this reason, software programs often have messages that are designed to be conversational rather than formal.

Chapter 9 mentions social capital because the development of friends and acquaintances increases the ability to receive information and support from these individuals. "Seeking information from acquaintances puts information giving and seeking into the social economics of the relationship; it is an exchange of favors, of revealing needs and providing assistance" (Donath, 2007, p. 15). Thus, building networks of friends through social networking software also builds social capital. Social capital operates on many levels, "affecting the relationship quality of individual community members as well as the viability of the community as a social and economic entity" (Mathwick, Wiertz & Ruyter, 2007, p. 832).

As discussed, all of the characteristics of social media are necessary in the building of social capital. People need to be aware of each other through their identity and sense of presence. User-generated content is a contribution that people make on the network and it can also build social capital. Our perception of being in a place is essential for online communication to work. We must feel as if we are meeting people in a place to exchange messages. Notification and awareness are the software systems that tells us when the messages arrive. We would not be able to build social capital online without interaction, which is key to building relationships and community. Demonstrating ethical behavior and trust through messages is necessary for people to exchange favors and build social capital.

Ideological Background of Social Networks

Social capital is a sociological concept that refers to social networking connections. Social networks are perceived as having value because of the social connections that they make. It is the idea of how people gain access to powerful positions through the direct and indirect use of social connections. The origin of the concept of social networking begins with L. J. Hanifan's 1916 article regarding local support for rural schools. The term social capital was used to refer to community and social cohesion. Hanifan wrote about people coming together in a community to improve living conditions. In contrast, some scholars (Drentea &

Moren-Cross, 2005) contend that social capital can be traced back to the works of Marx, who wrote about capital emerging from social relationships.

Sociologist Pierre Bourdieu used the term in 1972 in his *Outline of a Theory of Practice*, and the term has also been used by sociologists James Coleman and Barry Wellman. "Bourdieu became interested in how members of the middle and upper classes were able to capitalize on material and human resources inherent in networks and social groups to advance their own interests" (Alfred, 2009, p. 3). His idea of social capital stresses the resources that people use for their own personal advantage. The program LinkedIn uses this philosophy. Bourdieu's argument is social capital is an aspect of a wider system of subjective belief and structural relationships. These beliefs and relationships are related to the inequalities of power and resources. Bourdieu's contribution to the concept of social capital is the interconnection between social capital and social inequalities.

In contrast, Coleman (1988) used the concept of social capital to explore educational research in young children. "In Coleman's understanding (1988), social capital is a relational property of individuals and of the social groups they form" (Matei, 2004, p. 27). Coleman compared students in public and private schools. "He theorized that the private school students performed better because there was a stronger sense of community and norms that the parents, teachers, and students embraced" (Alfred, 2009, p. 4). Alfred (2009) further states that according to Coleman, "social capital is concerned with the social relationships, especially those embedded in the family and community, are useful in helping children develop their cognitive, as well as their social abilities" (p. 4). Coleman's investigations have implications for research on social networks because the findings of the National Science Foundation research conducted here showed that students did not build social capital. "The results indicate that the educational use of social media may not counteract poor social connections that are seen in face-to-face communication or elicit the same impacts seen in the use of social media sites such as MySpace and Facebook" (ScienceDaily, 2010, p. 1). Therefore, depending on family, community and educational background, students may or may not have the skills to build social capital.

Many social media advocates have argued that the use of social media tools in classroom settings could greatly enhance interaction and learning and assist shyer, more reserved students in becoming more involved, as has been seen in other online environments. For instance, students who do not speak in class may be avid online users. However, the National Science Foundation findings show that the incorporation of social media had no measurable impact on social connections, to the point that students did not consider other members of the class to be part of their social network. Thus, the students were not building social capital.

Contributions from "Pierre Bourdieu (1972) with regard to social theory, and then James S. Coleman (1988) in his discussions of the social context of education moved the idea into an academic context. Later, the work of Robert D. Putnam (2000) introduced the idea of social capital as a focal point for research and policy discussion. Robert D. Putnam connected the term social capital to concepts of democracy and political involvement (see www.bowlingalone.com). As a result, American culture views social capital as creating civic engagement.

> The networks that constitute social capital also serve as conduits for the flow of helpful information that facilitates achieving our goals. . . . Social capital also operates through psychological and biological processes to improve individual's lives. . . . Community connectedness is not just about warm fuzzy tales of civic triumph. In measurable and well-documented ways, social capital makes an enormous difference to our lives. (Putnam, 2000, p. 290)

The information that individuals exchange, helps to build social capital. In social networks, these individuals can be acquaintances or friends. Putman's (2000) "claim was that communities that exhibit high levels of social capital exhibit a higher quality of life, and that quality of life decreases with reductions in social capital" (Kavanaugh & Patterson, 2001, p. 498). Moreover, Putnam did not believe that community computer networks would help build social capital. Today, "social network theorists . . . view social capital as a private good that can be obtained by individuals and used for their personal benefit" (Mathwick, Wiertz & Ruyter, 2007, p. 834), which fits with Bourdieu's use of the term.

The four components that Bourdieu, Coleman, and Putman agree on as being components of social capital are networks, resources, norms and trust (see Alfred, 2009). The networks that we build are both online and off. Norms is the subject of chapter 7: Social norms are the rules that a community considers to be appropriate, and inappropriate, including values, beliefs, attitudes and behaviors. Resources are both social resources and structural resources that are made available through social ties. The core assumption guiding social capital research is that the goodwill of others toward us is a valuable resource to be harnessed. Instead of goodwill, Mathwick, Wiertz, and Ruyter (2007) describe volunteerism, which is based on "habits of the heart." Additionally, goodwill includes sympathy, forgiveness, and trust from friends.

Trust

Trust and social norms are the foundations of social capital because these characteristics are necessary to bond people together. Social trust becomes a generalized norm of the community. People need to believe that the information they are receiving from others, is truthful. For instance Beem (1999) states:

> Trust between individuals thus becomes trust between strangers and trust of a broad fabric of social institutions; ultimately, it becomes a shared set of values, virtues, and expectations within society as a whole. Without this interaction, on the other hand, trust decays; at a certain point, this decay begins to manifest itself in serious social problems... The concept of social capital contends that building or rebuilding community and trust requires face-to-face encounters. (p. 20)

As stated in chapter 9, trust is the commitment that we make to others and the belief that others will meet their commitment to us. Research has shown (Cassell & Bickmore, 2000; Meshel, 2005; Rosenbloom, 2000) that trust can be built into software and online networks of people. Moreover, we need to be able to trust the people that develop the software and also trust those that we meet online. "Trust, obligations, or information do not exist in absence of individuals exercising or transacting them" (Matei, 2004, p. 27). Just like face-to-face communities, online groups can trust each other. Counter to Beem's statement above, written before social networking was widely established, people can also build communities online (see Rheingold, 1993). Wellman, Haase, Witte and Hampton (2001) found that the Internet could supplement the building of social capital because it creates new methods of communication. "Much of America's economic power to [build] abundant social capital in the form of trust and a basic level of habitual honesty" (Boyd, 2003, p. 297). By using computer-mediated communication to build social capital, the Internet has now become embedded into every day life.

Types of Social Capital

Before examining social capital on the Internet, it is important to make a distinction between two types of social capital—bridging and bonding. Bridging social capital is the type of social capital that brings people or groups together that previously did not know each other. Research studying bridging social capital examines characteristics of a social system, including trust, norms, and networks. These studies explore the collective effectiveness of a society.

Bonding social capital brings people who know each other closer together (see Yuan & Gay, 2006). "Bonding social capital refers to resources that people can gain from their ties with people from the outside" (p. 1067). Research on bonding social capital examines the characteristics of interpersonal networks and "how people can have access to different kinds of mutual aid, and different forms of social support through them" (Mebane, et al. 2008).

Individuals can build social capital with both people within a group or those outside it. Research has found that bridging and bonding ties with people in the same group and bridging ties with people from outside the group are sources for task-related resource exchange and non-task-related social support. However, the reasons for this are very different. Additionally, bonding social capital will reinforce group cohesion. When people are comfortable talking to each other, they are more likely to create new knowledge. Additionally, the density of the link in and outside of the group leads to the formation of new knowledge.

In online games, we find both types of social capital. Members of gaming communities engage in "bridging social capital—the loose connections between relative strangers that lead to diverse networks and information streams—or bonding social capital, which is traditional social, emotional, and substantive support" (Williams et al., 2006). Games enable people both people who are face-to-face friends and strangers to come together and play. Strangers often meet when the games are connected to the Internet.

Social Capital on the Internet

Wellman, Quan-Haase, Witte and Hampton (2001) examined the Internet and social capital. Specifically, they examined how social network contacts influence social capital in terms of organizational and political participation, and community commitment. In terms of community, they state: "greater use of the Internet may lead to larger social networks with more weak ties and distasteful interaction with some of these ties, resulting in lower commitment to the online community" (p. 449). Distasteful interactions are the result of misbehavior on the Internet. The more time individuals spend online the more likely they are to encounter disagreeable people, which can result in the lowering of online community allegiance. As a result, the Internet may or may not help to build social capital.

These researchers found that the Internet supplements network capital by extending face-to-face and telephone contact. In particular, the Internet is a method for friends who are socially and geographically dispersed to stay in touch with each other. In addition, Wellman, Quan-Haase, Witte and Hampton (2001) found that Internet use increases participatory capital. "The more people are on the Internet, and the more they are involved in online organizational and political activities, the more they are involved in offline organizational and political activity" (p. 450). In total, the results of this research suggest, "that the Internet is increasing interpersonal connectivity and organizational involvement. However, increased personal involvement can reduce commitment to community. It should be noted that community commitment has been on a decline and this started to occur before the development of the Internet (see Putnam, 2000).

Conversely, "some researchers argue that the Internet can be seen as a social-capital building technology because existing social networks can take advantage of the information distribution aspects of the network to become more effective and connected communicators" (Kavanaugh & Patterson, 2001, p. 498). This is a concept that many people have about social networks. For instance, Kavanaugh and Patterson (2001) examined the impact of the Blacksburg Electronic Village on the local community. The researchers anticipated that higher levels of community involvement would occur as use of the Internet increased. However, their findings were not supported. Instead, the research supported Putnam's belief that community computer networks would not help to build social capital.

Although, the building of social capital could not be linked with local community involvement, Kavanaugh and Patterson (2001) found that the Internet is used for social-capital-building activities. "It is this talk or social capital building among community members that builds the social networks and social trust on which community involvement and eventually quality of life thrive" (p. 507). They suggest that people in the future will have the opportunity to learn social-capital-building communication behaviors. At the present time, it does not appear that people are transferring their social capital skills to online environments.

In contrast, Mathwick, Wiertz, and Ruyter (2007) found that peer-to-peer problem solving (p. 3) communities use the network to build social capital. "Information resources and social support systems emanate from social capital" (p. 845). Thus, the support that can be provided online builds social capital. "Clearly, a support group provides social capital that is an embedded community activated for purposeful action" (Drentea & Moren-Cross, 2005, p. 924). Several other studies support the findings that online networks can build social capital. Sum, et al. (2008) state: "older adults who were trained to use the Internet reported having high levels of social connectivity, high levels of perceived social support, and generally more positive attitudes towards ageing" (p. 215). Alfred (2009) discovered that female-dominated networks and websites are found to be more supportive than mixed gendered networks. Our National Science Foundation research supports this finding because females did not send any negative messages to either males or females. Males did sent negative messages, which were mostly directed at males. Thus, the female style of online communication seems to be more positive and supportive.

In contrast to the above findings, Matei (2004) found that when examining forty-eight states in the United States, the Internet strengthens offline interaction. The states are viewed as individualized social units of the American polity. Social capital as a concept does not only reside on an individual level. The researcher investigated the relationship between social capital and the emergence of online community. Her research questions were: 1) "Do states with higher levels of social capital have a higher propensity to create regional online communities?"; and 2) Is there an association between social capital and Yahoo! Group activity?" (p. 33). Both questions resulted in positive associations. This research focused on determining whether or not there is a positive association between online and offline social phenomena. Geographic units tend to generate a number of online groups. Moreover, ethnically homogenous states are more likely to generate online groups.

As a means for measuring social capital on the Internet, Williams (2006) developed the Internet Social Capital Scales, or ISCS. The scales are "an attempt to theorize, create, and validate a series of scales to measure social capital in online and offline contexts" (p. 610). The scales contain ten items and they have been found to be valid and reliable. "The ISCS can be used for the broad application of 'the Internet,' or it can be used for more specific social Internet activities such as e-mail, chat rooms, game play, etc." (p. 611). Game play and the use of social capital is the topic of the next section.

Games and Social Capital

A study of the social life of Guilds in *World of Warcraft*, was conducted by Williams et al. (2006). Included in the study was how people in guilds build social capital. The study examined the social dynamics of players within the in-game organizations known as guilds. Both bridging and bonding social capital behaviors are found in *World of Warcraft* because it is "populated with a range of social experiences ranging from ephemeral impersonal groups to sustained and deep relationships that extend offline" (p. 340).

Ideas of space and place are important concepts for game worlds because games form a vibrant place for people to meet and interact. The game space is determined by software code. The software program itself governs walls and travel abilities, such as the ability to walk or fly. As a result, software can limit the behaviors of individuals in the game both through planned and unplanned ways. "The structure and rule set of the game world have a clear impact on what kinds of people play, what they do, and how and why they interact" (Williams et al., 2006, p. 340). In contrast, the players themselves create a place to play, interact, and build social capital.

The formations of guilds in *World of Warcraft* differ by goals, size, and membership. A social guild is one where the game's goals are secondary to the social interactions that are formed between people. In contrast raiding guilds, the most glamorous in *World of Warcraft*, organize team events of around forty people that typically last between 2 and 8 hours. "To perform well, each player must act in the best interests of the group, requiring a high degree of familiarity and practice" (Williams et al., 2006, p. 345). Finally, a role-play guild is one that allows it members to pretend to be their characters. Players are expected to be in character when they are socializing or raiding other guilds.

The smaller guilds are ones that develop the strongest bonding social capital in *World of Warcraft*, It is because people in smaller guilds often know each other from face-to-face contacts from outside the game. "Roughly 75 percent of small guilds feature some founding unit of real-life family and friends" (Williams et al., 2006, p. 346). Medium guilds progress from tightly knit groups to large and less personal ones. Huge guilds are slightly less sociable because they must rally their members into a formal organization. "Players in formally structured guilds tend to have a more social experience than others" (p. 354). Thus, it is more likely that players will build social capital in smaller guilds than in larger ones. The small guild promotes more social interaction with people known outside of *World of Warcraft*.

Social Capital and Self

Advocates of social capital theory argue that building relationships can increase one's sense of self, the topic of chapter 2. Mead (1932) argued that the self arises through social interactions with objects and other people. These interactions can be online or off because people can build relationships through both face-to-face and online encounters, such as representations through avatars.

"Social capital is said to be an intangible force that helps to bind society together by transforming self-seeking individuals into members of a community with shared interests" (Mathwick, Wiertz & Ruyter, 2007, p. 832). The rewards of being a part of a social network and the benefits of using the connections, helps to build self-esteem. For instance, "women must develop a sense of ego identity to negotiate life's course and maintain positive interactions to reap the benefits of social capital resources inherent in communities of support" (Alfred, 2009, p. 7). Social interactions can help to build our self-esteem, this includes our interactions to gain social capital. How we present ourselves to others is important in the process of building social capital. Individuals need to present themselves as being reliable and trustworthy. These are traits that our news broadcasters also need to communicate to audiences.

Social Capital, Politics, and News

Social media has had a major impact on politics and the ways in which news is reported. Former CNN reporter, Rich Sanchez (2010) states: "We don't just report the news, we listen to you and we talk to each other, through social media, and list your concerns while gathering the facts you need to know to better understand what's going on" (p. 4). Sanchez successfully incorporated Twitter into the news coverage of disasters when individuals started sending tweets during his newscast. Additionally, people are encouraged to send homemade videos to the network. Individuals are now part of the daily news by communicating through social networks, such as Twitter, Facebook, and YouTube. Moreover, news interviews can be posted to YouTube and many of these interviews have gone viral.

For instance, politicians will announce their candidacy through YouTube, rather than on national television. Candidates such as Howard Dean and Barack Obama have used social media successfully. Dean used the network to collect money and Obama used it to collect people. Their use of social media may have taken the Democratic Party by surprise. But, there is no doubt that social media played a central role in Obama's election. But, use of the Internet actually began in the election of President Clinton, who used discussion lists to organize people and rallies. Most people start the trend of using the Internet for politics with the campaign of Howard Dean. Dean demonstrated that the network can be a powerful tool for raising money for election campaigns.

In contrast, Obama hired Chris Hughes, a co-founder of Facebook, to develop Web-based networking tools for use in political campaigns. This move set a new standard for political campaigning. Obama "used social media to raise money, to interact with people, to hear what they were talking about, to respond to them and to get them out to vote" (Sanchez, 2010, p. 14). As a result, social media clearly established itself as an important tool for political campaigns. The use of social media for campaigns illustrates the power of the medium to create and support social capital.

Social Capital in Education

The building of social capital can be the result of learning interactions because they take place in a cultural context. The key characteristics needed to build social capital in education are reciprocity, trust, shared norms, and values. As discovered in the National Science Foundation grant, instructors need to plan to maximize learning interactions by designing a constructivist style of learning. In addition to constructing knowledge through interactions, students need to be made aware of how educational interactions can help to build their social capital. "An individual's knowledge and skills are not enough to develop social capital in the classroom . . . [students] must be able and willing to interact in new ways, in new contexts, and with new people" (Alfred, 2009, p. 11).

Many of today's students are using Facebook and other social networks in their personal lives. Ellison, Steinfield and Lampe (2007) studied students to see if there was a relationship between social networking sites and the ability to maintain connections with others. They introduced the concept of "maintained social capital," which is bridging relationships or maintaining relationships with people who are acquaintances as opposed to close friends. For instance, many college students use social networks to maintain relationships with high school acquaintances. For first year college students, keeping relationships with high school friends helps the student to make the transition between high school and college.

The researchers found that "participants overwhelmingly used Facebook to keep in touch with old friends and to maintain or intensify relationships characterized by some form of offline connection, such as dormitory proximity or a shared class" (Ellison, Steinfield & Lampe, 2007, p. 1162). A new finding was that students use social networks as a way to connect with offline contacts instead of meeting new people online. This is an offline to online movement flow, which suggest that professors need to develop social capital behaviors in the classroom and these behaviors may be carried into online relationships. For instance, turning a face-to-face classmate into an online friend helps to build social capital for individuals.

Conclusion

Social networking is both a technical and social phenomena. The idea of social capital can be traced back to the writings of Hanifan and Marx. However, Coleman and Putnam popularized the term. On the Internet, Wellman and the researchers he works with popularized the idea of social capital. Today, we can use computer-mediated communication to build social networks and social capital because the Internet increases interpersonal activity.

Online environments, such as *World of Warcraft*, create places for people to interact and build social capital. We can find both building and bonding social capital in this environment because people and their goals for the game are so diverse. Personal backgrounds can influence whether or not people build strong or weak ties through social networks.

Similarly, students who come from different types of educational, social, and community backgrounds will have different skills in building social capital. Professors need to be aware that students don't necessarily build social capital when social networking software is introduced into the classroom. Students have difficulty moving their social skills into education and professional contexts,

Today, we can use computer-mediated communication as a method for building social capital. Even in gaming environments, people build both bonding and bridging relationships. These relationships are the key to building trust that is need to develop social capital.

Conclusion

Social networks can be used to make the classroom more social by introducing guest speakers and industry experts into a class. Moreover, these networks provide additional communication channels for students to interact with each other and teachers.

Although social networks are a relatively new software application, their existence is based on many years of Internet behavior. As a result, we can look to the past thirty years of Internet use to better understand its use today. Moreover, behaviors examined in face-to-face relationships can be applied to online ones. For instance, the work of Erving Goffman (1959) and his ideas of front and back stage can be applied to behavior. These concepts can be used to examine what is happening in today's classrooms. As students take cell phone calls, curse online, and exhibit unruly behavior in virtual classrooms, teachers can see how backstage behavior is filtering into front stage behavior in class.

When discussion lists, Second Life, and course management systems are used for educational purposes, some of these behaviors and misbehaviors are transferred to the classroom environment. Professors need to be fully aware of how these online tools influence a course. Additionally, the professor needs an understanding of the topics covered in this book—social media, self identity, online community, space versus place, awareness and notification, Second Life, ethical issues, social norms, trust, remix culture and social capital.

This may seem a lot to learn before teaching an online course, but knowing something about these topics can help you to analyze the advantages and disadvantages of introducing computer-mediated communication into your classroom. This is especially true for the changes that can occur in student behavior. Removing people form their words can cause students to be rude, critical, and disrespectful. Sometimes a teacher wonders if the student realizes that he or she can read their words.

Social norms are just one part of the mix needed to understand Internet behavior. The inter-relationship between all of the issues above is necessary. These topics fall into three overlapping categories: social, technical, and usability. At times, the social factors may seem to override the other two. On one hand, the themes of self-identity, community networks, ethical issues and trust seem to be clearly in the category of social. However, the software shapes the nature of these social interactions. For instance, self-identity is conveyed through text or an avatar depending on the software program. Trust can be helped or hindered by the computer's interface.

On the other hand, awareness and notification, and space and place appear to be technical issues. The difference between space and place on the Internet are more than the meanings of words and technology. Place is embedded with feelings and human emotion. If people did not feel as if the Internet created a place for them to meet, individuals would not be able to socialize and build friendships online.

Additionally, the chapter on trust includes information on user interfaces and how software engineers design automated chats. Remix culture also could not happen without user-friendly interfaces that make the digital tools easy for people to use. Usability is a major issue for software programs that want to be adopted by large groups of people. Content creation depends on easy to use software that is available to many users.

In terms of ethics, the student responses in chapter 8, illustrate how norms are changing in online interaction. Students are neutral about the sharing of videos and music online, which is often a violation of copyright. Also, they are neutral on the issues of using proper grammar and spelling, along with cursing. Using poor grammar and cursing online can filter into the classroom. Several incidents in the book have described how this can happen, for instance the quotes from students in chapters 2 and 6.

Adding social networking to the mix of issues described above occurs primarily on a social level. When we introduce these tools into the classroom, students don't always make the connection between the social and professional use of the technology. As professors and teachers, we cannot assume that students know how to use these tools for the purposes we intend. Although students may use Facebook, YouTube, and Second Life for pleasure, educators need to instruct them on how these tools can be put to work to build social capital and gain professional skills.

Facebook

Facebook can be used as a case study to further illustrate the concepts discussed in this book. Sanchez (2010) states that "Twitter, Facebook, and MySpace have changed the way we communicate to each other. Now they are changing what we, together, communicate to the world" (p. 5). Mark Zuckerberg was aware that Facebook could make a powerful impact on culture. The program was originally designed "to build pathways for sharing between people who already know each other in the real world—it can have a potent emotional power" (Kirkpatrick, 2010, p. 13). The emotional bonds formed through Facebook are important for building Facebook communities. Additionally, Facebook creates a place for people to gather and build a community.

As information was shared in the community, Zuckerberg knew that Facebook would mean that people are increasingly living their lives in public. In fact, some "people view [Facebook] as a platform for narcissism rather than a tool for communication" (Kirkpatrick, 2010, p. 13). This is because people can post so much information about themselves.

Presenting yourself to the world begins with a profile of information about yourself. Basic information includes relationship status, interests, political views, and religion. Lanier argues that people create a form of self-reductionism when they create a Facebook profile. Lanier (2010) states:

> You fill in data: profession, marital status, and residence. But in this case digital reduction becomes a causal element, mediating contact between new friends. That is new. It used to be that government was famous for being impersonal, but in a postpersonal world, that will no longer be a distinction" (p. 69)

People now freely post a reduced description of themselves in social networks. The sharing can be public or private. Users can control their contact information. Abram and Pearlman (2010) state: "The Contact Information section lets you control who can see the various pieces of contact info you may have added to your profile—such as phone number or e-mail address" (p. 74).

However, some users forget to use these setting and they place compromising pictures on social networks (see Barnes, 2006). For example, young people have been surprised that parents and schools are looking at their pages. Similarly, college students have mixed reactions to future employers using Facebook as a recruitment tool. The program makes people wonder about how much self-disclosure is appropriate to put online. The privacy settings in Facebook enable users to share information with one person or the whole world. For instance, Baym (2010) speaks to the multiple ways users can share information on Facebook:

> In these sites [MySpace, Facebook, YouTube, and Flickr] people can create personal accounts, upload their own materials, and share them with others publically or only amongst approved recipients. Social network sites are unique in combining multiple modes of communication and, hence, in the breadth of and control over social cues they provide. (p. 17)

The sharing of information, especially videos is part of remix culture. Facebook supports the exchange of remixed materials. People are notified about materials that you post on Facebook. On Facebook, people are notified about birthdays, tagged photos, wall messages, and replies to posts. Facebook even sends messages to your e-mail account to make sure that you are aware of what is happening in your Facebook account. The notification feature is very robust in Facebook, which makes the program more personal.

> The success of Facebook and other SNSs are relationship maintenance tools comes from their wide but selective reach: people can communicate with multiple weak ties simultaneously. Messages can be delivered to all friends via status updates, for instance, or select friends through wall posts. Equally, if not more importantly, people can share photographs. As of this writing, SNS may facilitate a sense of connection. (Baym, 2010, p. 135)

Facebook is a social network that focuses on building personal relationships. Trust is built by the use of real names. Trusting people on the Internet depends on knowing the identity of the other person. For instance, accepting a friendship invitation will automatically connect you to that person and people want to know who they are connected to. Originally the relationships were designed to be with real world friends. As a result, Facebook requires individuals to use their real names. Although it requires real names, people do misbehave and use false ones.

> Facebook requires real names. One analysis of 4,540 Facebook profiles of students at Carnegie Mellon University (USA) Gross & Acquisti, 2005) found that 89 percent of user names seemed to be real. Only 8 percent were clearly false and just 3 percent partial; 80 percent had pictures that made them identifiable. However, Facebook's system for recognizing authenticity is flawed, resulting in multiple profies bearing the names of celebrities, businesses, or websites. (Baym, 2010, p. 109)

Successfully connecting with others requires a person to use behavior that follows social norms. The book *Facebook for Dummies*, has a list of behavior patterns for Facebook developers. These behaviors are similar to the ones described in chapter 7. These include:

- Don't spam.
- Be useful.
- Be social.
- Be clear about what you do.

- Be competitive.
- Listen to your users.
- Be reliable. Be fast.

People developing software for Facebook should follow the rules listed above to ensure that Facebook users will respond positively to their software. By making the social norms available to developers, Facebook tries to ensure the popularity of the program.

Facebook and Media Ecology

Postman (1995) contends that ethical values are embedded in every technology. Sean Parker, an early Facebook employee states: "[Facebook] was 'Let's build something that has lasting cultural value and try to take over the world'" (cited in Kirkpatrick, 2010, p. 47). The problem was that no one knew exactly what that meant. Zuckerberg wanted to design a software program that was simple and easy to use. The many notification systems designed in Facebook make people aware of the program and their social connections. Zuckerberg has a good understanding of how to create software that engages individuals. However, his view of sharing information has led to unanticipated privacy issues, a topic that Facebook struggles with. The cultural value of Facebook has positive and negative influences as described above. One of these consequences is the use of Facebook for activism and protests. The notification features make it easy to contact numbers of people, instead of one or two.

Looking at social networks from a media ecological perspective, forces us to examine the advantages and disadvantages of introducing computer applications into society. For instance, Facebook has been a central communication tool in the Middle East to foster revolt. Additionally, Facebook has problems with privacy issues, an idea that is directly related to how the software was developed. Moreover, Facebook is a popular social communication tool used by young people. Postman (1995) was particularly concerned about how social media influence educational media. While social networking is a tool used by many young people, professors need to have an understanding about the technology and think about the possible consequences of introducing these social tools into education. Our National Science Foundation research shows that social media can be unexpected and not perform the way we anticipate. Using the questions Postman asked in chapter 6 is one way to start examining how social tools can be used to socialize the classroom.

Appendix

Appendix A

1. Mentioning a spoiler in a book or movie without warning people.
   Mean: 2.231 Median: Somewhat Disagree

2. Use of untitled subject headers or misleading message subjects.
   Mean: 2.808 Median: Somewhat Disagree

3. Frequent spelling and grammar errors.
   Mean: 3.269 Median: Mildly Disagree

4. 1337 speak or the use of shortcuts in messages (r u there?).
   Mean: 3.962 Median: Neutral

5. Posting of messages that are advertisements or spam within message threads.
   Mean: 1.808 Median: Strongly Disagree

6. Posting sexually explicit material on someone's wall or in a discussion forum.
   Mean: 1.846 Median: Strongly disagree

7. Cursing or using adult language while communicating in a social networking site.
   Mean: 3.654 Median: Neutral

8. Using systems for personally investigating individuals and obtaining personal information.
   Mean: 3.600 Median: Neutral

9. Performing employee searches and background checks using social software.
   Mean: 3.840 Median: Mildly Disagree

10. Requesting friends and acquaintances to use P2P music and movie sharing systems online.
    Mean: 3.920 Median: Neutral

11. Sharing MP3 and Video files online with friends and family.
    Mean: 5.200 Median: Mildly Agree

12. Sharing MP3 and Video files online with complete strangers.
    Mean: 4.120 Median: Neutral

13. Forwarding online chain letters.
    Mean: 1.680 Median: Strongly Disagree

Appendix B

1. Going through a person's friend list and "friending" those people without knowing who they are.
   Mean: 2.302 Median: Somewhat Disagree

2. Would you date someone you met online?
   Mean: 3.913 Median: Neutral

3. Would you buy a car online?
   Mean: 3.913 Median: Neutral

4. Would you buy a textbook?
   Mean: 6.478 Median: Strongly Agree

5. Would you buy a living creature?
   Mean: 3.522 Median: Mildly Disagree

6. Would you adopt a child through an online service?
   Mean: 2.217 Median: Strongly Disagree

7. Would you swap an Apartment online?
   Mean: 3.304 Median: Neutral

8. Would you book a vacation online?
   Mean: 5.870 Median: Somewhat Agree

9. Would you buy your prescriptions online?
   Mean: 3.739 Median: Neutral

10. Would you buy your glasses online?
    Mean: 3.522 Median: Neutral

11. Would you trust e-mails from your bank or the government online?
    Mean: 4.913 Median: Somewhat Agree

12. Would you share your Social Security number online?
    Mean: 2.636 Median: Somewhat Disagree

13. Would you trust someone from Nigeria?
    Mean: 2.000 Median: Somewhat Disagree

14. Would you buy clothes online?
    Mean: 5.500 Median: Somewhat Agree

15. Would you purchase something from a site that does not have a hacker safe icon?
    Mean: 3.227 Median: Mildly Disagree

16. Would you prepay for services online?
    Mean: 4.273 Median: Mildly Agree

17. Would you buy jewelry online?
    Mean: 3.909 Median: Neutral

18. Would you buy undergarments online?
    Mean: 3.909 Median: Neutral

19. Would you donate to charity online?
    Mean: 4.091 Median: Neutral

20. Would you share with someone your personal secrets online?
    Mean: 3.955 Median: Neutral

21. Would you build a romantic relationship online?
    Mean 3.455 Median: Neutral

22. Would you buy food online?
    a. Mean: 4.227 Median: Neutral

23. Would you trust an IQ quiz online?
    Mean: 3.773 Median: Neutral

24. Would you pay your credit card online?
    Mean: 5.500 Median: Somewhat Agree

25. Would you donate money to a legal defense fund online?
    Mean: 3.273 Median: Neutral

26. Would you ever meet someone in real life after meeting them online for 1 month?
    Mean: 3.909 Median: Neutral

27. Would you ever meet someone in real life after meeting them online for 1 year?
    Mean 5.091 Median: Mildly Agree

28. Would you ever buy something online after reading a review? (never have seen the product before in real life)
    Mean: 4.955 Median: Mildly Agree

Bibliography

Abram, Carolyn and Leah Pearlman, *Facebook for Dummies, 3rd Edition*. Hoboken, NJ: Wiley Publications, 2010.

Adams, Tyrone and Norman Clark, *The Internet: Effective Online Communication*. Orlando, FL: Harcourt College Publishers, 2001.

Alfred, Mary V., "Social Capital Theory: Implications for Women's Networking and Learning." *New Directions for Adult and Continuing Education*, no. 122, (2009, Summer): 3–12.

Anderson, Terry, Liam Rourke, Randy D. Garrison and Walter Archer, "Assessing Teaching Presence in a Computer Conferencing Context." *Journal of Asynchronous Learning Networks 5*, no. 2 (2001). www.aln.org (accessed February 8, 2005).

Anton, Corey, *Communication Uncovered: General Semantics and Media Ecology*. Fort Worth, TX: Institute of General Semantics, 2011

Associated Press. "Last Internet Provider in Egypt Goes Dark." *The Washington Post* (2011, January 31). www.Washingtonpost.com (accessed January 31, 2011)

Bannan, Karen J., "It's Catching." *Adweek* 41, no. 23 (2000): IQ20.

Barnes, Susan B. and Lance Strate, "The Educational Implications of the Computer: A Media Ecology Critique." *The New Jersey Journal of Communication* 4, no. 2 (1996).

Barnes, Susan. B., "Douglas C. Engelbart: Developing the Underlying Concepts for Graphical Interfaces and Contemporary Computing." *The IEEE Annals of the History of Computing Journal, 19 (3)*, (1996), 16–26.

Barnes, Susan, "Developing a Concept of Self in Cyberspace Communities," in *The Emerging Cyberculture*, edited by Stephanie B. Gibson and Ollie O. Oviedo, 169–201. Cresskill, NJ: Hampton Press, 2000.

Barnes, Susan B. *Online Connections: Internet Interpersonal Relationships*. Cresskill, NJ: Hampton Press, 2001.

Barnes, Susan B., *Computer–Mediated Communication: Human–to–Human Communication Across the Internet*. Boston, MA: Allyn & Bacon, 2003.

Barnes, Susan B., "A Privacy Paradox: Social Networking in the United States." *First Monday* 11, no. 9, (2006): 0–14. www.firstmonday.org/issues/issue11_9/barnes/index.html (accessed September 18, 2007).

Barnes, Susan B. "Alan Kay: Transforming the Computer into a Communication Medium." *IEEE Annals of the History of Computing*, 29:2, pp. 18-30, 2007.

Barnes, Susan B., "Interpersonal Communication," in *Reflections on Blended Learning: Rethinking the Classroom,* edited by M. Starenko, 76–78. Rochester, NY: Lulu Press, 2008.

Barnes, Susan B. and Neil Hair, "From Banners to You Tube: Using the Rear-View Mirror to Look at the Future of Advertising." *International Journal of Internet Marketing and Advertising, 5:*3, 223-239 , 2009.

Barrett, Edward, *Sociomedia: Multimedia, Hypermedia, and the Social Construction of Knowledge.* Cambridge, MA: The MIT Press, 1992.

Baym, Nancy, "The Emergence of On–line Community," in *Cybersociety 2.0.* edited by S. G. Jones, 5–68. Thousand Oaks, CA: Sage Publications, 1998.

Baym, Nancy, *Tune in, Log on.* Thousand Oaks, CA: Sage Publications, 2000.

Baym, Nancy, *Personal Connections in the Digital Age.* Malden, MA: Polity Press, 2010.

Beem, C., *The Necessity of Politics: Reclaiming American Public Life.* Chicago: University of Chicago Press, 1999.

Beniger, James R., "Personalization of Mass Media and the Growth of Pseudo–Community." *Communication Research* 14, no. 3 (1987): 352–371.

Bias, Randolph G., "The Pluralistic Usability Walkthrough: Coordinated Empathies," in *Usability Inspection Methods*, Nielsen, Jakob, Mack, R.L. (eds.) pp. 63–76. Wiley, New York, 1994.

Bolter, Jay D., *Writing Space: Computers, Hypertext, and the Remediation of Print.* Mahwah, NJ: Lawrence Erlbaum Associates, Inc., 1991.

Bolter, Jay D. and Diane Gromala., *Windows and Mirrors: Interaction Design, Digital Art, and the Myth of Transparency.* Cambridge, MA: The MIT Press, 2003.

Borges, José A., Israel Morales, Nkstor J. Rodrigues, "Page Design Guidelines Developed Through Usability Testing," in *Human Factors and Web Development,* Forsythe C., Grose, E., Ratner, J. (eds.) pp. 137–152. Lawrence Erlbaum Associates, Mahwah, NJ, 1998.

Bostrom, Robert and Stephen Heinen, "MIS Problems and Failures: A Socio–Technical Perspective." *Part I: The Causes. MIS Quarterly* 1, no. 2 (1977): 17–32.

Bostrom, Robert and Stephen Heinen, "MIS Problems and Failures: A Socio–Technical Perspective." *Part II: The Application of Socio–Technical Theory. MIS Quarterly* 1, no. 3 (1977): 11–28.

Bourdieu, Pierre, *Outline of a Theory of Practice.* Cambridge, UK: University of Cambridge, 1972.

boyd, danah and Nicole B. Ellison, "Social Network Sites: Definition, History, and Scholarship. *Journal of Computer–Mediated Communication 13*, 2008: 210–230.

Boyd, Josh, "The Rhetorical Construction of Trust Online." *Communication Theory* 13, no. 4 (2003): 392–410.

Bruner, Jerome S., *The Culture of Education.* Cambridge, MA: Harvard University Press, 1996.

Bruner, Jerome S., *Toward a Theory of Instruction.* Cambridge, MA: Harvard University Press, 1966.

Bryant, Alison J., Ashley Sanders–Jackson, and Amber M. K. Smallwood, "IMing, Text Messaging, and Adolescent Social Networks." *Journal of Computer–Mediated Communication* 11, no. 2 (2006). www.jcmc.indiana.edu/vol11/issue2/Bryant.html (accessed February 17, 2006).

Buffardi, Laura E. and Keith W. Campbell, "Narcissism and Social Networking Websites." *Perspectives in Social Psychology Bulletin 34* (2008): 1303–1314.

Bugeja, Michael, *Interpersonal Divide: The Search for Community in a Technological Age.* New York: Oxford University Press, 2005.

Bumgarner, B. A., "You Have Been Poked: Exploring the Uses and Gratifications of Facebook Among Emerging Adults." *First Monday* 12, no. 11, (2007): 1–16. www.unic.edu/htbin/cgiwrap/bin/ojs/indes.php/view (accessed January 30, 2008).

Burnett, Ron, *How Images Think.* Cambridge, MA: The MIT Press, 2004.

Burnette, Daarel, "Online Threats Terrify Students." *The Courier–Journal,* Sunday April 29, 2007. courier–Journal.com (accessed April 29, 2007).

Bynum, Terrell Ward, "Ethics and the Information Revolution," in *Readings in Cyber Ethics,* edited by R. A. Spinello and H. T. Tavani, 9–25. Boston, MA: Jones and Bartlett Publishers, 2001.

Byrne, Dara N., "Public Discourse, Community Concerns, and Civic Engagement: Exploring Black Social Networking Traditions on BlackPlanet.com. *Journal of Computer–Mediated Communication 13,* no. 1 (2007). www.jcmc.indiana.edu/vol13/issue1/byrne.htm (accessed January 29, 2008).

Carroll, John M., Dennis C. Neale, Philip L. Isenhour, Mary Beth Rosson, and Scott McCrickard, "Notification and Awareness: Synchronizing Task–Oriented Collaborative Activity." *International Journal of Human–Computer Studies 58,* (2003): 605–632.

Case, Tony, "The Digital Hot List 2007." *Adweek,* (2007). www.adweek.com (accessed December 27, 2007).

Cassell, Justine and Bickmore, Timothy, "External Manifestations of Trustworthiness in the Interface." *Communications of the ACM* 43, no. 12 (2000): 50–54.

Cassell, Justine and Dona Tversky, "The Language of Online Intercultural Community Formation." *Journal of Computer–Mediated Communication 10,* no. 2 (2005). jcmc.indiana.edu/vol10/issue2/cassell.html (accessed Feburary 14, 2008).

Cathcart, Robert. R. and Gary Gumpert, "The Person–Computer Interaction: A Unique Source," in *Intermedia: Interpersonal Communication in a Mediated World, 3rd Edition,* edited by G. Gumpert and R. R. Cathcart, 323–332. New York: Oxford University Press, 1986.

Cavazos, Ed A. and Gavino Morin, *Cyber–Space and the Law.* Cambridge, MA: The MIT Press, 1994.

Ceruzzi, Paul. E., *A History of Modern Computing.* Cambridge, MA: The MIT Press, 1998.

Cheuk, Bonnie, "Social Networking Analysis: Its Application to Facilitate Knowledge Transfer." *Business Information Review 24,* no. 3 (2007): 170–176.

Cheung, Lily S., "A Constructivist Approach to Designing Computer Supported Concept–Mapping Environment." *International Journal of Instructional Media* 33, no. 2 (2006): 153–164

Cirlot, J. E., *A Dictionary of Symbols*. New York: Philosophical Library, 1962.

Clements, Douglas H. and Julie Sarama, "Research on Logo: A Decade of Progress." *Computers in the Schools 14,* no. 1/2 (1997): 9–45.

Cohill, Andrew. M. and Andrea L. Kavanaugh. *Community Networks: Lessons from Blacksburg Virginia, Second Edition*. Norwood, MA: Artech House, Inc., 2000.

Coleman, James. S., *Foundations of Social Theory*, Cambridge, MA: Belknap Press, 1998.

Collins, Allan and Richard Haverson, *Rethinking Education in the Age of Technology*. New York, NY: Teachers College Press, 2009.

Copeland, Michael, "The Missing Link." *Business 2.0 7,* no. 11 (December 2006): 118.

Copeland, Libby, "Putting the I in Advertising." *Washington Post,* (2007, May 7). www.washingtonpost.com (accessed May 7, 2007).

Coyne, Richard, *Designing Information Technology in the Postmodern Age*. Cambridge, MA: The MIT Press, 1995.

Crumlish, Christian, *The Power of Many: How the Living Web is Transforming Politics, Business, and Everyday Life*. San Francisco, CA: Sybex, 2004.

Cummings, Thomas and Suresh Srivasta, "The Management of Work: A Socio–Technical Systems Approach. Technical Report, Kent State University (1977).

De Vise, Daniel, "Wide Web of Diversions Gets Laptops Evicted from Lecture Halls." *The Washington Post,* March 9, A01, 2010.

Degraffenreid, Scott, "Resistance is Futile! Millennials Hit the Workforce" and "Getting Gamers: Painting the Target!" 2006 and 2007. www.neessarymeasures.com (accessed April 24, 2007).

DeHoff, J., "Creating a Metaverse One World at a Time: Avatar–based Marketing." *Infinite Vision Media,* 2006. www.infinitevisionmedia.blogspot.com/2006/06/avatar-basedmarketing (accessed November 26, 2007).

Delevoy, Robert L., *Symbolists and Symbolism*. New York: Rizzoli International Publications, 1982.

Dewey, John, *Reconstruction in Philosophy*. Boston, MA: Beacon Press, 1920/1948.

Dibbell, Jullien, *My Tinylife: Crime and Passion in a Virtual World*. New York: Henry Holt and Company, 1998.

Dohney–Farina, Stephen, *The Wired Neighborhood*. New Haven, CT: Yale University Press, 1996.

Donath, Judith S., "Identity and Deception in the Virtual Community," in *Communities in Cyberspace*, edited M. A. Smithe and P. Kollock, 29–59. New York: Routledge, 1999.

Donath, Judith, "Signals in Social Supernets." *Journal of Computer–Mediated Communication* 13, no. 1 (2007): 0–21. www.ascuse.org/jcmc?vol3/issue/1/donath .html. (accessed January 29, 2008).

Doring, Nicola, "Personal Home Pages on the Web: A Review of Research." *Journal of Computer–Mediated Communication* 7, no. 3 (2002): 0–22. www.ascuse.org/jcmc?vol3/issue/1/doring.html. (accessed March 28, 2006).

Dourish, Paul, "Re–Space–ing Place: 'Place' and 'Space' Ten Years On." *CSCW'06*, November 4–8, 2006. Banff, Alberta, Canada, 2006.

Dourish, Paul and Victoria Bellotti, "Awareness and Coordination in Shared Spaces." *Proceedings of the ACM Conference on Computer–Supported Cooperative Work*, 107–114. Toronto, Canada: ACM Press, 1992.

Downes, Stephen, "Hacking Memes." *First Monday 4*, no. 10 (1999). www.first monday.org. (accessed September 19, 2006).

Dozier, John W. and Sue Scheff, *Google Bomb*. Deerfield Beach, FL: Health Communication, Inc., 2009.

Drentea, Patricia and Jennifer L Moren–Cross, "Social Capital and Social Support on the Web: The Case of an Internet Mother Site." *Sociology of Health & Illness*, (2005): 920–943.

Du, Helen S. and Christian Wagner, "Learning with Weblogs: Enhancing Cognitive and Social Knowledge Construction." *IEEE Transactions on Professional Communication 50*, no. 1 (2007): 1–16.

duLac, J. Freedom, "At 10, Dance–Dancing His Way to Gunness Record." *The Washington Post,* February 2, 2011. www.washingtonpost.com. (accessed February 2, 2011).

Dyson Ester, *Release 2.0: A Design for Living in the Digital Age*. Broadway Books, New York, 1997.

Egert, Christopher, "The Integrated Online Seminar System: An Architecture and Implementation of a Media–Centric Environment for Web–Based E–Learning" (Doctoral dissertation, University at Buffalo, 2003). *Dissertation Abstract International* 64, no. *08B* (2003): 3899.

Eijkman, Henk, "Web 2.0 as a Non–Fundamental Network–Centric Learning Space. Campus–Wide Information Systems 25, (2008): 93–104.

Ellison, Nicole B., Charles Steinfield, and Cliff Lampe, "The Benefits of Facebook 'Friends:' Social Capital and College Students' Use of Online Social Network Sites." *Journal of Computer Mediated Communication*, 12 (2007), 1143–1168.

Fischer, Roger, *Microlearning with Mobile Weblogs*, (2005). www.microlearning.org/micropapers/MLproc_2005_fischer.pdf (accessed November 24, 2007).

Fleischer, Peter, "Some Ruled of Thumb for Online Privacy. Peter Fleischer: Privacy. . ?" (2007) www.peterfleischer.blogspot.com/2007/05/some-rules-of-thumb-for-online–privacy.html. (accessed May 7, 2007).

Forsythe C., E. Grose, and J. Ratner, (eds.) *Human Factors and Web Development*. Mahwah, NJ: Lawrence Erlbaum,1998.

Friedman, Batya, Peter H. Kahn Jr., and Daniel C. Howe, "Trust Online." *Communications of the ACM* 43, no. 12 (2000): 34–40.

Friedman, Thomas L., *The World is Flat*. NY: Farrar, Straus and Giroux, 2005.

Galkin, William S., "Privacy: What is it?" *Computer Law Observer*, issue 14 (May 1996), http://www.awcircle.com/issue14.html (accessed December 23 1997).

Gao, Fei, and David Wong, Student Engagement in Distance Learning Environments: A Comparison of Threaded Discussion Forums and Text–

Focused Wikis." *First Monday Journal* 13, no. 1 (2008). www.uic.edu (accessed April 21, 2008).

Gardner, Howard, *Frames of Mind*. New York: Basic Books, 1983.

Garfield, Bob, "The YouTube Effect." *Wired*, (December 2006): 222–227.

Garrison, Randy D. and Heather Kanuka, "Blended Learning: Uncovering its Transforative Potential in Higher Education." *Internet and Higher Education* 7: 95–105, 2004.

Garton, Laura, Caroline Haythornthwaite, and Barry Wellman, "Studying Online Social Networks." *Journal of Computer–Mediated Communication 3*, no. 1 (1997): 1–30 www.ascuse.org/jcmc//vol13/issue1/garton.html. (accessed February 13, 2004).

Garvin, Keith, "Teen Tells How He was Lured into Child Porn." *ABC News* (April 5, 2006). www.abcnews.com (accessed April 5, 2006).

Gibson, William, *Neuromancer*. New York: Ace Books, 1984.

Giese, Mark, "Self Without Body: Textual Self–Representation in an Electronic Community." *First Monday* 29. (1998). www.firstmonday.org (accessed April 14, 2000).

Goffman, Erving, *The Presentation of Self in Everyday life*. Garden City, NY: Doubleday and Company, 1959.

Goffman, Erving, *Frame Analysis*. Boston, MA: Northeastern University Press, 1974.

Goldbeck, Jennifer, "The Dynamics of Web–Based Social Networks: Membership, Relationships, and Change." *First Monday 12*, no. 11 (2007): 1–14. www.firstmonday .org (accessed January 30, 2008).

Gombrich, Ernst. H., *The Sense of Order*. Ithaca, NY: Cornell University Press, 1984.

Graham, Gordon, *The Internet: A Philosophical Inquiry*. London: Routledge, 1999.

Grassian, Esther and Rhonda B. Trueman, "Stumbling, Bumbling, Teleporting and Flying . . . Librarian Avatars in Second Life." *Reference Sciences Review 35*, no. 1 (2006): 84–89.

Gronstedt, Anders, "Second Life: The 3 D Web World is Slowly Becoming Part of the Training Industry." *Training and Development*, (August 2007): 44–49.

Gross, Ralph and Alessandro Acquisti, "Information Revelation and Privacy in Online Social Networks." *WPES'05, Association of Computing Machinery*, (2005): 71–80.

Grossman, Lev, "Power to the People." *Time Magazine*, (December 2006–January 2007): 42–58.

Gulati, Girish J., "Members of Congress and Presentation of Self on the World Wide Web." *Press/Poloitics* 9 (1) (2004): 22–40.

Gumpert, Gary and Robert R. Cathcart, *Intermedia: Interpersonal Communication in a Mediated World, 3rd Edition*. New York: Oxford University Press, 1986.

Halavais, Alexander, *Search Engine Society*. Malden, MA: Polity Press, 2009.

Hale, Claudia L., "A Constructivist Approach to Meaning: In Defense of Interpretation. *National Communication Association* (Alta Conference on Argumentation)," (1985): 523–534. Communication & Mass Media Complete database (accessed April 14, 2008).

Halper, Sachiko, Kevin Kelly, and Wen Hao Chang, "A Reflection on Coursestream System: A Virtual Classroom Streaming System Designed for Large Classes."

TechTrends: Linking Research & Practice to Improve Learning 51, no. 2 (2007): 24–27.

Halsey III, Ashley, "U.S. Teens Report 'Frightening' Levels of Texting While Driving." *The Washington Post* (November 17, 2009). www.washingtonpost.com (accessed November 17, 2009).

Hamelink, Cees J., *The Ethics of Cyberspace.* London: Sage, 2000.

Hampton, Keith and Barry Wellman, "Long Distance Community in the Networked Society. *American Behavioral Scientist 45,* no. 3 (2001): 476–495.

Hanifan, Lyda Judson., "The Rural School Community Center." *Annals of the American Academy of Political and Social Science* 67 (1916): 130–138.

Hanlin–Rowney, Amber, Ken, Maria Eugenia Aba Lara, Deborah Quinn, Ken Roffmann, Tracie Tyson Kuntzelman Nichols, and Linda Welsh, "Online Collaborative Inquiry as a Framework for Exploring Transformative learning." *Journal of Transformative Education Online 4,* no. 4 (2006): 320–334.

Hargittai, Eszter, "Whose Space? Differences Among Users and Non–Users of Social Networking Sites." *Journal of Computer–Mediated Communication, 13,* no. 1 (2007): 276–297. www.blackwell–synergy.com. (accessed January 25, 2008).

Harper, Ben D., and Kent L. Norman, "Improving User Satisfaction: The Questionnaire for User Interaction Satisfaction Version 5.5," in *Proceedings of the 1st Annual Mid–Atlantic Human Factors Conference,* pp. 224–228. Virginia Beach, VA, 1993.

Harrison, Steve and Paul Dourish,"Re-place-ing Space: The Roles of Place and Space in Collaborative Systems. *Computer Supported Cooperative Work '96.* Cambridge, MA, 1996.

Hayles, Katherine N., *Writing Machines.* Cambridge, MA: MIT Press, 2002.

Haythornthwaite, Caroline, Michelle M. Kazmer, Jennifer Robins, and Susan Shoemaker, "Community Development Among Distance Learners: Temporal and Technological Dimensions." *Journal of Computer-Mediated Communication 6,* no. 1 (2000).www.ascusc.org/jcmc/vol16/issue1/. (accessed January 25, 2008).

Healy, Jane M., *Endangered Minds.* New York: Simon & Schuster, 1990.

Hennig–Thurau, Thorsten, Kevin P. Gwinner, Gianfranco Walsh, and Dwayne Gremler, "Electronic Word–of–Mouth via Consumer–Opinion Platforms: What Motivates Consumers to Articulate Themselves on the Internet?" *Journal of Interactive Marketing 18,* no. 1 (2004): 38–52.

Hiltz, Starr Roxnne, Barry Wellman, "Asynchronous Learning Networks as a Virtual Classroom." *Communications of the ACM* 40, no. 9, (1997), 44—49.

Hirshberg, Peter, "On TV and the Web." *TED talk.* (2007, December). www.ted.com/index.php/talks/peter_hirshberg_on_tv_and_the_web.html (accessed January 21, 2009).

Hof, Robert D. "The Power of Us." *BusinessWeek,* June 20, 2005, 75–76.

Holzwarth, Martin, Janiszewski, Chris, & Neumann, Marcus, "The Influence of Avatars on Online Consumer Behavior." *Journal of Marketing* 70 (October 2006): 19–36.

Hoppough, Suzanne, "Image Doctor." *Forbes 179,* no. 60 (February 26, 2006). www.Forbes.com (accessed February 14, 2010).

Horn, Stacey, *Cyberville: Clicks, Culture, and the Creation of an Online Town*. New York: Warner Books, 1998.

Horton, Donald and R. R. Wohl, "Mass Communication and Para–Social Interaction: Observation on Intimacy at a Distance," in *Intermedia: Interpersonal Communication in a Mediated World, 3rd Edition* edited by G. Gumpert and R. R. Cathcart, 185–206. New York: Oxford University Press, 1986 [1956].

Howe, Jeff, "The Hit Factory." *Wired* 13, no. 11 (2005): 200–205, 218.

Huffaker, David A. and Sandra L. Calvert, "Gender, Identity, and Language Use in Teenage Blogs." *Journal of Computer–Mediated Communication 10*, no. 2 (2005).

Hughes, Matthew, Susie Ventura, and Dando, Mark. "Assessing Social Presence in Online Discussion Groups: A Replication Study." *Innovations in Education & Teaching International 44*, no. 1 (2007): 17–29.

Humphreys, Lee, "Mobile Social Networks and Social Practice: A Case Study of Dodgeball. " *Journal of Computer-Mediated Communication* 13 (2008): 341–360.

Irwin, Harry, "Attribution, Constructivism, and Images in Interpersonal Communication." *Communicator 13*, (1983): 62–79. Communication & Mass Media Complete database. (accessed April 14, 2008).

Ivory, Melody Y., Rashmi R. Sinha, Marti A. Hearst, "Empirically Validated Web Page Design Metrics," in: Proceedings of the *SIGCHI Conference on Human Factors in Computing Systems*, 3 (1), (2001), pp. 53–60. Seattle, WA: ACM Press.

Janson, Anthony F., *History of Art, Fifth Edition*. Upper Saddle River, NJ: Prentice Hall, 1995.

Jarvenpaa, Sirkka L. and Dorothy E. Leidner, "Communication and Trust in Global Virtual Teams." *Journal of Computer–Mediated Communication 3*, no. 4 (1998): 1–30. www.aascusc.org. (accessed October 27, 2000).

Jenkins, Henry, *Convergence Culture*. New York: New York University Press, 2006.

Jennings, Nancy and Chris Collins, "Virtual or VirtuallyU: Educational Institutions in Second Life." *International Journal of Social Sciences 2*, no. 3 (2008): 180–186.

Johansen, Robert, David Sibbet, Suzyan Benson, Alixia Martin, Robert Mittman, and Paul Saffo, *Leading Business Teams: How Teams Can Use Technology and Group Process Tools to Enhance Performance*. Reading, MA: Addison–Wesley (1991).

Johnson, Stephen, *Interface Culture: How New Technology Transforms the Way We Create and Communicate*. San Francisco: HarperEdge, 1997.

Jones, Steve G. *Cybersociety: Computer–Mediated Communication and Community*. Thousand Oaks, CA: Sage, 1995.

Jones, Steve G., *CyberSociety 2.0: Revisiting Computer–Mediated Communication and Community*. Thousand Oaks, CA: Sage Publications, 1998.

Jones, Quentin, "Virtual-Communities, Virtual Settlements & Cyber-Archaeology: A Theoretical Outline." *Journal of Computer-Mediated-Communication* 3, no. 3 (1997): 1–26.

Kakutani, Michiko, "Texts without Content." *The New York Times* (March 17, 2010). www.nytimes.com (accessed March 17, 2010).

Kang, Cecilia, "Google, Twitter Team Up for Egyptians to Send Tweets via Phone." *The Washingon Post*, January 31, 2011. www.washingtonpost.com (accessed January 31, 2011).

Kang, Cecilia, "Clinton Urges Egypt to Unblock Twitter, Facebook." The Washingon Post, January 27, 2011.www.washingtonpost.com (accessed January 27, 2100).

Katz, James. E. and Ronald E. Rice, *Social Consequences of Internet Use*. Cambridge, MA: The MIT Press, 2002.

Kavanaugh, Andrea J. and Scott J. Patterson, "The Impact of Community Computer Networks on Social Capital and Community Involvement." *American Behavioral Scientist 45*, no. 3 (2001): 496–509.

Kay, Alan C., "User Interface: A Personal View," in *The Art of Human-Computer Interface Design* edited by B. Laurel, 191–207. Boston, MA: Addison-Wesley, 1990.

Kay, Alan, and Adele Goldberg, "Personal Dynamic Media," in *The New Media Reader* edited by N. Montfort and N. Wardrip–Fruin, 393–404. Cambridge, MA: MIT Press, 2003 [1977].

Kazmer, Michelle M., "Beyond C U L8R: Disengaging from Online Social Worlds." *New Media Society* 9, no. 1 (2007): 111–138.

Kelton, AJ, "Second Life: Reaching into the Virtual World for Real-World Learning." *Research Bulletin, Educause Center for Applied Research 17,* (2007): 1–13.

Kennedy, Elizabeth, "Syrians call for Protests on Facebook and Twitter." *The Washingon Post,* February 1, 2011. www.washingtonpost.com. (accessed February 1, 2100).

Kilgannon, Corey, "Teenagers Misbehaving, for all Online to Watch." *The New York Times* (February 7, 2007). www.nytimes.com (accessed February 13, 2007).

Kim, Kyung-Hee and Haejin Yun, "*Cying* for Me, *Cying* for Us: Relational Dialectics in a Korean Social Network Site." *Journal of Computer–Mediated Communication 13*, no. 1 (2007): 298–318. www.blackwell-synergy.com. (accessed January 25, 2008).

Kirkpatrick, David, *The Facebook Effect*. New York: Simon & Schuster, 2010.

Kollock, Peter, "Design Principles for Online Communities." *PC Update* 15(5), (1998) 58–60.

Kuchinskas, Susan, "Brave New World." *Adweek* 47, no. 35 (2006): SR6.

Lamb, Annetta and Larry Johnson, "Want to be My 'Friend'? What you Need to Know About Social Technologies." *Teacher Librarian* 34, no. 1 (October, 2006): 55–57.

Lange, Patricia G., "Publicly Private and Privately Public: Social Networking on YouTube." *Journal of Computer-Mediated Communication 13*, no. 1 (2007): 361–380.

Lanier, Jaron, *You are Not a Gaget*. New York: Alfred A. Knopf, 2010.

Larson, Malene C., "Understanding Social Networking: On Young People's Construction and Co–Construction of Identity Online," in *Online networking: Connecting People,* edited by K. Sangeetha, 197–216. Hyderabad, India: The Icfai University Press, 2008.

Lee, Judith Y., "Charting the Codes of Cyberspace: A Rhetoric of Electronic Mail," in *Communication and Cyberspace* edited by L. Strate, R. Jacobson, and S. Gibson, 275–296. Cresskill, NJ: Hampton Press, 1996.

Lenhart, Amanda, *Adults and Social Network Sites.* Washington, DC: Pew Internet Data Memo (January 14, 2009). www.pewinternet.com (accessed June 2, 2009).

Lenhart, Amanda, Susan Arafeh , Aaron Smith, and Alexandra R. Macgill, "Writing, Technology and Teens." *Pew Internet and American Life Project*, 2008.

Lenhart, Amanda, John Horrigan, and Deborah Fallows, "Content Creation Online." *Pew Internet & American Life Project*, (2004, February 29): 1–16.

Lenhart, Amanda and Mary Madden, "Teen Content Creators and Consumers." *Pew Internet & American Life Project*, (November 2, 2005): 0–21.

Lenhart, Amanda, Mary Madden, and Hitlin, Paul. *Teens and Technology: Youth are Leading the Transition to a Fully Wired and Mobile Nation.* Washington: Pew Internet & American Life Project, 2005. www.pewinternet.org (accessed November 12, 2006)

Lenhart, Amanda., Madden, Mary, Alexandra R. Macgill, and Aaron Smith, "Teens and Social Media: The Use of Social Media Gains a Greater Foothold in Teen Life as they Embrace the Conversational Nature of Interactive Online Media." *Pew Internet and American Life Project*, 2007.

Lenhart, Amanda, Susan Arafeh, Aaron Smith, Alexandra R. Macgill, "Writing, Technology and Teens." Report, *Pew Internet and American Life Project*, 2008.

Lessig, L. (2008). Remix: Making Art and Commerce Thrive in the Hybrid Economy Available as a free Creative Commons Attribution-NonCommercial-NoDerivs (by–nc–nd) licensed download, 6.

Lessig, Lawrence, *Remix: Making Art and Commerce Thrive in the Hybrid Economy.* New York: Penguin Press, 2008.

Levinson, Paul, *Electronic Chronicles.* Tallahassee, FL: Anamnesis Press, 1992.

Levinson, Paul, *The Soft Edge.* New York: Routledge, 1997.

Lévy, Pierre, "'The Art and Architecture of Cyberspace,' Collective Intelligence," in *Multimedia from Wagner to Virtual Reality* edited by R. Packer and K. Jordan, 370–379. New York: W.W. Norton & Company, 2001.

Levy, Stephen, *Hackers.* New York: Doubleday, 1984.

Levy, Steven, "How Many Friends is Too Many?" *Newsweek*, May 17, 2008.

Licklider, J. C. R. and Robert Taylor, "The Computer as a Communication Device." *Science and Technology* [Online], April 1968.

Livingstone, Sonia, "Taking Risky Opportunities in Youthful Content Creation: Teenagers' Use of Social Networking Sites for Intimacy, Privacy, and Self–Expression." *New Media Society 10*, no. 3 (2008): 393–411.

Lohr, Steve, "Reluctant Conscripts in the March of Technology." *The New York Times* (September 17, 1995): E16.

Lombard, Matthew and Theresa Dutton, "At the Heart of it All: The Concept of Presence." *Journal of Computer Mediated Communication* 3, no. 1 (1997): 1–43.

Lüders, Marika, "Conceptualizing Personal Media." *New Media & Society* 10, no. 5 (2008): 683–702.

Macdonald, Janet, "Assessing Online Collaborative Learning: Process and Product." *Computers & Education* 40, no. 4 (2003): 377–391.

MacMillan, Douglas, "A Twitter Code of Conduct." *BusinessWeek*, (May 8, 2009). www.businessweek.com. (accessed May 9, 2009).

Madden, Mary, "Online Video." *PEW Internet & American Life Project Report*, (July 25, 2007). www.pewinternet.org (accessed March 28, 2010).

Madden, Mary and Amanda Lenhart, "Teens and Distracted Driving." *Pew Internet Life Project*, (November 16, 2009). www.pewinternet.org (accessed December 28, 2009).

Mann, Denise, "Medical Students Reckless on Internet, Sometimes at Patients Expense." *CNN Health*, (September 22, 2009). www.cnnhealth.com (accessed January 27, 2010).

Matei, Sorin, "The Impact of State–Level Social Capital on the Emergence of Virtual Communities." *Journal of Broadcasting & Electronic Media* 48, no. 1 (March 2004): 23–40.

Mathwick, Charla, Caroline Wiertz, and Ko De Ruyter, "Social Capital Production in a Virtual P3 Community." *Journal of Consumer Research* 34, (2007): 832–849.

Mayer, Richard E., Roxana Moreno, Michelle Boire, and Shannon Vagge, "Maximizing Constructivist Learning from Multimedia Communications by Minimizing Cognitive Load." *Journal of Educational Psychology 91*, no. 4 (1999): 638–643.

McArthur, David and Matthew Lewis, *Untangling the Web: Applications of the Internet and Other Information Technologies to Higher Learning.* Rand Paper # MR–975–IET, (1998): 1–75. www.rand.org/publications/MR/MR975 (accessed August 2, 1998).

McCaffery, Larry, *Storming the Reality Studio: A Casebook of Cyberpunk and Postmodern Fiction*. Durham, NC: Duke University Press, 1992.

McConnell, Ben and Jackie Huba, "Book Excerpt: Giving Up Control and Other Scary Lessons." *BrandWeek*, (December 4, 2006). www.brandweek.com (accessed December 12, 2006).

McGrath, Ben "It Should Happen to You: The Anxieties of YouTube Fame." *The New Yorker* (October 16, 2006): 86–95.

McLuhan, Marshall, *Understanding Media*. New York: Signet Books, 1964.

McLuhan, Mashall and Bruce R. Powers, *The Global Village*. New York: Oxford University Press, 1989.

McMillan, David W., David M. Chavis, "Sense of Community: A Definition and Theory." *Journal of Community Psychology* 14 (1986): 6–23

Mead, George H., *The Philosophy of the Present*, edited by A. E. Murphy. LaSalle, IL: The Open Court Publishing Co., 1932.

Mead, George H., *Mind, Self, and Society*, edited by C.W. Morris. Chicago: The University of Chicago Press, 1934.

Mebane, Minou, Rita Porcelli, Amalia Iannone, Carlo Attanasio, and Donata Francescato, "Evaluation of the Efficacy of Affective Education Online Training in Promoting Academics and Professional Learning and Social Capital." *International Journal of Human–Conputer Interaction*, 24, no. 1 (2008): 68–86.

Melillo, Wendy, "We the People . . . Have a Lot to Say." *Adweek 48*, no. 11 (March 12, 2007): 20–22.

Meloncon, Lisa, "Exploring Electronic Landscapes: Technical Communication, Online Learning, and Instructor Preparedness." *Technical Communication Quarterly* 16, no. 1 (2007): 31–53.

Meshel, Jeffrey W., *One Phone Call Away*. New York: Portfolio, 2005.

Meyrowitz, Joshua, *No Sense of Place: The Impact of Electronic Media on Social Behavior*. New York: Oxford University Press, 1986.

Miller, Hugh and Jill Arnold, "Self in Web Home Pages: Gender. Identity and Power in Cyberspace," in: *Towards CyberPsychology: Mind, Cognition and Society in the Internet Age*, pp. 74–94. Amsterdam, IOS Press, 2003.

Mitchell, William J. *The Reconfigured Eye*. Cambridge, MA: The MIT Press, 1992.

Morris, Tee, *All a Twitter: A Personal and Professional Guide to Social Networking With Twitter*. Indianapolis: *Cue Publishing*, 2009.

Murphy, Karen L. and Mauri P. Collins, "Communication Conventions in Instructional Chats." First Monday (Online), 2 (11), 1997.

National Science Foundation Award #0633401 "Theoretical and Applied Approaches to Teaching Social Networking in STEM Education. *National Science Foundation,* (March 8, 2007). www.nsf.gov/awardssearch/showAward.do?AwardNumber=o633401.

Negroponte, Nicholas, *Being Digital*. New York: Random House, 1995.

Neo, Mai, "Learning with Multimedia: Engaging Students in Constructivist Learning." *International Journal of Instructional Media 34*, no. 3 (2007): 149–158.

Nielsen, Jakob, "Usability Engineering." Morgan Kaufmann Publishers, San Francisco, 1993," in: Nielsen, Jakob, Mack, R. L. (eds.) *Usability Inspection Methods,* pp. 25—62. New York: Wiley, 1994.

Nielsen, Jakob. *Designing Web Usability*. Indianapolis: New Riders Publishing, 2000.

O'Leary, Noreen, "They Want the World (And They Want it Now)." *Adweek* 26, no. 49 (2005): 4.

O'Sullivan, Patrick B., "What You Don't Know Won't Hurt Me: Impression Management Functions of Communication Channels in Relationships." *Human Communication Reports 26*, no. 3 (2000): 403–431.

Ong, W. J., *Orality and Literacy: The Technologizing of the Word*. New York: Methuen, 1982.

Packer, Randall and Ken Jordan, *Multimedia: From Wagner to Virtual Reality*. New York: W. W. Norton & Company, 2001.

Papacharissi, Zizi, "The Virtual Geographies of Social Networks: A Comparative Analysis of Facebook, LinkedIn and ASmallWorld." *New Media Society,* 11, no. 1 *and* 2 (2009): 199–220.

Papert, Seymour. *The Connected Family*. Atlanta, GA: Longstreet Press, 1996.

Paris, D. C. "Is There a Professor in this Class?" in *Issues in Web-Based Pedagogy*, edited by R. A. Cole. Westport, CT: Greenwood Press, 2001.

Park, Namkee, Kwan Min Lee and Pauline Hope Cheong, "University Instructors' Acceptance of Electronic Courseware: An Application of the Technology Acceptance Model." *Journal of Computer-Mediated Communication 13*, no. 1 (2007): 163–186. jcmc.indiana.edu. (accessed April 21, 2008).

Pegoraro, Rob. "Vodafone, France Telecom Reportedly Restore Service in Egypt." *The Washingon Post,* January 31, 2011. www.washingtonpost.com. (accessed January 31, 20112011,).

Peirce, Charles, S., *The Essential Peirce*, edited by The Peirce Edition Project. Bloomington, IN: Indiana University Press, 1998.

Phillips, Gerald. M. and Nancy J. Metzger, *Intimate Communication.* Boston: Allyn and Bacon, 1976.

Picciano, Anthony G., "Beyond Student Perceptions: Issues of Interaction, Presence and Performance in an Online Course." *Journal of Asynchronous Learning Networks* 6, no. 1 (2002): 21–40.

Pokin, Steve, "Pokin Around: A Real Person, A Real Death." *St. Charles Journal*, Tuesday November 23, 2007.

Postman, Neil, "The Reformed English Curriculum," in *High School 1980: The Shape of the Future in American Secondary Education*, edited by A. C. Eurich, 160–168. New York: Pitman Publishing, [1970] 1980.

Postman, Neil, *Teaching as a Conserving Activity.* New York: Dell Publishing, 1979.

Postman, Neil, *The Disappearance of Childhood.* New York: Vintage Books, 1982/1994.

Postman, Neil, *Amusing Ourselves to Death.* New York: Viking, 1985.

Postman, Neil, *Technopoly: The Surrender of Culture to Technology.* New York: Alfred A. Knopf, 1992.

Postman, Neil, *The End of Education.* New York: Alfred A. Knopf, 1995.

Prensky, Marc, "Digital Natives, Digital Immigrants." *On the Horizon NCB University Press* 9, no. 5 (October, 2001a).

Prensky, Marc, "Do They Really *Think* Differently?" *On the Horizon NCB University Press* 9, no. 6 (December, 2001b).

Prensky, Marc, *Teaching Digital Natves.* Thousand Oaks, CA: Corwin.

Proserpio, Luigi and Dennis A. Gioia, "Teaching the Virtual Generation" *Academy of Management Learning & Education* 6, no. 1 (2007): 69–80.

Putnam, Robert, *Bowling Alone: The Collapse and Revival of American Community*, New York: Simon & Schuster, 2000.

Reeves, Byron and Clifford Nass, *The Media Equasion: How People Treat Computers, Televisions, and New Media Like Real People and Places.* Stanford, California: University Press, 1996.

Rheingold, Howard, *The Virtual Community.* Reading, MA: Addison–Westley Publishing Company, 1993.

Rheingold, Howard, "Virtual Community," in *The Community of the Future* edited by F. Hesselbein, M. Goldsmith, R. Beckhard and R. F. Schubert, 115–122. Reading, MA: Addison–Wesley Publishing Company, 1998.

Rheingold, Howard, *Smart Mobs: The Next Social Revolution.* Cambridge, MA: Basic Books, 2002.

Roland, M., "Discussing Social Media." *Many 2 Many*, (2004). [Online Blog]. www.corante.com (accessed April 9, 2005).

Rosenbloom, Andrew, "Trusting Technology." *Communications of the ACM* 43, no. 12 (2000): 31–32.

Rourke, Liam, Terry Anderson, D. Randy Garrison, and Walter Archer, "Assessing Social Presence in Asynchronous Text–Based Computer Conferencing." *Journal of Distance Education 14*, no. 2 (2001). cade.athabascau.ca/vol14.2/rourke_et_al.html (accessed February 10, 2005).

Russo, Tracy C. and Joy Koesten, "Prestige, Centrality, and Learning: A Social Network Analysis of an Online Class." *Communication Education* 54, no. 3 (2005): 254–261.

Rymaszewski, Michael, Wagner James Au, Mark Wallace, Catherine Winters, Corey Ondrejka, and Benjamin Batstone–Cunningham, *Second Life: The Official Guide*. Indianapolis, IN: John Wiley & Sons, 2007.

Sadoski, Mark and Allan Paivio, "A Dual Coding Theoretical Model of Reading," In *Theoretical Models and Processes of Reading* 5th ed., edited by R. B. Ruddell and N. J. Unrau, 1329–1362. Newark, DE: International Reading Association, 2004.

Sanchez, Rick, *Conventional Idiocy*. New York: Celebra, 2010.

Schau, Hope Jensen, & Gilly, Mary C., "We Are What We Post? Self–Presentation in Personal Web Space." *Journal of Consumer Research, Inc.,* 30, December 2003.

Schrock, Andrew, "Examining Social Media Usage: Technology Clusters and Social Network Site Membership." *First Monday* 14, no. 1 and 5 (January 2009).

Schuler, Douglas, "Community Networks: Building a New Participatory Medium." *Communications of the ACM* 37, no. 1 (1994): 39–51.

ScienceDaily. (2010, May 5). "New Study Examines Use of Social Media in the Classroom." www.sciencedaily.com (accessed May 6, 2010).

Seelye, Katherine, "YouTube Passes Debates to a New Generation." *New York Times*, June 14, 2007.

Selfe, Cynthia, "Technology and Literacy: A Story about the Perils of not Paying Attention." *National Council of the Teachers of English, Keynote Address,* (1998): 1–23. www.ncte.org/forums/selfe/. (accessed August 23, 1998).

Shah, Dhavan V., Jack M. McLeod, and So-Hyang Yoon, "Communication, Context, and Community." *Communication Research*, 28: 4, 464–506. 2001.

Shneiderman, Ben, "Education by Engagement and Construction," in *Sociomedia: Multimedia, Hypermedia, and the Social Construction of Knowledge* edited by E. Barrett, 13–26. Cambridge: The MIT Press, 1992.

Shneiderman, Ben, *Designing the User Interface: Stratigies for Effective Human–Compter Interaction, 3rd ed.* Reading, MA: Addison–Wesley, 1998.

Shneiderman, Ben, "Designing Trust into Online Experiences." *Communications of the ACM* 43, no. 12 (2000): 57–59.

Shenk, David. *Data Smog: Surviving the Information Glut*. San Fransico, CA: Harper Edge, 1997.

Short, John A., Ederyn Williams, and Bruce Christie, *The Social Psychology of Telecommunications*. New York: John Wiley & Sons, 1976.

Sipress, Alan, "Does Virtual Reality Need a Sheriff?" *Washington Post* (June 2, 2007): A01.

Slater–Lawrence, Michael, "Facilitating the Self–Formation of Collaborative Groups, Online." *Proceedings of the Sixth International Conference on Advanced Learning Technologies*, (2006). ieeexplore.ieee.org. (accessed April 21, 2008).

Slevin, James, *The Internet and Society*. Cambridge, UK: Polity, 2000.

Smith, Mark K., "Social Capital." *The Encyclopedia of Informal Education* (2000–2009). www.infed.org/biblio/social_capital.html. (accessed April 21, 2008).

Sohlenkamp, Markus, Ludwin Fuchs, and Andreas Genau, "Awareness and Cooperative Work: The POLITeam approach." *Proceedings of the Thirtieth Annual Hawaii International Conference on Systems Science,* IEEE, 1997.

Spinello, Richard A., *Cyber Ethics: Morality and Law in Cyberspace.* Boston, MA: Jones and Bartlett Publishers, 2000.

Spinello, Richard A. and Herman T. Tavani, *Readings in Cyber Ethics.* Boston, MA: Jones and Bartlett Publishers, 2001.

Staff, (June 14, 2007) "YouTube Passes Debates to a New Generation." *New York Times* [Online]. www.nytimes.com (accessed June 14, 2007).

Starenko, Michael, *Reflections on Blended Learning: Rethinking the Classroom.* Rochester, NY: Lulu Press, 2008.

Starenko, Michael, Karan Vignare, and Joeann Humbert, "Enhancing Student Interaction and Sustaining Faculty Instructional Innovations Through Blended Learning," in *Blended Learning: Research Perspectives* edited by A. G. Picciano, and C. D. Dziuban, 161–175. The Sloan Consortium, (2007).

Stephenson, Neil, *Snow Crash.* New York: Bantam Books, 1992.

Stone, Allucquere R., "Will the Real Body Please Stand Up?: Boundary Stories About Virtual Cultures," in *Cyberspace: First Steps,* edited by M. Benedikt, 81–118. Cambridge, MA: The MIT Press, 1991.

Strate, Lance, "Cybertime," in *Communication and Cyberspace,* edited by L. Strate, R. Jacobson, and S.B. Gibson, 351–377. Cresskill, NJ: Hampton Press, 1996.

Strate, Lance, "The Varieties of Cyberspace: Problems in Definition and Delimitation." *Western Journal of Communication* 63, no. 3 (Summer, 1999): 382–412.

Sullivan, Bob "Kids, Blogs and Too Much Information: Children Reveal More Online than Parents Know," (2005). www.msnbc.msn.com/id/7668788/print/1/displaymode/1098/. (accessed 21 March 2006.)

Sum, Shima, Mark R. Mathews, Mohsen Pourghasem, and Ian Hughes, "Internet Technology and Social Capital: How the Internet Affects Seniors' Social Capital and Wellbeing." *Journal of Computer–Mediated Communication,* 14 (2008), 202–220.

Telegraph U. K., "Teenagers 'Spend an Average of 31 Hours Online.'" *Telegraph Media Group,* 2009. www.telegraph.co.uk/technology/4574792/Teenagers-spend-an-average-of-31-hours-online.html. (accessed April 17, 2009).

The New London Group, "A Pedagogy of Multiliteracies: Designing Social Futures." *Harvard Educational Review* 66, no. 1 (1996): 60–92.

The New Media Consortium, "Spring 2007 Survey: Educators in Second Life." *The New Media Consortium* (Spring, 2007): 0–30.

Tong, Stephanie T., Brandon Van Der Heide, Lindsey Langwell, and Joseph B. Walter, "Too Much of a Good Thing? The Relationship Between Number of Friends and Interpersonal Impressions on Facebook." *Journal of Computer-Mediated Communication* 13, (2008): 531–549.

Trippi, Joe, *The Revolution Will Not be Televised: Democracy, the Internet, and the Overthrow of Everything.* New York: ReganBooks, 2004.

Tsukayama, Hayley, "Your iPhone and iPad are Tracking You, Researchers Say." Washington Post [Online], April 20, 2011. www.washingtonpost.com/blogs/faster forward/post/your-iphone...g-you-researchers-say/2011/04/20/AFhL4BCE_blog.html?wpisrc=nl_tech. (accessed April 20, 2011).

Tuman, Joseph S., "Old Rules May Not Apply Anymore." In *Real Law@ Virtual Space* edited by S. J. Drucker and G. Gumpert, (151–165). Cresskill, NJ: Hampton Press, 1999.

Turkle, Sherry, *The Second Self.* New York: Simon & Schuster, 1984.

Turkle, Sherry, "Computer as Rorschach," in *Intermedia: Interpersonal Communication in a Mediated World, 3rd Edition* edited by G. Gumpert and R. R. Cathcart, (439–459). New York: Oxford University Press, 1986.

U.S. Fed. News, American Time Use Survey—2006 results, *U.S. Fed News*, June 28, 2007.

Valauskas, Edward J., "Les Networkia: Understanding the Internet Community." *First Monday* [Online], 4, 1996.

Valiathan, P. (2002). Blended Learning Models. *Learning Circuits*. www.astd.org/lc. (accessed June 8, 2008).

Van Der Gaag, Martin and Tom A. B. Snijders, *The Resource Generator: Social Capital Quantification with Concrete Items* (2004). [Online Research Report] www.xs4all.nl/~gaag/workRG_paper.pdf. (accessed May 8, 2005).

Vazire, Simine and Sammuel D. Gosling, "e–Perceptions: Personality Impressions Based on Personal Websites." *Journal of Personality and Social Psychology* 87 (1), 2004: 123–132.

Vogt, Carlton, "Private Space or Public: Just What Sort of Creature is the Internet." The Yourdon Report Discussion Group, 2006 [online] tech.groups.yahoo.com/group/TYR/massage/2107.

Vygotsky, Lev S., *Mind in Society*. Cambridge, MA: Harvard University Press, 1978.

Vygotsky, Lev S., *Thought and Language*. Cambridge, MA: Harvard University Press, 1986.

Walther, Joseph B., "Computer-Mediated Communication: Impersonal, Interpersonal, and Hyperpersonal Interaction," *Communication Research* 23, no. 1 (February, 1996): 3–43.

Walther, Joseph B., Anderson, J. F., and Park, D. W., "Interpersonal Effects in Computer-Mediated Interaction: A Meta-Analysis or Social and Antisocial Communication." *Communication Research* 21 (4) (1994), 460–487.

Warlick, David F., *Redefining Literacy 2.0,* 2nd ed. Columbus OH: Linworth Books, 2009.

Waskul, Dennis and Mark Douglass, "Cyberself: The Emergence of Self in On–Line Chat." *Information Society* 13, no. 4 (1997): 375–297.

Weiner, Norbert, *The Human Use of Human Beings: Cybernetics and Society*. Garden City, NY: Doubleday Books, 1954.

Wellman, Barry, "Physical Place and Cyberplace: The Rise of Personalized Networking." *International Journal of Urban and Regional Research*, 25(2), 227–252, 2001.

Wellman, Barry, Anabel Q. Haase, James Witte, and Keith Hampton, "Does the Internet Increase, Decrease, or Supplement Social Capital?" *American Behavioral Scientist* 45, no. 3 (2001): 476–495.

Weizenbaum, Joseph, *Computer Power and Human Reason*. New York: W. H. Freeman and Company, 1976.

Wharton, Cathleen, John Rieman, Clayton Lewis, and Peter Polson, "The Cognitive Walkthrough Method: A Practitioners Guide," in *Usability Inspection Methods*, Jakob Nielsen, R. L. Mack, (eds.) pp. 105—140. New York: Wiley, 1994.

Wheeler, Steve, "Information and Communication Technologies and the Changing Role of the Teacher." *Journal of Educational Media* 26, no. 1 (2001): 7–17.

Whittle, David B., *Cyberspace: The Human Dimension*. New York: W. H. Freeman and Company, 1997.

Willard, Nancy E., *The Cyber Ethics Reader*. New York: McGraw-Hill, 1997.

Williams, Amanda L. and Michael J. Merten, "Adolescents' Online Social Networking Following the Death of a Peer." *Journal of Adolescent Research* 24, no. 1 (2009): 67–90.

Williams, Amanda and Dourish, Paul. "Imagining the City: The Cultural Dimension of Urban Computing." *Computer*, (2006): 38–43.

Williams, Demitri, "On and Off the Net:' Scales for Social Capital in an Online Era." *Journal of Computer-Mediated Communication* 11 (2006), 593–628.

Williams, Demitri, Li Xiong, Yuanyuan Zhang, Nick Yee, and Eric Nickell, "From Tree House to Barracks." *Games and Culture* 1, no. 4 (2006): 338–361.

Williams, Sean D., "Part 1: Thinking Out of the Pro-Verbal Box." *Computers and Composition* 18, no. 1 (2001): 21–32, 22.

Wise, J. Macgregor, *Exploring Technology and Social Space*. Thousand Oaks, CA: Sage Publications, 1997.

Whitaker, L. A., "Human Navigation," in *Human Factors and Web Development*, Chris Forsythe, Erick Grose, and Julie Ratner, (eds.) pp. 63–74. Lawrence Erlbaum Associates, Mahwah, NJ, 1998.

Wojtowicz, Peter, *I Blog, Therefore I Am*. Bloomington, IN: AuthorHouse, 2005.

Wolverton, Brad, "Hazing Photos Spur Debates on Complicity of Coaches." *The Chronicle of Higher Education*, LII(3), June 2, 2006: Al & A33.

Wood, Andrew F. and Michael J. Smith, *Online Communication: Linking Technology, Identity & Culture*. Mahwah, NJ: Lawrence Erlbaum Associates, 2001.

Wood, Julia T., *Spinning the Symbolic Web: Human Communication and Symbolic Interaction*, 2nd edition. Noorwood, NJ: Ablex Publishing Corporation, 1995.

Wynn, Eleanor and James E. Katz, "Hyperbole Over Cyberspace: Self–Presentation and Social Boundaries in Internet Home Pages and Discourse." *The Information Society* 13 (1997): 297–327.

Yuan, Y. Connie and Geri Gay, "Homophily of Network Ties and Bonding and Bridging Social Capital in Computer–Mediated Distributed Teams." *Journal of Computer-Mediated Communication*, 11, (2006): 1062–1084.

Zettl, Herbert, "Back to Plato's Cave." In *Communication and Cyberspace*, Lance Strate, Ron Jacobson, and Stephanie B. Gibson (eds). Cresskill, NJ: Hampton Press, 1996.

Index

About the Author

Susan B. Barnes, PhD, is a full professor in the College of Liberal Arts and associate director of the Lab for Social Computing at the Rochester Institute of Technology. She has received numerous grants for both applied and theoretical research on the impact of computers in society. Her publications include *Online Connections: Internet Interpersonal Relationships* (2001, Hampton Press, winner Dorothy Lee Award) and *Computer-Mediated Communication: Human-to-Human Communication Across the Internet* (2003, Allyn & Bacon), *Introduction to Visual Communication* (2011, Peter Lang), *Web Research: Selecting, Evaluating & Citing* with Marie Radford and Linda Barr (2002, Allyn & Bacon), and *Mediated Interpersonal Communication* with E. A. Konijn, S. Utz, M. Tanis (2008, Routledge). This last book was the winner of a CHOICE Award.

Dr. Barnes has written articles and book chapters for numerous publications on the topics of internet relationships, social networking, and visual communication. She received a National Science Foundation grant to examine the use of social networking in education. In 2009, she was awarded the prestigious Wilson Award for a top communication scholar from the New York State Communication Association.

www.ingramcontent.com/pod-product-compliance
Ingram Content Group UK Ltd.
Pitfield, Milton Keynes, MK11 3LW, UK
UKHW020125290926
15471UKWH00003B/291

9 780739 188231